TAC RECON

US Air Force Tactical Reconnaissance
Combat Operations from WWI to the Gulf War

TERRY M. MAYS

SCHIFFER MILITARY
4880 Lower Valley Road Atglen, PA 19310

Designed by Christopher Bower
Cover design by Brenda McCallum
Type set in GeoSlab703 Md BT /Minion Pro

ISBN: 978-0-7643-6523-2
Printed in India

Published by Schiffer Publishing, Ltd.
4880 Lower Valley Road
Atglen, PA 19310
Phone: (610) 593-1777; Fax: (610) 593-2002
Email: Info@schifferbooks.com
Web: www.schifferbooks.com

For our complete selection of fine books on this and related subjects, please visit our website at www.schifferbooks.com. You may also write for a free catalog.

Schiffer Publishing's titles are available at special discounts for bulk purchases for sales promotions or premiums. Special editions, including personalized covers, corporate imprints, and excerpts, can be created in large quantities for special needs. For more information, contact the publisher.

We are always looking for people to write books on new and related subjects. If you have an idea for a book, please contact us at proposals@schifferbooks.com.

Dedication

---| |---

For my dad,
SMSgt. Edgar M. Mays (USAF, Ret.),
proudly a "Voodoo Medicine Man" and a "Phantom Phixer,"
and
the air and ground crews of the USAF Tactical Reconnaissance
from World War I to the Gulf War

---| |---

Contents

Preface

I was "born into" United States Air Force reconnaissance. My father served as the maintenance crew chief on RB-47 and RB-57 aircraft in Japan (Johnson and Yakota Air Bases) when I was born there. One of my earliest photos is of my dad holding me while sitting in the cockpit of an RB-57. He went on to serve as a crew chief on the RF-101 Voodoo and deployed in support of the Air Force reconnaissance mission during the Cuban Missile Crisis. He later deployed to Vietnam in 1965 as the squadron commander's crew chief in the first RF-4C squadron introduced into the Vietnam War. Later in the 1970s, he returned to RB-57s before they were phased out of the Air Force.

The author with his father on an RB-57 in Japan during 1959. "RB" is the acronym for "reconnaissance bomber."

An examination of United States Air Force tactical reconnaissance has been on my back burner for many years. I heard many tales related to reconnaissance operations from my father as I grew up. Sometimes on weekends he would take me into a hangar for a closer view of the aircraft. Climbing inside an RB-57 with its unique crew cockpit is still a fond memory.

Through my dad I had opportunities to meet and chat with many of the reconnaissance pilots followed in this book. Air Force reconnaissance is a small world, and both pilots and maintenance personnel often remained in this narrow field for many years, if not their entire careers. Over my lifetime, those reconnaissance pilots have included those who flew in World War II, the Korean War, the Cuban Missile Crisis, operations over Laos, and the Vietnam Conflict. I also met reconnaissance pilots who have flown designated tactical reconnaissance aircraft in America's conflicts since World War I. Alas, drones and reconnaissance pods that can be attached to nearly any fighter now perform these missions and have replaced the manned tactical reconnaissance squadrons.

The mention of my dad's name was enough to grant me access to attend gatherings of RF-101 pilots. Col. Clyde East, who flew tactical reconnaissance in World War II, the Korean War, briefly in Vietnam immediately after the Tonkin Gulf Incident and served as my dad's squadron commander during the Cuban Missile Crisis, was very gracious. Before he passed away, he granted me the opportunity to speak with him at any time whenever my dad's name was mentioned. It was truly an honor to do so. Those familiar with Air Force history have probably heard of the annual "Gathering of Eagles" programs of the Gathering of Eagles Foundation at the Air Command and Staff College. The Gathering brings famous pilots from around the world together to share memories, meet others, and raise funds for local youth programs. Col. East participated in the fifth Gathering in 1986, along with Paul Tibbets (commander of the "Enola Gay"); Charles "Chuck" Yeager (the first pilot to break the sound barrier); astronaut Alan B. Shepherd; Francis Gabreski (who earned the distinction of "ace" in both World War II and the Korean War); Benjamin O. Davis Jr. (one of the original twelve members of the Tuskegee Airmen and a World War II ace); and there were others of equal distinction. One could say the achievements of Col. East as a reconnaissance pilot in World War II, the Korean War, and the Cuban Missile Crisis certainly kept him in good company.

Thanks to my dad's reputation among pilots, I was able to personally meet Cuban Missile Crisis RF-101 pilots John Leaphart, Tom Curtis, Bill Bernert, Joe O'Grady, Chuck Lustig, Doug Yates, B. J. Martin, and Jerry Rogers. Nearly every pilot on this list also flew reconnaissance missions during the Vietnam War. Some flew in the Korean War, and at least one, in addition to Colonel East, flew in World War II. This group of men represented the core of American tactical reconnaissance pilots in World War II, the Korean War, the Cuban Missile Crisis, and the Vietnam War.

Accordingly, this book is dedicated to my dad, SMSgt. Edgar M. Mays. Through him I developed a deep respect and interest in United States Air Force tactical reconnaissance. His name and reputation opened so many doors to meet and socialize with the reconnaissance pilots to whom I also dedicate this book. And . . . he forgave me for joining the Army instead of the Air Force.

This book is nearly completely written on the basis of my research of primary source material, which includes military records from each conflict, personal interviews, and autobiographical notes. I'm a firm believer in taking the reader into the historical record and, hopefully, making it live again. This book features many passages from these sources. I'm not the one telling the story; rather, my goal is to help the reader live the stories in the passages developed by those who were there. In other words, allow me to help them speak to all of us. This book resulted from many trips to the United States Air Force archives and interviews with those who either flew the reconnaissance aircraft or maintained them. This book is their story and is dedicated to their grit and courage. The pilots faced the same hazards as fighter pilots did, but their planes were often not armed. In come conflicts, they fought and defended each other as fighter pilots. In other conflicts, they went into combat low and fast to secure the reconnaissance needed by commanders. The enemy knew they were coming sooner or later . . . and were often waiting for them with all calibers and ranges of small arms, antiaircraft artillery, antiaircraft missiles, and fighter aircraft. Tactical reconnaissance pilots were often shot down in higher percentages than pilots of other aircraft were. Many are still "missing in action—presumed dead" today from recent conflicts. Yet, they would go up and do it again. Their maintenance personnel worked in the rain and cold during every conflict. My dad told me stories of working long hours on an aircraft and then sleeping in a ditch for a little rest while the plane was on a mission. He would postflight the plane upon its return. Then he would be lying prone in a revetment, as Viet Cong mortars were being fired, attempting to "zero in" the coordinates to put a round squarely inside the revetment. He told me that after an attack, he would walk around his location and pick up the shrapnel pieces. In the Air Force, shrapnel became foreign object debris, or FOD, that must be collected since it could be sucked into a jet engine and damage it. I still have a small box of mortar shrapnel he brought home from Vietnam.

Deciding how to assemble the narrative for this book proved to be an interesting challenge. The source material is nearly all primary historical documents and personal interviews from World War I to the Vietnam and Southeast Asian conflict. However, each conflict was quite different in length and amount of American air reconnaissance involvement. Because of that, one standard style does not suffice for every book chapter. For example, while it is possible to cover the Korean War on a month-by-month basis, this format does not work well with other conflicts. Intensive American military involvement in World War I lasted less than twelve months and the total American reconnaissance involvement in Southeast Asia lasted fourteen years. The Air Force deployed one tactical reconnaissance group in the Korean War yet many in World War II. This presents complications in any attempt to follow each war via examination of every reconnaissance group or squadron. This would work well in the Korean War but would need multiple volumes for World War II.

The solution was to assemble this book by a means that provided a unique structure for each conflict based on its length and number of reconnaissance units deployed to support it. Because each conflict and its associated reconnaissance structure was unique in some way, each chapter is unique in how it follows the employment of American reconnaissance aircraft to support it. World War I is examined by military campaigns. This reflects the ever-growing involvement of the United States in the conflict and the related increase in reconnaissance assets over an approximate ten-month period that witnessed the utilization of American troops on the line.

World War II is examined first by theater—Pacific, western European, and North African / Mediterranean. With so many units flying tactical reconnaissance, the narrative turns to trace specific units for a week or month at a time during campaign phases as examples of what all of the reconnaissance units in that particular theater were experiencing as the war progressed. With this format, the chapter is able to follow Army Air Force reconnaissance through various stages of World War II. Therefore, each section follows one or two reconnaissance units through operations in a particular stage of the war based on specific campaigns in specific theaters.

The Korean War represents a mobile war of approximately six months followed by a near stalemate along the original North Korean–South Korean border for the next two and a half years. The chapter follows the one Air Force tactical reconnaissance Group on a monthly basis during the mobile period of the war followed by the early stalemate. Then it shifts to a general overview of the reconnaissance situation for the last year of the war.

The war in Southeast Asia lasted in one form or another for fourteen years. Its chapter follows this progress in terms of general aviation campaigns: Laos, Operation Rolling Thunder, campaigns in South Vietnam, Operation Line Backer I, Operation Line Backer II, and then the ceasefire to the Mayaguez incident.

A Cold War chapter covers specific contingency and crisis operations that included American Air Force tactical reconnaissance support, including the 1958 Lebanon Crisis, 1958 Taiwan Crisis, 1965 Dominican Republic Crisis, and 1962 Cuban Missile Crisis.

The final chapter briefly examines the limited final use of specific tactical American reconnaissance aircraft in the Gulf War. This chapter also briefly examines the introduction of reconnaissance pods and the growth in the number of reconnaissance drones, which have replaced specific Air Force reconnaissance aircraft at the tactical level as visual and photographic assets. Today, nearly any tactical aircraft can be mounted with a reconnaissance pod for these duties.

Acknowledgments

There are many individuals who have contributed to this book and a complete list would be extensive. At the same time, I would like to highlight the contributions of a few. First I would like to thank some of the reconnaissance pilots and others who patiently provided me with many hours of their time to answer questions and relate their personal stories. These include Clyde East, John Leaphart, Tom Curtis, Bill Bernert, Joe O'Grady, Chuck Lustig, Doug Yates, B. J. Martin, Jerry Rogers, Don Dessert, the family of Morgan Beamer, Eric Yocum (15th TRS Association), and my dad, Edgar M. Mays. Bucky Weston, a USAF veteran of the Vietnam War, assisted with proofreading. Susan Weston provided valuable assistance and encouragement throughout the writing process. Tom Curtis read the manuscript from the point of view as a retired USAF reconnaissance pilot who flew missions during the Cuban Missile Crisis and Vietnam War. The Citadel Foundation awarded grant support for two visits to the USAF archives. At the same time the USAF Historical Research Agency cooperated more than I could have hoped in this project. Finally, but not least, Fugee Two and Zoomee offered their support by sleeping in a chair next to me during many long nights of writing.

CHAPTER 1
Introduction to USAF Tactical Reconnaissance

I made a "May Day" call after observing fragments of the aircraft separating, and indications showed that any minute there would be an explosion and loss of control.

—Capt. John Rogers, 45th Tactical Reconnaissance Squadron

The RF-101 Voodoo reconnaissance jet roared across its North Vietnamese target at minimum altitude on February 8, 1967. Instead of guns blazing, the aircraft completed its mission with cameras rolling. The pilot, Capt. John Rogers of the 45th Tactical Reconnaissance Squadron (TRS), pulled his plane skyward as he completed the camera run and banked the RF-101 toward the coast and the relative safety of the Gulf of Tonkin. Glancing down at a highway, Rogers noticed a convoy of North Vietnamese trucks. "While observing the trucks, I felt several hits which I first interpreted as turbulence," recalled the pilot. Fire warning lights flashed in the cockpit, alerting Rogers that more than turbulence had rocked his aircraft. North Vietnamese antiaircraft gunners had found their mark as the reconnaissance jet passed overhead. He pulled the plane up and to the left in an effort to reach the Gulf of Tonkin where recovery would be easier if forced to eject from the damaged aircraft. "I made a 'May Day' call after observing fragments of the aircraft separating, and indications showed that any minute there would be an explosion and loss of control."

Over the water, Rogers pulled his ejection seat handle and exited the dying aircraft. The pilot remembered feeling safe because he had made it to the Gulf of Tonkin, where the US Navy would be able to retrieve him. Ejecting over land would have added considerable difficulties to a rescue attempt resulting in his probable capture by North Vietnamese forces and incarceration in a prisoner-of-war (POW) camp. His relief quickly waned while descending in his parachute harness. Several small North Vietnamese sampans (small boats utilized for fishing and coastal transportation) were heading toward his location. Looking out toward the open ocean, Rogers could see a US Navy destroyer steaming toward his location as well. A race had developed to see who would be the first to reach the American pilot. Rogers glanced skyward. Another RF-101 circled overhead, obviously keeping track of the downed pilot's position while Navy A-1Es approached from the east. The A-1E Skyraider, a large slow single engine propeller aircraft, carried considerable ordnance and could loiter over a downed pilot providing cover while rescue teams moved into the area. The A-1Es dived upon the North Vietnamese sampans and thwarted their attempt to reach Rogers. Ten minutes later the Navy destroyer pulled alongside the pilot and fished him from the water with a hoisting device.[1] Just another day on the job for a United States Air Force (USAF) reconnaissance pilot during the early years of the Vietnam War.

Books and articles about the American contributions to the air campaigns between World War I and the Vietnam War tend to concentrate on engagements with German, Japanese, Korean, or North Vietnamese fighters. However, reconnaissance aircrews are often forgotten in these tales of air-to-air battles and high-intensity bomber missions. Reconnaissance crews frequently flew unarmed, and often alone, over targets—including some of the most heavily defended areas in each conflict. Yet they have received little attention because, instead of destroying fighters or dropping ordnance, they were shooting film.

During the Vietnam War, tactical reconnaissance aircrews were the unsung heroes of the air war. They were more likely to have been listed as killed in action (KIA) or missing in action (MIA) after the return of the POWs in 1973 than were the aircrews of any other type of USAF aircraft operating over North Vietnam. RF-4C Phantom II crews, flying the reconnaissance version of the F-4 fighter, faced a 45 percent chance of being listed as KIA or MIA if downed over North Vietnam or North Vietnamese waters. The average for aircrews of all other types of USAF aircraft operating over North Vietnam was 38 percent. Vietnam-era reconnaissance pilots deserve the respect that they have rarely received in the postwar years. This latter statement is true for the tactical reconnaissance air crews in America's earlier conflicts.

In World War I, American tactical reconnaissance crews were armed and often needed to defend each other from enemy fighters eager to down them and prevent the return of reconnaissance information back to Allied lines. In World War II, visual reconnaissance aircraft sometimes retained their weapons, but many to most flew unarmed. In the Korean and Vietnam Wars they flew unarmed. Often the phrase "Alone, Unarmed, and Unafraid" is applied to reconnaissance pilots in recognition of long, dangerous missions over enemy territory where speed and stealth are often their only measures of defense.

Signal Corps #1 (Wright Flyer Model A), the world's first military aircraft. Purchased for testing as an Army observation asset.

When can we identify the birth of American tactical air reconnaissance? Ask five people, and one might receive seven answers . . . it depends on how one defines "tactical," "air," and "reconnaissance." The armies of the Union and Confederate states employed balloons for aerial reconnaissance during the American Civil War. While they did not roam the battlefield, they did rise in altitude to provide a better view of troop movements behind enemy lines. The American Army dispatched a Signal Corps balloon to Cuba during the Spanish-American War. The crew in the balloon basket provided a similar service by reporting on the movement and disposition of Spanish troops during the battles for Santiago. The United States was one of the first customers for the aircraft designed by Wilbur and Orville Wright after their first heavier-than-air flights in 1903. The American Army not only purchased a couple of the earliest aircraft but also sent officers to be trained in the operation of the aircraft by the Wrights. Their purpose: experimentation with the use of heavier-than-air reconnaissance on the battlefield. Unlike balloons, aircraft can move about the battlefield to examine objectives and troops in different locations. Or is the birth of American tactical reconnaissance the establishment of the First Aero Squadron on March 5, 1913? At this point, the Army boasted its first aircraft squadron that was permanently designated for observation purposes. Of course, there are those who might say the birth of tactical air reconnaissance was the deployment of eight aircraft of the First Aero Squadron into Mexico with General John Pershing's expedition to track and eliminate the bandit gang of Pancho Villa, who had raided the American town of Columbus, New Mexico, on March 9, 1916. Having looked at the question of "air" and how and when we conquered its hold on us in cooperation with gravity, one could question the term "tactical." Are we looking at reconnaissance as intelligence gathering of the immediate battlefield or as deep reconnaissance into the enemy's homeland? Or what is "reconnaissance"? Do we begin with the first visual intelligence gathering from the air or the ability to produce photographs that record our observations? No answer is correct, and no answer is wrong but rather depends upon how one views the progression of American aerial observation from the time of the balloons of the Civil War until the American entry into World War I. However, whatever direction one takes for the birth of tactical air reconnaissance, it was present in World War I, and that conflict forms the beginning of our examination. This narrative begins with the deployment and formation of American observation squadrons in World War I with the stated purpose of conducting reconnaissance along and behind the battlefield in support of the ground troops. This will change throughout history as aircraft operational ranges increased.

As mentioned, American tactical air reconnaissance pilots have flown either armed or unarmed depending upon the conflict and specific model of aircraft. Capt. Rogers flew unarmed during his RF-101 photographic reconnaissance missions in the Vietnam War. Many American reconnaissance pilots flew unarmed in World War II as well. However, the United States did employ the P-51 Mustang fighter in the visual reconnaissance role in some squadrons. These pilots flew armed and could defend themselves, although this could be controversial at times. There were those who believed the long-range tactical reconnaissance pilots needed to defend themselves if attacked by fighters deep in enemy territory. But there were also those who argued the best defense for reconnaissance pilots was to arrive at and return from the objective fast and alone. This provided the best opportunity for not being spotted and not depleting precious fuel in a dogfight.

While John Rogers flew unarmed in Vietnam, Lt. J. E. Conklin flew his reconnaissance missions armed twenty-three years earlier. In the early afternoon of D-day on June 6, 1944, Conklin downed a German Fw 190 fighter while on a visual reconnaissance over a highway route in France. Conklin and other pilots of the 67th Tactical Reconnaissance Group (TRG) flew with missions to serve as the eyes of the Army and look for the movement of German troops on rail and roads toward the beach areas. The beachhead held by Allied forces was tenuous in the early afternoon, and German reinforcements needed to be intercepted, if possible, before arriving at the coast. The visual reconnaissance pilots dispatched their intelligence by radio for fighter bombers to engage the German forces. The official Group Operations Report records the mission and presents a means for us to visualize the sortie:

Lt. Joseph E. Conklin, pilot in the lead ship [of a two-plane flight], took off at 1100 hours for visual reconnaissance over route YX5 in France. Departed English coast in the vicinity of Beachy Head and entered French coast near Trouville . . . At 1212 hours, encountered intense accurate light flak from two flak towers, light house type with windmill vase, at la Loupe, VR 7080. One silenced by 2 sec. bursts, strikes observed around panels in top. At 1220 hours intense accurate light flak or m/g [machine gun] fire from 8 flak towers scattered through woods at VR 4916 (near Ecloanes). Three are light house type, five wooden tripod type. Two of the tripod type fired on, one hit. Moderate inaccurate light flak from Auffon area. At 1225 hours at Dreux airfield, three silver FW-190s with yellow and black or white and black checkerboard on rudder. Two at end of landing run on SW-NE runway. Attacked the remaining FW 190 which was on its final approach with wheels down. Opened fire at approximately 400 yards and closed to 50 yards with two long bursts. The enemy aircraft started smoking after the first burst and after the second burst, exploded and hit the ground. At 1240 hours at R 5750, about 50 MET [medium equipment transporter] heading NW, believed half-track personnel carriers, stationary. Some personnel inside and around but not heavily loaded. At 1245 hours at VR 9756, Etrepagny airfield, camouflage netted building size of blister hangar in NE corner of field—fired into by lead pilot. Lead man returned to base and landed at 1335 hours. No. 3 man had become separate and he returned alone, landing at 1350 hours.[2]

Our look at United States Air Force tactical reconnaissance begins even earlier with World War I.

CHAPTER 2
World War I

The work is directly for the man on the ground, for it is these pictures which will tell him what there is to be overcome in the territory in front of him, thus saving many lives.

—*Capt. Daniel Morse, 50th Aero Squadron*

On April 6, 1917, the United States declared war on Germany following years of internal debate on whether the country should become actively involved in the European war. The country's military was not prepared for a war—especially one in which the belligerents had three years to develop new and improved military technology in the hopes of turning the tide of the stalemate that evolved after 1914.

Advancements in aviation during the first three years of World War I left the United States dreadfully behind the European states in terms of aircraft technology and development. The American Jenny aircraft of the 1916 Mexican Expedition were woefully underpowered and not prepared to face the rigors of aerial combat, and the American aircraft industry was not prepared to "catch up" and produce advanced aircraft in sufficient numbers to meet the American military demands. As a result, it was understood that the American military needed to acquire Allied aircraft that were currently in the production stage. This placed American air units in competition for the limited aircraft produced by the British and French air industry. On July 29, 1918, following the three German spring and summer offensives of that year, a recommendation to Gen. John Pershing, the commander in chief of the American Expeditionary Forces, called for a goal of 356 aircraft squadrons by the end of June 1919. With this plan, the balance of unit types reflected the current and projected manpower declines of continued warfare experienced by the French and British. The plan included 147 pursuit, 110 bombardment, and 101 observation squadrons. However, this plan was modified the following month to a more manageable 202 squadrons, with 101 of these being observation squadrons. Hence, one is reminded that the original mission of aircraft in warfare was observation.[1]

The first observation aircraft provided for the newly arriving American observation squadrons were often underpowered and secondhand. These included the French SPAD S.X1 and the British Sopwith 1½ Strutter. As newer aircraft became available, the American observation squadrons received two of the best models flown in the last two years of the wars: the French Salmson 2A2 and the British de Havilland DH-4. Both of the latter aircraft carried two crew members with a pilot sitting in the front behind the engine and an observer/gunner who flew in a separate area about two-thirds of the way along the aircraft from its nose. The pilot not only flew the aircraft but also could fire a machine gun mounted on top of the engine. The firing mechanism was synchronous with the turning of the propeller, allowing the guns to fire through the turning blades without hitting them. The observer made notes on what the crew spotted, operated a camera if carried on the mission, and could fire a single or dual machine gun mounted at his cockpit. Because of that, the lone observer plane packed as much firepower as a pursuit plane, although not as maneuverable. Many German pursuit pilots fell to the rear gun of an observer aircraft during the war.

Reviewing firsthand records and autobiographies of American air crews leads to one quick conclusion. If it were possible to have all of them sit in a room and ask them which of the two planes (or the French Breguet 14, which could be found in much smaller numbers among American squadrons) provided the best service to American crews, one would probably encounter a debate at best and a serious argument at worst. Crews tended to be fiercely loyal to whichever aircraft they preferred, including possibly the Breguet.

1st Aero Squadron Salmson SA2

The Salmson 2A2 first flew in 1917 and became the most widely utilized observation aircraft in American observation squadrons. The French designed the plane (as well as the Breguet 14) knowing the inadequacies of the British Sopwith 1½ Strutter that populated not only British squadrons but also many of its own squadrons, Belgian squadrons, and the earliest arriving American squadrons. The Salmson boasted a 231 hp Salmson 9Za 9-cylinder water-cooled radial piston engine that could reach a speed of 117 mph at sea level, a range of 310 miles, and a service ceiling of 20,500 feet. It carried a single Vickers machine gun on top of the engine and a dual Lewis machine gun on the ring around the rear cockpit. Comparing this with the Sopwith 1½ Strutter, the latter could attain a speed of 100 mph with a 130 hp Clerget engine and a ceiling of 15,500 feet and operate at a range of 230 miles.

The Salmson's main competition for the love of the American aircrews was the de Havilland DH-4, built under license in the United States and mounting the famous American Liberty engine (built from a Rolls Royce design) loved by many of the pilots in the war. A DH-4 with a 400 hp Liberty engine could attain an impressive 143 mph, a range of

De Havilland DH-4

Handheld Graflex camera utilized by some American observers

Handing a camera to a reconnaissance observer in a 91st Aero Squadron Salmson 2A2

470 miles, and a ceiling of 22,000 feet. It carried a single machine gun for the pilot and another on the cockpit ring for the observer. The third aircraft, the Breguet 14, was the least utilized in combat by the American observation units. During the war, a large variety of engines were mounted on the plane. The engines typically mounted in the planes assigned to American bombardment and observation crews carried a 400 hp Liberty engine, providing a speed of approximately 121 mph, a range of 560 miles, and a ceiling of 20,300 feet.

The United States also entered the war with a deficiency in cameras for aerial photography. In fact, the best camera lenses at this time were constructed in Germany. After a review of available cameras, the United States military settled on the DeRam model manufactured in France, although other cameras, including an American Graflex model, were utilized until these were more widely available.

American mobile photographic developing lab and a collection of aerial reconnaissance cameras

Duties of Observer Missions

The aircrews of the American observation squadrons of World War I performed many reconnaissance related tasks, and photographing German positions represented just one of these assignments. AES observation squadrons performed a host of duties ranging from scouting and reconnaissance, artillery call for fire and fire adjustment, photography, and ground support, among other functions. The variety of possible missions either directly aided the American and other Allied units on the ground or indirectly supported them by providing their headquarters units with intelligence information related to the battlefield or enemy rear area situation.

As a result of being directly connected with aiding the troops on the ground, many AES observation air crews expressed sincere satisfaction with their duties. Having read many autobiographies, letters, and memos from these aircrews, it is quite interesting to come across so few comments from crews longing for service with pursuit squadrons. Films and novels tend to portray the pursuit pilots as the "Knights of the Air," longing to engage enemy pilots in aerial duels. Yet the observation aircrews frequently wrote of their satisfaction in taking care of the troops below them. At the same time, there needs to be a caveat added here that many of these observation aircrews ended the war with the downing of German planes credited to them, and a couple of them returned home as aces. This is also something not portrayed well in films and novels where the lowly scout observation planes were nearly always easy prey for the "Knights" in pursuit planes. As will be discussed later in this chapter, attacking an observation plane carrying a rear-mounted Lewis machine gun could be quite detrimental to a pursuit pilot.

Capt. Daniel P. Morse Jr., the commander of the 50th Aero Squadron, offers a fine tribute to not only his satisfaction but also the work performed by all of the AES observation squadrons in support of the "doughboys" on the ground:

> The pleasing part of observation work to me is the fact that it is constructive, so far as warfare can be. We were always trying to save the lives of our own men by spotting the enemy so that our troops could keep them at a disadvantage; by serving as a means of communication from the front lines to the rear when communication was cut; by reporting the position of our own front line troops so that our artillery wouldn't fire on our own troops; by taking pictures of the enemy's lines and back areas so that the infantry would not go over the top blind; and by many other ways.[2]

Morse was quite proud of his unit's work on behalf of the infantry. He wrote the following in reference to the squadron's aerial photography efforts:

> Here again the work is directly for the man on the ground, for it is these pictures which will tell him what there is to be overcome on the territory in front of him, thus saving many lives. You can well imagine from the foregoing that the observation end of aviation is the most important of all aviation. The pilots and observers are always in direct touch with everything going on in their sector and on each side, and therefore it is most interesting . . . Needless to say, the pilots and observers and the enlisted men who kept the machines in order and the quarters in condition deserve a world of credit, too.[3]

Assembling an official list of duties for the AES observation squadrons is not as easy as one would think. An examination of World War I documents and aircrew autobiographies presents an inconsistent list of the duties assigned to AES observation squadrons. This is due to the nature of the AES in World War I. Looking back to the 1916 Expedition in Mexico, we find a fledgling air service attempting to conduct its main—and essentially only—mission in the military: scouting and reconnaissance of what lies in front of a military force. Just over one year later, the same air service faced the realities of changing technology and its employment strategies in warfare. Observation aircraft did not simply fly ahead of the military force and report back to the commander upon landing anymore. American aircraft can only be classified as being in a military technological revolution since 1914. They now faced the challenges presented by an opponent keen to destroy them and to prevent them from returning with their information. The opposing force worked to deceive and misdirect the observation aircrews with fake emplacements or to camouflage them from view. Ground troops hurled antiaircraft artillery which would burst and send pieces of metal in all directions into the sky, in hopes of hitting a pilot or observer or strike the engine or fuel tank. Soldiers fired machine guns and rifles from the ground at low-flying aircraft. Groups of enemy fighter aircraft actively hunted the observation planes.

Lt. Col. H. A. Toulmin Jr., the former chief of the Coordination Staff of the AES in World War I, offered a view of the observation squadron missions from his perspective. He placed the duties into two distinct categories: intelligence (photography, radio, and visible signals) and artillery fire control.[4] Yet these two compact categories do not cover many of the missions known to have been flown by the AES observation squadrons. In the end perhaps the best way to understand the types of missions flown by the AES observation squadrons is to review the autobiographies of the pilots and observers assigned to the squadrons rather than rely on planning documents and views from higher headquarters. The examination of several autobiographical pieces written by pilots and observers reveals a much broader list of missions that can be placed into the following categories: artillery support, reconnaissance, infantry liaison, ground support, photography, protection of other aircraft, and propaganda.

Panels utilized to communicate with reconnaissance aircraft flying over a ground unit

Artillery Support

Capt. Morse of the 50th Aero Squadron referred to Artillery Support missions in terms of two categories: "surveillance" and "indirect fire adjustment." The former involved a type of mission of opportunity, in which the crew scouted an area, and if they encountered a target of opportunity, they would radio a designated artillery battery for a fire mission. Morse outlined a typical surveillance mission.

On each mission, in observation, the pilot and observer have something definite to do. They might start off on a surveillance. They would then send down their "call letters" on the way out to the front by their wireless, and by the time they arrived, the artillery unit for which the call was meant would be in readiness. It would have its "panel"—a piece of white cloth of various sizes and shapes according to the unit using it—out, and the plane would fly over the spot and, on seeing the panel, send down its "understood letters" in code. Then, going over the enemy lines, they might see a convoy of trucks on a road not visible from the ground on our side of the lines. The wireless would then send its call letters to the artillery and the coordinates of the spot where the trucks were. The artillery shot according to those directions, and if the shots fell away from the target, the observer sent down his code letters to tell the artillery at what distance from the target his shots fell.[5]

First Lieutenant Smart of the 135th Aero Squadron bragged on the artillery observation and adjustment skills of his observer, Lieutenant Sheets:

> Sheets was an excellent observer who seldom missed spotting a shell burst. After we had successfully completed a few of these *reglages*, the artillery units asked for him when an operation of this kind was necessary. Most of the *reglages* were arranged with the artillery the day or night before they were to take place. We knew where our battery was located and also where the battery's panneau station was located. The two were not necessarily at the same location, but were not far apart.[6]

Reconnaissance

General reconnaissance duties included looking for objectives or targets as they appeared. In other words, a pilot flew over an assigned area of territory to see if he could spot any movement or emplacement of the enemy forces. Sometimes missions could be assigned just because he was available over the battlefield. Lt. Morse noted:

> Or the mission might be a "reconnaissance." The plane would then proceed directly over the enemy's lines within the section assigned it and the observer would try to see all he could. Opportunity might come up for him to direct the artillery, as in the surveillance plane, but if not he flew over the enemy lines and reported everything he saw, or did not see. For instance, he reported whether a certain road between two specific towns were "active"—much traffic on it—or the actual amount of trucks, artillery, horses, troops, etc., seen, or whether he had seen absolutely nothing. The latter, strange as it may seem, is just as important to know about the enemy's actions as is the former. If the observer saw anything especially important, such as troops about to attack or appearing about to, he wirelessed down certain letters and numerals which, when translated from the code, meant that the enemy was about to attack at a certain place. When the mission was completed, the plane flew over the headquarters of the division for which the plane was working and dropped a written message stating all particulars as to what was seen, the exact place, the exact time and the height at which the plane was flying and signed it with the observer's name and the name of his pilot. This message was dropped on a previously designated spot marked by a divisional panel, of specific shape. A duplicate message was also dropped at the Corps headquarters, also marked on the ground by a panel of specific shape. Upon returning to the squadron field, still another duplicate report was made out and that telephoned into Corps headquarters. Corps headquarters telephoned that to the division interested if it had

not already received the one dropped. Thus at least one of the messages reached the division if those that were dropped were lost. The division sent the information contained in the report to the lower commands in the division, and each lower command issued such orders to those below it as it deemed necessary from the information received from the plane. It can be seen that, theoretically at least, the information from the plane reaches the troops in the front line in some form or other. In actual operations, however, the theoretical does not always happen, but at least the staff of the division know conditions and issue orders accordingly.[7]

Infantry Liaison

These missions provided contact between the troops on the ground and their commanders who might not know their specific locations, how fast they are progressing, whether they are pinned down or blocked, or if they are heading in a wrong direction. The reconnaissance planes on these missions sought American soldiers in a particular battle sector and then returned with reports on their location and movement.

Capt. Morse of the 50th Aero Squadron noted:

There were a few times during attacks that the 77th Division got information of their advanced troops for as long a period as eighteen hours only through the reports our pilots and observers brought in, and that our reports were always taken as authentic and a deciding factor when any doubt appeared. The importance of this can only be fully realized by those who have been through some real war, but the value to the man fighting on the ground can be seen when the doughboys have gone over the top and no more is heard from them until the aeroplane brings back word.[8]

Two air crew members of the 50th Aero Squadron received Medals of Honor for discovering and maintaining contact with the "Lost Battalion" during the Meuse-Argonne Offensive at the end of the war. Both men died performing duties which will be reviewed later in this chapter. They were the only observation air crew members awarded the Medal of Honor during World War I.

The 90th Aero Squadron, an early arriver in the American Toul Sector, flew numerous infantry contact missions in support of newly arrived American divisions conducting training near Chaumont:

On August 4, the first Infantry Contact mission was assigned to the 90th, the work of which it was later to do so much, and by which it gained its reputation of being a "Shock Squadron." A "coup de main" by the Infantry was being carried out northeast of Flirey. Lieutenants White and Sherrick were detailed to carry out the mission at dawn and report on the attainment of the objective four kilometers beyond the old German lines. In spite of extremely bad weather conditions, a contrary wind and low clouds with frequent showers, the mission was quite successful, and valuable information as to the progress of the raid was brought back.[9]

An infantry liaison or contact flight could also involve what is now known as a ground support mission. During infantry attacks some observation aircraft could be assigned to fly above them and fire their machine guns at German positions when spotted. These actions served to not only attempt to suppress the Germans but also alert the advancing infantry to their locations. Films and depictions of World War I have many people thinking the entire Western front was a "no-man's-land" of vegetation, bare terrain dotted with shell holes, and the rotting corpses of men and animals between two lines of trenches. While true in many, many areas—especially in the middle years of the war—in actuality, much of the western front consisted of terrain covered in vegetation rather than of a dirt or mud moonscape . . . more or less depending upon earlier battles. This is especially the case in 1918 in locations where the front had been pushed by the Allies toward southeast Belgium and Germany itself. Low-flying aircraft could often spot enemy troops and/or gun emplacements on the far sides of hills or along vegetation during the advances of friendly infantry. The machine gun(s) manned by the observer would then serve as a ground support weapon to suppress and mark the positions.

1Lt. Laurence Smart, a pilot with the 135th Aero Squadron, viewed these ground support attacks as dangerous but also as a way to aid his fellow American soldiers in the infantry. He noted in his memoirs:

> It was a nasty but necessary job. The pilot would fly just over the heads of the infantry as they went over the top in an attack. We would look for any strong points of resistance, such as machine gun emplacements, artillery batteries, or troop movements. Whenever possible, we would strafe such objects with our machine guns. After about an hour and a half of this type of mission, we would return to our field. Flying right under barrages was about as dangerous a mission as possible. The plane would rock and buck all the time. The fury of the battle was right under the plane and you really had a grandstand seat for the drama of "Hell on Earth" but it was not in any way enjoyable.[10]

Aerial photograph of a village

Photography

Aerial photography of the battlefield conditions and terrain provided valuable intelligence to commanders before, during, and after combat. While the pilot flew the plane, the observer in the rear operated the large cameras which were usually mounted on the side of the plane at his station. Upon completing a photographic series of an objective, the plane returned to its base, where a courier picked up the film or film plates and took them to a location for processing. More on this type of mission will be presented throughout this chapter.

Protection missions involved flying aerial gun support for a squadron-mate performing any of the other four tasks. Pursuit planes were rarely available, especially in the early period of the American deployment to France, to provide protection for the observation squadrons against German fighter aircraft. This is not as bad as it first appears because many observation crews desired to scoot over the front line in small numbers to avoid the attention of patrolling German aircraft. For this reason, it was common for observation aircraft to provide cover for another assigned to a reconnaissance or spotting mission. The observer (and gunner) in the latter aircraft was busy with his assigned mission, and the pilot concentrated on keeping the plane on a course that provided his observer with the best views of the potential targets. The other observer aircraft flew cover and searched for any German aircraft that could interfere with the mission. In a scramble back to the Allied lines, a pair or trio of observers with machine guns could put up a stern fight, and many German fighters fell to their machine guns while chasing the observer aircraft. 1Lt. Smart of the 135th Aero Squadron remembered these pairings:

> Initially, we used two planes to go along as protection from E.A. [enemy aircraft] because the observer, who was taking the photographs, could not watch for enemy aircraft as well while concentrating on getting good photographs. The pilot would be flying at a constant altitude and keeping the correct course. Theoretically, we were supposed to have pursuit plane protection, but we never did receive it. Our pursuit squadrons never did reach their desired strength to take on missions of this kind. Most of the pilots and observers preferred to go alone. It was thought more planes attracted too much attention. This made the job more dangerous, but it was up to the pilot and his observer to make the decision.[11]

Spring and Summer 1918 German Offensives

Two months after the American declaration of war, the country deployed the First Division to France. The infantry division was not prepared or properly trained for immediate entry into the front lines although its soldiers exhibited an enthusiasm for their mission. The first-activated National Guard unit, the 29th Division, arrived another three months later, in September 1917. Despite the hopes of the Allied powers that had been fighting since 1914, massive American reinforcements would obviously not be arriving until 1918.

The year 1917 did not end well for the Entente powers. The United States maintained only one full division on or near the front line although others were in training or still forming. The number of American soldiers arriving each month tended to be much smaller than required to quickly build a force sufficient in size to counter the number of German soldiers on the western front or to transport them from the eastern front. French soldiers faced serious morale issues and were near open revolt against their commanders following poorly conceived offensives in 1917. The British Expeditionary Force (BEF) suffered many casualties in its own failed 1917 offensives. The Russian military collapsed, leading to political upheaval and eventually to the Bolshevik Revolution in November 1917. Germany viewed the slow mobilization, training, and deployment of American combat troops, and problems faced by France and Great Britain, as opportunities to secure a quick, full, or partial victory before the eventual arrival of the former in large numbers. With the Russian revolution in November 1917, and the new government's official surrender in March 1918, Germany could free some troops from occupation duties and release them to the western front in a final attempt to end the war before the arrival of the full American army.

German general Erich Ludendorff launched three offensives during a three-month period between March and May 1918 to separate the British and French troops on the western front, destroy military and civilian morale, and force, at minimum, a withdrawal of the British from the war effort or, even better, a complete surrender of London and Paris to Berlin. The first, Operation Michael, seized more territory near the town of St. Quentin (on the Somme River) in a two-week period than the Allies had slowly reacquired in all of the fighting across the entire western front since 1914. The Germans attacked on March 21 and steadily pushed Entente troops while gaining ground retaken by the latter after the initial 1914 German offensive halted. Approximately 2,200 American personnel including three AES pursuit squadrons eventually aided the Entente defensive efforts. The Entente effort to halt the offensive cost approximately 254,000 casualties (including seventy-seven Americans) with the Germans suffering approximately 239,000 casualties. Fighting raged until April 5.

On April 7, the German army launched Operation Georgette against the BEF at Ypres. The German army planned to reach the English Channel and thereby isolate the BEF from the rest of the Entente forces to the south as well as cut their supply lines to the channel ports in hopes of forcing Great Britain from the war. The British dug in their heels following huge losses and held. Casualty estimates for both sides vary but can be stated to be approximately 82,000 British, 30,000 French, and 86,000 German soldiers. A limited number of American support troops did aid the British in this effort.

The Germans launched the third prong of the trio of operations, Operation Blucher-Yorck, on May 27. They initially made solid headway against the Entente forces. The American 1st and 2nd Divisions were training when the German offensive hit the French lines. German successes resulted in French units ceasing training oversight of the American units and moving forward. The American divisions moved forward as well. The 1st Division fought at the Battle of Cantigny as part of the Entente efforts to halt and turn the German offensive. By the time the Entente halted the offensive they amassed approximately 137,000 casualties and the Germans lost approximately 130,000 casualties. The combined German casualties from the three offensives along with two minor offensives extending from Operation Blucher-Yorck resulted in a critical loss of manpower for the German army as the size of the American Army continued to grow. The Entente powers offered the Germans little time to regroup and recover. They launched what some refer to as the "Hundred Days Offensive," which exploited the German losses and exhaustion through a series of offensives lasting from August 8 to the armistice on November 11. The majority of World War I AES operations, in particular tactical reconnaissance in support of the ground troops, occurred in this 100 day window of time.

United States Participation in the Allied Efforts to Halt Germany, May–July 1918

The 1st and 12th Aero Squadrons led the entry of American observation squadrons into combat with American ground forces. The 1st Aero Squadron flew general intelligence gathering visual reconnaissance missions and its first exchange of gunfire with German planes occurred on April 12. Later that month, it joined the newly formed 1st Observation Group along with the 12th Aero Squadron and the 88th Aero Squadron. The latter unit became operational at the end of May but did not join the 1st Observation Group until July 6. The AEF declared the 90th and 91st Aero Squadrons operational in June.

Cantigny, Château-Thierry, Belleau Wood, and Vaux represent some of the earliest battles in which American units participated in large numbers. All four battles placed American units in support of their Allies, the British and French, during their summer counterattacks to halt and turn the German offensives. At Cantigny on 28 May, the American 1st Division successfully led a counterattack to neutralize a small German-held salient in the lines following their offensive southeast of Amiens.

Farther south and two days later the US 3rd Division held the Germans on the Marne River opposite the small town of Château-Thierry. The Germans occupied Château-Theirry and Vaux the next day while the Americans continued to hold the southern bank of the Marne. The Allied defense now held the Germans in a salient that stretched from Soissons in the northwest, southeastward to Rheims, and then to the point of the triangle at Château-Thierry and along the Marne. The initial counterattack operations commenced on June 6, with the attack on Belleau Wood by the US 2nd Division, which included US Marines. The small forest lay northwest of Château-Theirry and permitted the Americans to check the German advance in that corner of the salient in cooperation with other Allied forces.

General William (Billy) Mitchell visited the 12th Aero Squadron on the same day to observe American observation operations. He wrote the following in his memoirs after seeing Benjamin Porter Harwood of the 12th Aero Squadron return from a June 2 mission:

Hardly a plane of our observation aviation returned without having entered into combat. I was on the observation airdrome at Frenceille one day when a pilot, with Harwood as observer, landed from a reconnaissance flight. Harwood had seven or eight bullet holes through his flying suit, several slight wounds on his body and the tip of his nose was shot off. In spite of this, he made an excellent report of his mission and observed, 'The only thing that bothered me was the way the German incendiary bullets made the fur in my flying suit smell when they went through it.'[12]

Plans called for an Allied counteroffensive to begin on July 18. During this phase, the 12th Aero Group provided visual and photographic reconnaissance in support of Allied operations. Benjamin Porter Harwood of the 12th Aero Squadron received the Distinguished Service Cross for his actions while flying a protective mission for a photographic plane as the Allied troops prepared to counterattack. His citation reads:

For extraordinary heroism in action near Château-Thierry, France on July 5, 1918. Lieutenant Harwood volunteered with another plane to protect a photographic plane. In the course of their mission they were attacked by seven enemy planes (Fokker type). Lieutenant Harwood accepted the combat and kept the enemy engaged while the photographic plane completed its mission. His guns jammed and he himself was seriously wounded. After skillfully clearing his guns, with his plane badly damaged, he fought off the hostile planes and enabled the photographic plane to return to our lines with valuable information.[13]

The 88th Aero Squadron provided corps-level reconnaissance support as the Allied forces moved northward after the actions around Belleau Wood. Their duties also included protective flights to cover more experienced French aerial photographic crews.

The Final Report of the Signal Corps on AES operations during this engagement summed up the German air opposition in the area quite succinctly:

At Château-Thierry the enemy had a powerful aggregation of pursuit squadrons. In addition, there were many squadrons which carried out the work of observation, army day and night reconnaissance, and bombardment. Here, for the first time in the history of the observation squadrons of the 1st Corps group, it became a daily occurrence to encounter enemy pursuit patrols in numbers varying from 7 to 20 in a single patrol. These hostile pursuit forces were equipped with the latest types of fast scout airplanes, and among the squadrons there encountered by the Americans were some of the best of the German pursuit aviation.[14]

The 1st and 12th Aero Squadrons completed a shifting of airfields in the salient area on June 29, in preparation for Allied operations beginning the next day. Much of the information points included in the 2nd Division's preattack intelligence report of June 29 to capture Vaux were developed from the work accomplished by the two American observation squadrons during the month of June. The section on "Trenches" in the division's intelligence report opens with: "Parts of the trenches at the southeastern edge of the town are visible on aeroplane photographs."[15]

July opened with the American attack on Vaux. The 1st and 12th Aero Squadrons performed infantry contact missions on the first day and then tended to concentrate on artillery support, visual reconnaissance, and photographic reconnaissance until mid-July. During this period, American observation squadrons devised the tactic of sending armed reconnaissance aircraft to accompany and protect the plane conducting photography. Pursuit squadrons were busy with their own duties and tended to oppose flying cover for the observation planes, which placed them at risk of being attacked by higher-flying German fighters. The AES did not completely abandon this pursuit-plane protection and worked diligently to develop new tactics before the St. Mihiel Offensive. Plans called for an Allied counteroffensive to begin on July 18. During this phase, the 12th Aero Group provided visual and photographic reconnaissance in support of Allied operations.

Aerial photograph of Vaux. Note the craters around the village.

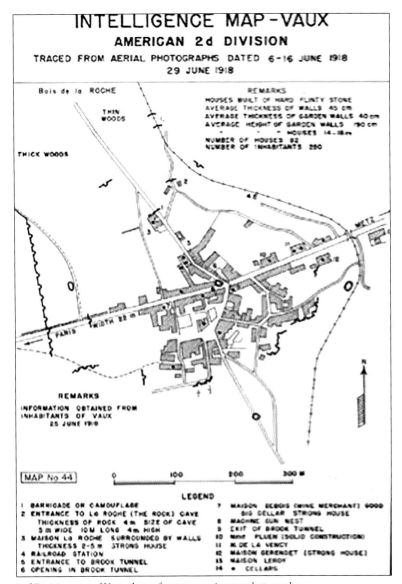

2nd Division map of Vaux, drawn from reconnaissance photographs

American divisions played a decisive role in halting the German advance along the Marne and Champagne in cooperation with primarily French, but also British, forces between July 15 and 17. In particular, American troops performed well alongside the French defending the strategically important city of Rheims. From July 18 to August 6, these American troops assisted in the Allied counteroffensives that pushed the Germans from the Marne to the Vesle River. American forces seized Château-Thierry and Vaux before continuing to the north. Officially, the offensive lasted until August 6.

Lt. Joseph Palmer of the 88th Aero Squadron received the Distinguished Service Cross for his actions during the campaign. The citation reads:

The President of the United States of America, authorized by Act of Congress, July 9, 1918, takes pleasure in presenting the Distinguished Service Cross to Second Lieutenant (Field Artillery) Joseph A. Palmer, United States Army Air Service, for extraordinary heroism in action while serving with 88th Aero Squadron (Attached), 15th Field Artillery Regiment, US Army Air Service, A.E.F., near Fismes, France, 11 August 1918. John W. Jordan, second lieutenant, 7th Field Artillery, observer; Roger W. Hitchcock, second lieutenant, pilot; James S. D. Burns, deceased, second lieutenant, 165th Infantry, observer; Joel H. McClendon, deceased, first lieutenant, pilot; Charles W. Plummer, deceased, second lieutenant, 101st Field Artillery, observer; Philip R. Babcock, first lieutenant, pilot; and Louis G. Bernheimer, first lieutenant, pilot. All of these men were attached to the 88th Aero Squadron, Air Service. Under the protection of three pursuit planes, each carrying a pilot and an observer, Lieutenants Bernheimer and Jordan, in charge of a photo plane, carried out successfully a hazardous photographic mission over the enemy's lines to the River Aisne. The four American ships were attacked by 12 enemy battle planes. Lieutenant Bernheimer, by coolly and skillfully maneuvering his ship, and Lieutenant Jordan, by accurate operation of his machine-gun, in spite of wounds in the shoulder and leg, aided materially in the victory which came to the American ships, and returned safely with 36 valuable photographs. The pursuit plane operated by Lieutenants Hitchcock and Burns was disabled while these two officers were fighting effectively. Lieutenant Burns was mortally wounded and his body jammed the controls. After a headlong fall of 2,500 meters, Lieutenant Hitchcock succeeded in regaining control of his plane and piloted it back to his airdrome. Lieutenants McClendon and Plummer were shot down and killed after a vigorous combat with five of the enemy's planes. Lieutenants Babcock and Palmer, by gallant and skillful fighting, aided in driving off the German planes and were materially responsible for the successful execution of the photographic mission.[16]

The successful Allied efforts to halt the offensives resulted in heavy losses of German manpower. The Allies turned to the "Hundred Days Offensive" to immediately exploit German losses on the battlefield. American tactical reconnaissance squadrons played a major support role in the growing American military effort within this campaign from August 8 to the armistice on November 11.

St. Mihiel Offensive, September 12–16, 1918

As the AEF prepared for the offensive, the Army and Corps Observation Groups received slightly different missions. Each would perform Visual (day and night) reconnaissance, photographic reconnaissance, command reconnaissance, and artillery adjustment. The Corps Observation Group received the additional mission for infantry and artillery liaison since its squadrons flew in support of specific infantry divisions. The diversity of missions performed by the observation squadrons can be seen in which staff members or commanders selected the specific missions for the aircraft. At the army and corps levels, the G-2 (intelligence section) oversaw visual and photographic reconnaissance missions, the G-3 (operations section) directed command reconnaissance, and the artillery commander directed artillery adjustment missions. At the corps level, the observation squadrons were attached to specific divisions and division commanders assumed responsibility for infantry liaison missions while the division artillery commanders performed the same function for artillery liaison.[17]

Eleven observation squadrons prepared for operations with the First Army in the St. Mihiel offensive. Six of these were experienced in combat operations and included the 1st, 12th, 90th, 91st, and 135th Observation Squadrons. A caveat must be added here to note that the combat experience of the latter squadron was only two weeks and the most experienced squadron (the 1st) held only four months of combat flying. The five inexperienced observation squadrons were the 8th, 9th (night reconnaissance), 24th, 50th, and 104th. In an attempt to delineate responsibilities between the aircraft observation squadrons and as well as the balloon observation companies, additional instructions provided to corps commanders called for them to designate a specific aircraft squadron to each division commander who would then have authority to designate their missions. One aircraft observation squadron was assigned to the corps artillery to perform photographic operations and adjust cannon fire when the assigned balloon observation company was not able to fulfill its mission due to weather conditions or enemy antiballoon actions. The AEF placed the same system at the divisional level—balloon observation companies assumed first-line responsibility to work with divisional artillery fire adjustment.[18]

The AES established a mission priority list based on preparation phases from the St. Mihiel Offensive. The first phase (Preparation) included "maximum photographic reconnaissance" and night observation missions when enemy forces were suspected of being on the move after sundown. The second phase (Night Preceding the Attack) did not involve specific observation missions other than the night flights of the Preparation phase. Night bombardment squadrons were designated for missions throughout the night. The third phase (Day of the Attack) and the fourth phase (Exploitation) involved the full range of day missions assigned to observation squadrons. Night missions of the 9th Aero squadron continued after the first day of the attack.[19]

Pursuit squadrons received similar instructions. However, their missions included special emphasis on the fact that although their primary objective in the offensive was to "search out enemy aircraft, and attack them with the object of causing maximum casualties and inflicting the greatest possible damage to his air Service and with a further object of obtaining a definite moral superiority," they also held a very important secondary responsibility "to place Corps Observation Aviation in a position where it will be and will feel that it is protected."[20] However, the pursuit squadrons operated under a 15 kilometer limit for their operations while many reconnaissance targets of the observation squadrons were farther than 15 kilometers from the front lines. This placed an immediate constraint on protection for the observation squadrons even before the offensive commenced. First Pursuit Wing authorized its aircraft to escort observation planes up to the 15 kilometer limit and meet them there upon return, but the observation crews would be on their own while performing assigned missions beyond the point. Aerial protection fell upon sending multiple aircraft or flying alone.[21]

Each division issued its own set of more detailed instructions for the observation squadron assigned to it. As an example, which shows expanded missions, the 5th Division issued the following Operations Order Annex segment to the 12th Aero Squadron:

The 12th Aero Squadron (18 planes-Aerodrome: Toul) is assigned to the 5th Division for all aviation duties. This squadron will be charged with the following: Visual reconnaissance. Surveillance. Infantry contact patrols. Adjustment and control of fire of divisional Artillery, Alert planes for special missions, Photographic missions required by the 1st Army Corps, Protection of tanks from hostile aeroplane. Position of front line troops will be staked out when called for by aeroplanes. A dropping ground will be established near each P. C., (exact location designated later) where panels may be displayed for signalling to aeroplanes. The Division liaison officer will provide teams of special observers at the dropping ground to watch for aeroplane signals and a relay of runners to deliver messages to the Division P. C. The aero squadron will keep 2 planes constantly on the alert from 112 hour before dawn throughout the hours of daylight, and will receive its orders direct from the Division Commander by telephone, radio or special courier or through the Chief of the Aviation Service, 1st Army Corp . . . Planes returning from missions of any kind will drop messages, giving full reports of the results of their missions, at the Division P. C. The squadron will keep a surveillance plane constantly over the divisional sector of attack throughout the hours of daylight, and will be in continual communication by radio with the division P. C., and the artillery battalion assigned for fugitive targets. division artillery commander.[22]

Further instructions included details for plane-infantry communications including the meaning behind white-panel combinations laid upon the ground for observation aircraft to see; three-letter radio telegraphy codes for the airplanes to send to ground stations; and signaling flares, simply called "fireworks," in the operations orders. An example of the 12th Aero squadron's fireworks signals (carried in the observer's area) and their meanings as assigned by the 5th Division is as follows:

Signals Made by Infantry Aeroplane (by fireworks)

I am the Aeroplane of Right Division	1 cartridge of one star
I am the Aeroplane of the 5th Division	2 cartridges each of two stars
I am the Aeroplane of the left Division	2 cartridges each of 1 star
Where are you (call for marking out line)	1 cartridge of six stars
Understood	1 cartridge of three stars
Threatened counter attack in my direction	1 caterpillar
Anti-tank gun at this point	Yellow smoke[23]

Gen. Pershing wanted to launch the offensive before the middle of September or earlier, if possible, because of the coming rainy season in the area, which would turn the terrain to mud and delay movement of the army. At the same time, the Germans were under pressure to adjust the existing front lines because of the large number of casualties from the three spring offensives. By September 9, a date of September 12 had been set for the opening of the offensive. On the other side, the Germans had already begun the initial stages to shorten their lines when the Americans (550,000) and French (110,000) attacked. The AES observation squadrons were allocated to Army and Corps elements as First Army (24th and 91st), I Corps (1st, 12th, and 50th), IV Corps (8th, 90th, and 135th), V Corps (88th, 99th, and 104th), and the French Night Bombardment Group (9th). Not only did the Americans and French outnumber the Germans in the St. Mihiel area but they far exceeded the number of German aircraft. In terms of just observation aircraft, the Germans operated approximately 120 planes in the area at the time of the offensive, and the Americans alone could place approximately 233 observation aircraft in the opening of the attack.

Information on the ground offensive will be seen across the following pages of this chapter while our primary examination moves into a day-by-day look at the work of the American observation squadrons. Each squadron established a daily flight schedule beginning with the opening of the offensive on September 12, which set takeoff intervals in order to relieve air crews and keep planes in the air for each particular mission. An example can be seen with the 90th Aero Squadron's September 12 schedule that covered the first quarter of the morning:

Headquarters 90th Aero Squadron
Observation Group-Fourth Army Corps
September 12, 1918
Infantry Contact Planes
(Equip each of these planes with one streamer on each wing).

Observer	Pilot	Plane No.	Time
Lt. Vinson, F. L.	Lt. Rohrer, L.E.	16	5:20
Lt. Loew, W. O.	Lt. Kinsley, W. E.	10	6:00
Lt. Shuss, P. B.	Lt. Livingston, J. W.	2	7:00
Lt. Sherrick, J. C.	Lt. White, M. O.	1	8:00

Reserve Lt. Neidecker, B. C. (Reserve pilot must be on field from 4:30 and plane ready).

Artillery or Counter Attack Planes

Lt. Walden, D. M.	Lt. Lee, M. G.	15	5:20
Lt. Sullivan, A. P.	Lt. Bovard, J. M. 1	1	7:00
Lt. Bogle, H. C.	Lt. Young, J. S.	19	6:00
Lt. Hayden, V. B.	Lt. Pierson, N. E.	14	8:00

(Reserve planes (c) and (d).)
(Equip planes 15-19-11 and 14 with two message containers.)

Command Planes

Lt. Francis, W. L.	Lt. Cowle, H. H.	3	5:00
Lt. Lake, H. A.	Lt. Conover, Harvey	4	5:20
Lt. Dorrance, G. M.		6	5:20

Reserve Artillery Plane

Lt. Parr, A. E.	Lt. Pike, G. M.	17	

Photographic Plane

Lt. Lindstrom, G. T.	Lt. Carver, Leland	12	

Lt. Broomfield will be in charge of the field and will report to Lieut. Gallop for instructions.

All Pilots not on the above schedule will be on the field ready to fly.

Observers will be at Group Headquarters excepting while on a mission and one half hour prior to time scheduled for departure.

By order of Lt. Gallop
Morton B. Adams, 1st Lt. Chief Observer[24]

Each of the observation squadrons launched aircraft on a similar type of schedule as reported by the 90th Aero Squadron. Reports began as the air crews made contact with the troops on the ground, generally via radio telegraph from the former and via white panels from the latter. Reports of casualties in the air also began to arrive. The 27th Aero Squadron (Pursuit) prepared a report from one of its pilots, Lt. Leo Dawson, who departed the airfield at 7:50 a.m. Upon his return, Dawson's report included the note, "Was fired at by machine guns and fired good bursts from both guns at troops on ground. I then turned and started out. Noticed a Salmson with American Cocardes on ground right side up. North east of Mihiel." This could be the first confirmed report of a downed American observation aircraft during the St. Mihiel offensive.

The coming rains that troubled Gen. Pershing's planning began just prior to the offensive. Rain during the night before the attack kept the 9th Aero Squadron on the ground and prevented them from conducting any night reconnaissance flights immediately before the artillery barrage.[25] The 24th Aero Squadron (First Army) launched one reconnaissance sortie in the morning rain while the 9th Aero Squadron (First Army) conducted seven visual reconnaissance and one message delivery sorties during the first day. They also reported scattered showers and poor visibility.[26] The corps-level observation squadrons flew numerous missions in support of the advancing divisions. For example, the 1st Aero Squadron (I Corps) flew two visual reconnaissance, two photographic, two artillery support, four infantry contact, and one unexplained general reconnaissance sorties on the first day. One of the photography missions collected ten pictures before being driven from the area by four attacking German pursuit planes. The other photography sortie returned early with only five pictures, due to the lack of visibility caused by rain. The general reconnaissance aircraft returned from its mission, but the Germans downed one of their two escorting pursuit planes. One of the infantry contact air crews reported difficulty finding their assigned American ground force because the troops had not been displaying their recognition panels. However, the crew noted they did fire upon German soldiers on horses and unsuccessfully chased a German two-seat observation plane. Another infantry contact mission ended early due to mechanical issues with the aircraft.[27]

50th Aero Squadron de Havilland DH-4

The observation squadrons assigned to I Corps lost four aircraft during the first day of the St. Mihiel offensive. German aircraft downed two planes of the 12th Aero Squadron within less than two hours. The first went down within Entente lines at 10:00 a.m. and might have been the plane spotted by the 27th Aero Squadron (pursuit) pilot during his patrol. Four German planes jumped the observation crew and shot down the plane, wounding the observer, which then crash-landed. The 12th Aero Squadron lost their second plane at 12:10 a.m. A German formation damaged the plane, forcing the pilot to land within Entente lines without casualties. The 50th Aero Squadron lost an aircraft, which did not return after a mission. The fourth plane (squadron not identified) crashed after a fight with German planes.

The pilot reported being lost in a rain storm and then being ambushed by multiple German fighters. The observation plane crashed after receiving substantial damage and caught fire upon hitting the ground. The pilot survived but with wounds and burns. Later that day, the observer had not yet been found. The 12th Aero Squadron reported that an aircraft was damaged in a duel with German pursuit planes, a wing and the fuel tank having been pierced by bullets. The pilot managed to bring the plane back safely despite the attack.[28]

Lt. Horace W. Mitchell, a pilot in the 8th Aero Squadron, flew with Lt. John W. Artz as his observer on the first day of operations. Mitchell noted an overwhelming number of Entente pursuit aircraft that morning. He later wrote, "Ours was the only plane on the expedition. The sky was full of Allied planes, so we needed no protectors. Our machine was a D.H.4. It was a very windy, rainy day." However, the Germans downed his aircraft with their "archie" batteries. In late November 1918, he wrote:

The wind was blowing from the southwest and was so strong that in a few minutes we were blown across the Moselle, where we were heavily "Archied." To get away from the Archies it was necessary to fly with the wind, and after getting away I turned a half north to recross the Moselle and come back over the battlefield to Beaumont. We were attacked by three German planes, two Fokkers and a Rumpler. In the fight that followed my front guns and motor were disabled and the observer slightly wounded. As we were only at an altitude of 2,000 feet and were flying behind the lines it was impossible to get back with the motor disabled. Therefore I landed. We were taken prisoners by German soldiers.[29]

Lt. Artz, wounded in the attack and crash, added the following details:

In the afternoon of September 12, 1918 while flying over the enemy's lines east of St. Mihiel, in the performance of my duty as an Aerial Observer, our airplane (D.H.4 Liberty) was attacked by several German airplanes. During the engagement, our engine was disabled, forcing us to land about twelve kilometers inside the German lines, near a village. The enemy continued firing until our plane had stopped moving on the ground and we were out of it. I received a flesh wound, during the attack. The pilot and I were immediately taken prisoners, searched, examined, my wound field dressed, and later in the afternoon we were taken to St. Avold.[30]

The V Corps Observation Group filed a very different "end of day" report due to two of its three observation squadrons being unable to conduct combat support missions on the first day of the attack. The 88th Aero Squadron had just been transferred from III Corps and had not arrived and established itself for operations yet. The 104th Aero Squadron was not able to transfer all of its aircraft and air crew to its assigned airfield for operations. A few had arrived by September 12, and they flew with the 88th and 99th Aero Squadrons.

The headquarters for the AES released the following summary of reconnaissance missions at 7:00 p.m. of September 12 (covering all operations the night of the eleventh and day of the twelfth):

Observation. Many successful visual reconnaissances were carried out during the course of the day. Information of the progress of the attack was reported regularly in spite of the adverse weather conditions which necessitated low liaison through the barrage. Accurate location of the front line was obtained. Reconnaissances of the 1st and 4th Corps located large convoys of enemy artillery and regulated fire of our artillery which inflicted material damage. A special mission in the region of Limey-Bouillonville-Thiaucourt was made by the Corps Observation Wing Commander (Major Brereton) with Captain Valois (Liaison Officer) as observer. Many observations of the progress of the attack were made. The information gained enabled the Wing Commander to employ his Wing very successfully in later reconnaissances. While maneuvering over Thiaucourt they were attacked by four Fokker E.A.'s. The jamming of the observer's gun forced them to land. The machine was crashed by striking wire entanglements. The Heavy Artillery Observation made twelve sorties for the adjustment of fire in the East Moselle Grouping. There were combats and two pilots and two observers are missing. The adjustments were not carried out.[31]

Maj. Brereton (retired in 1948 with the rank of lieutenant general, and he reappears in the next chapter) received the Distinguished Service Cross for his actions on September 12, as mentioned in the AES daily report. His citation reads:

General Orders: War Department, General Orders No. 15 (1919)
Action Date: 12 September 1918
Service: Army Air Service
Rank: Major
Unit: Corps Observation Wing, American Expeditionary Forces

Citation: The President of the United States of America, authorized by Act of Congress, July 9, 1918, takes pleasure in presenting the Distinguished Service Cross to Major (Air Service) Lewis Hyde Brereton (ASN: 0–3132), for extraordinary heroism in action while serving with Corps Observation Wing, Air Service, A.E.F., over Thiaucourt, France, 12 September 1918. Major Brereton, together with an observer, voluntarily and pursuant to a request for special mission, left his airdrome, crossed the enemy lines over Lironville, and proceeded to Thiaucourt. In spite of poor visibility, which forced them to fly at a very low altitude, and in spite of intense and accurate anti-aircraft fire they maintained their flight along their course and obtained valuable information. Over Thiaucourt they were suddenly attacked by four enemy monoplane Fokkers. Maneuvering his machine so that his observer could obtain a good field of fire, he entered into combat. His observer's guns became jammed, he withdrew until the jam was cleared, when he returned to the combat. His observer then becoming wounded, he coolly made a landing within friendly lines, although followed down by the enemy to within 25 meters of the ground. By this act he made himself an inspiration and example to all the members of his command.[32]

Lt. Dogan "Hump" Arthur and his observer/gunner Lt. Howard Fleeson, both assigned to the 12th Aero Squadron, also received the Distinguished Service Cross for shooting down their first German plane on the opening day of the offensive:

The President of the United States of America, authorized by Act of Congress, July 9, 1918, takes pleasure in presenting the Distinguished Service Cross to Captain (Air Service) Dogan H. Arthur, United States Army Air Service, for extraordinary heroism in action while serving with 12th Aero Squadron, US Army Air Service, A.E.F., in the St. Mihiel salient 12 September 1918. Lieutenant Arthur, pilot, and Second Lieutenant

Howard T. Fleeson, observer, executed a difficult mission of infantry contact patrol, without protection of accompanying battle planes, on the first day of the St. Mihiel offensive. After being driven back twice by a patrol of nine enemy planes, they courageously made a third attempt in the face of a third attack by the same planes, found the American lines, and after being shot down, but falling uninjured in friendly territory, communicated their valuable information to headquarters.[33]

Gen. Pershing ordered the Entente forces to push forward on September 13 after learning that at least two German divisions were moving to extract themselves from the already threatened salient. His aims included closing the salient to retreating German units and keeping his army ready to change missions and support the Meuse-Argonne Offensive, which was commencing in two weeks. Each observation squadron published a new roster and schedule for the second day of operations. The day's actions can be viewed in the end of day operations reports:

The 27th Aero Squadron

Pursuit squadron pilots reported their observation of the battlefield as they conducted their missions. Their information served as an additional resource to those already collected by the observation squadrons. One interesting example occurred on September 13, when 94th Aero Squadron (pursuit) pilot Eddie Rickenbacker (the leading American ace at the end of World War I, with twenty-six aerial victories credited to him) filed a report to his squadron, which was then forwarded as:

Time out: 9 h 50
Time in: 11 h 09
Max. Altitude: 300 m.
Mission: Vol. Patrol.
Weather: Poor.
Pilot: Lieut. Rickenbacker, P.L., Chambers.
· Lt. Rickenbacker Reports: Went up the lines from Vigneulles to Fresnes. Found American and French advance troops at Wadonville, Avillers and St. Benoit. I noticed French and American camions at the crest of the hills along the main road. I noticed about 500 Boche prisoners being marched back on the road from Hattonchatel by American soldiers. No new towns on fire in this section.
Lt. Chambers Reports: Same as observed by Lt. Rickenbacker.[34]

Three other American observation crews shot down German fighters during their missions on the first day of the offensive. The crews were lieutenants Wallace Coleman and Joseph Nathan; lieutenants John Curtin and Percival Hart; and Lt. George Ream with Lt. Joseph Nathan for the latter's second kill of the day as a pilot. All five of these officers flew with the 135th Aero Squadron. A single German fighter attacked Coleman and Nathan at approximately 9:30 a.m. and the latter utilized the observer's machine gun to bring it down. Nathan's second victory of the day occurred with Ream. The observer later wrote:

Having accomplished our mission we turned toward home, and just over Thiaucourt we were attacked from the clouds in front of and above us, by a formation of seven Fokkers. Having missed getting us in their first burst of fire as they dived, the whole formation turned and followed us for about six kilometres or more, being at no time more than 150 metres from us, and keeping up a steady fire. I fired more than 350 rounds from my guns and saw one of the leading planes go down in a nose dive. Finally when we were south of Flirely they left us. Our plane was pretty badly shot up, but neither of us was touched.[35]

Alas, the fog of war prevailed when Ream later claimed in the squadron the German plane fell to his forward machine guns. One can note that in the end, the combined efforts of both men resulted in the loss of a German fighter and the safe return of the observation crew. Hart later wrote a book on the squadron, in which he detailed the events leading to the destruction of the German fighter with Curtin as his observer.

Passing over Flirey they were attacked by a single Fokker, which dove on their tail. While Curtin maneuvered to keep Hart in a good position to continue firing his tracer bullets into the Hun plane's nose, six more Fokkers appeared at a higher level and dove to join the fight, just as the first Fokker fell, apparently out of control. Answering his observer's frantic signals to get going south in a hurry, Curtin dove with his motor full on and managed to increase the distance between his plane and the Boches until the latter turned north again, where they ran into a flight of six Spads. A dogfight ensued in which two of the American planes fell in flames, and the others broke off the engagement.[36]

The 135th Aero Squadron lost three aircraft on this first day of the offensive. Four crew members died in crashes, and two, lieutenants Fuller Landon and Brookhart, made an emergency landing in a field that they soon discovered was in Switzerland and not France. The pair were lost due to the poor weather that day. They spotted a small pasture adjacent to a small town and landed to determine their location. The area looked quite peaceful, without military activity, so they figured they were fairly southwest of the front lines. Farmers in the field informed the crew they were in Switzerland and that France was a five-minute drive by car. The two Americans quickly took off again, only to have their engine malfunction at 2,000 feet of altitude. Attempts to restart the engine failed, so Landon opted to set the plane down in another field below him. They soon discovered they had landed about a half mile inside Switzerland. Swiss soldiers approached the pair, and they learned why their engine had malfunctioned:

Some of the soldiers talked English and told us they had fired about four hundred rounds at us. It was the first we knew of it, so we began looking for results, and found that one bullet had gone through the water jacket and that all the water was gone. One went through my seat, but I could find no holes in my clothes. . . . The Swiss soldiers were very good to us, also the Swiss people.[37]

Landon and Brookhart were interned in Switzerland under liberal parole conditions until the end of the war in November.

Other observation squadrons experienced tough German opposition on the opening of the offensive as well. Lieutenants Young (pilot) and Bogle (observer) of the 90th Aero Squadron were forced to fly at approximately 50 meters in altitude due to the poor weather and challenges to their observation efforts. A German machine gun hit their radiator, resulting in a drop in height. The wheels nearly touched the ground, and German troops were exiting their positions in anticipation of capturing the crew. Young managed to keep his plane airborne and brought it down just behind the advancing American forces. In a bit of irony, they were able to provide their observation results directly to the troops on the ground upon landing and then headed toward the rear area before catching a ride on a vehicle. Bogle returned to the air later that day as the observer in another 90th Aero Squadron aircraft.[38] Some losses were mysteries at the time. A crew would depart the airfield and not return. The 50th Aero Squadron dispatched lieutenants Henry Stevens (pilot) and Edward Gardiner (observer) on a mission from which they did not return. The German Red Cross later reported that both men were dead. Speculation among the aircrews included the bad weather and winds as the likely culprits.[39]

24th Aero Squadron observer with camera in a Salmson 2A2

September 13

Weather conditions proved rainy and windy again on September 13, making flying, let alone observation, challenging. The 9th Aero Squadron (night) finally completed one reconnaissance sortie, which resulted in nothing to report during the night of September 12–13. Not only did the night observation squadron face the restrictions in visibility of night flying but the weather conditions hampered operations also. Daylight operations also faced restrictions in operations because of the weather. The 24th Aero Squadron, flying for 1st Army, did not fly any combat missions in support of Army assets. In addition, eleven of their twenty-two Salmson aircraft were grounded due to repair needs. In contrast to other areas, the squadron noted good visibility all day. They flew nine sorties for the day, but all were listed as test flights.[40]

I Corps Observation units faced poor visibility and rain throughout the day. The 1st Aero Squadron flew six sorties with two aircraft conducting reconnaissance missions, one for infantry contact, and three providing protection. One Salmson of the 1st Aero Squadron, flying with two other Salmsons for protection, returned without completing its reconnaissance mission due to the rain and low clouds, which obscured visibility of its assigned area. The infantry contact mission with the 2nd Infantry Division proved successful, with ground troops properly displaying panels for communication with the aircraft, which were then able to drop a message for them.[41] The 12th Aero Squadron conducted seven sorties with three planes designated for reconnaissance itself and the other four flying protection. One of the Salmsons providing aerial protection for this mission encountered problems and landed near Viéville-en-Haye. The second flight successfully completed its mission while the third group (one reconnaissance Salmson and one providing protection) encountered six German planes. The German fighters forced the reconnaissance Salmson to land near Pont-à-Mousson to avoid being shot down.[42] The 50th Aero Squadron reported seven sorties for the day. Five conducted reconnaissance and two made unsuccessful infantry contact flights. In both of the latter missions, personnel of the 90th Infantry Division would not display their identification and communication panels. One of the reconnaissance aircraft made a forced landing after encountering accurate German ground machine gun fire wounding the observer, Lieutenant Bellows, north of Pont-à-Mousson. Bellows died before his pilot, Lt. Morse, could return to their home field for medical assistance.[43]

V Corps observation squadrons encountered the same weather challenges as those of I Corps. The 99th Aero Squadron flew eight reconnaissance and one infantry contact missions throughout the day. Over half of these flew in rainy and/or cloudy conditions, restricting their visibility. The squadron reports do not indicate whether any of these flights were specifically designated for fighter protection.[44] The 104th Aero Squadron assumed flying duties with the Corps itself, and a detachment of the 88th Aero Squadron flew in support of the 26th Division. An interesting sample of the September 13 Summary of Reports for the 104th follows:

Lt. Reynolds, pilot, and Lt. Polley, observer, made reconnaissance of Rupt, Vigneulles, St. Benoit, Woel, Doncourt, and Combres. No enemy troops found. Many fires and explosions reported. Lt. Weeks, pilot, and Lt. Northup, observer, made reconnaissance of Corps front, nothing to report. Weather throughout the day was generally poor for observation work. Rain and low hanging clouds being very often encountered. No news of Lt. Johnston, missing since previous day. Lt. French and Vowles arrived from Luxeuil. On this day, Friday the thirteenth, the Squadron first operated as a separate unit over the front.[45]

Identification of the 88th Aero Squadron Operations Report for September 13 required a bit of investigation. The 88th also flew as part of the V Corps Observation Group. The officer who prepared the report forgot to include the squadron identification number in the document. Tracing the names of the air crews led the way for locating the document with names that matched the roster. The 88th Aero Squadron document records three reconnaissance missions and one infantry contact mission. During the latter flight, the infantry did not display their identification and communication panels. As with other squadrons, the poor weather prevented artillery support operations. During one flight, Lt. Philip Babcock encountered a German Halberstadt aircraft near Vigneuelles. The Halberstadt was a two-seat plane developed as a bomber and an escort fighter. In the hands of a good pilot, the plane could be highly maneuverable and an excellent scrapper against single-seat pursuit fighters. Lt. Babcock engaged the Halberstadt he encountered and fired eighteen rounds with the forward fuselage machine gun. He did not report any hits, and the German pilot did not accept combat, flying into the clouds to make an escape from the area.[46] Babcock piloted one of the four 88th Aero Squadron planes ambushed in the dogfight by twelve German fighters on August 11, as recorded earlier in this chapter.

The IV Corps Observation Group daily report is not immediately available for research but can be assembled from the consolidated report of First Army:

> Observation. In spite of extremely low clouds a great number of visual reconnaissance missions were made by all branches of Observation. The First Army Observation Group carried out twenty reconnaissance missions far back in the enemy lines, bringing back very important information concerning the direction and intensity of the enemy's movements. Only one enemy plane was encountered by the Army Observation Group in the course of the day, and that occurred over Metz at 15:30 when a single Fokker attempted to force the mission back over the lines. This enemy plane was shot down just south of Metz. Corps Observation performed a great number of infantry liaison patrols establishing the location of our advancing front lines during the entire course of the day. Accurate location was also given of a number of very important enemy targets, including convoys of enemy artillery, troop concentrations, ammunition dumps and machine-gun nests. A special mission by the 4th Corps Observation Group at 13:30 returned with important information concerning the Hindenburg line. This mission was made at an altitude of only 100 meters, but in spite of extremely active anti-aircraft fire, completed its mission, and returned unmolested by enemy aircraft. The 4th Corps made a great number of successful reconnaissance missions returning with valuable information concerning the movement of enemy troops and trains, also located our advancing front lines by means of infantry panels. This mission was also successful in locating a number of enemy batteries. A special mission by Command Airplanes was made over the front lines, and brought back tactical information of importance to the Army Command.[47]

Apparently, the German plane noted as having been shot down was not verified by a second source. Victory records from World War I do not credit any of the observation squadrons with a confirmed kill of a German plane on September 13.

Corps level reporting added more detail to the 50th Aero Squadron loss of Bellows noted earlier. Pilot Lt. Dave Beebe, with observer Lt. Franklin Bellows, received a long-distance mission. Beebe needed to keep the plane at a low altitude to avoid very poor weather conditions, which in turn provided a German machine gunner the opportunity to put a few rounds into the aircraft and strike Bellows.

September 14

The Allied forces achieved the main objectives of the St. Mihiel Offensive on September 13, after two days of fighting. Weather conditions for September 14 were cloudy but better in most areas than they had been the first two days. The next three days entailed consolidation of their positions as the German troops continued to withdraw. Observer air operations mirrored the first two days of the offensive. The 9th Aero Squadron conducted one day and one night reconnaissance operation.[48] The 24th Aero Squadron flew one reconnaissance, three protective, and one special flight for First Army.[49]

The observation squadrons in First Corps were more active, with having the infantry divisions to assist. The 12th Aero Squadron suffered a tragic accident when a plane returning from a reconnaissance mission struck the cable of an observation balloon. Both the pilot and observer died in the crash.[50] The V Corps area remained hot for the observation crews who encountered numerous German fighters, resulting in casualties for the 99th Aero Squadron during two photographic missions about 10 kilometers behind German lines as reported by the Corps aviation group:

1. During the day the two photographic missions with a total of nine planes were dispatched. At ten o'clock a photographic mission of the corps area from Harville to Lachaussee was undertaken by Observer Lt. Hill and Pilot Lt. Kahle of the 99th Aero Squadron. This plane was attacked by from three to five enemy planes over Lachaussee and in the combat Lt. Hill was killed, a bullet piercing his heart. Lt. Kahle succeeded in bringing the plane back to the field. Although the photo magazine was badly damaged by gun fire thirteen good photos were obtained. A protection plane for this mission, Pilot Lt. Edwards, Observer Lt. Davis, was also attacked and was forced to land. Plane was slightly damaged by machine gun fire. Pilot and Observer were uninjured.

2. A second photographic mission, Pilot Lt. Markam and Observer Lt. Nee1 of the 99th Aero Squadron, took off at twelve o'clock and photographed the region immediately in advance of the Corps area. This mission was protected by a formation of four Salmson planes. They were attacked by two different enemy patrols during which a general defensive fight occurred. Lt. Neel fired three hundred rounds at a Fokker triplane scout and believes he succeeded in shooting it down. This happened at 1300 o'clock over Chambley and confirmation is requested. Protection plane from the 88th Aero Squadron, Pilot Captain Littauer and Observer Lt. Boyd, was also attacked. The Observer was seriously wounded in foot and elbow and plane was forced to land within our own lines. Seventeen good photographs were taken.[51]

91st Aero Squadron Salmson 2A2. Note the forward machine gun on the nose of the aircraft and the twin guns mounted at the observer's cockpit.

At least three teams of 91st Aero Squadron crews engaged in dogfights with German fighters. Although American observation squadron aircraft did not shoot down any German planes on September 14, the German army reminded the 91st Aero Squadron that it could still pack a punch with antiaircraft artillery. However, the 91st Aero Squadron apparently did not inform them of the arrival of a green pilot named Lt. Paul Coles. German guns downed lieutenants Paul Hughey and Kenyo Roper in the early morning of the fourteenth. Later that morning, Coles flew his first combat mission across the lines, and the German gunners were waiting for him. George Kenney, the future World War II commander of the 5th Air Force in the Pacific, describes best what happened to Coles:

> The antis [antiaircraft guns] on this day gave one of the new men, Coles, a chance to distinguish himself. One of the Archie bursts tore off half of both lower Wings, but although the ship became almost unmanageable. Coles succeeding in bringing it back to the field and making a good landing. For his first trip over the lines his coolness was remarkable, his first words on landing being, "How long will it take to put on another pair of wings? 1 like to fly that boat, she handles so well."[52]

September 15

Allied forces continued to consolidate and strengthen their positions on the fifteenth. German troops still resisted but maintained a withdrawal toward a new defensive system, often known as the Hindenburg Line. I and V Corps observation squadrons maintained a busy schedule. The 91st Aero Squadron conducted numerous photographic missions near the Hindenburg Line on the fifteenth and sixteenth. Visibility improved for the air crews, and a number of missions were flown, with most being general reconnaissance, although the 208th Aero Squadron conducted as many artillery missions as reconnaissance that day. The 104th Aero Squadron lost a plane and pilot when hit by German antiaircraft fire after becoming separated from a group of 99th Aero Squadron aircraft. The observer survived the crash and was located by French soldiers.[53]

The five days of the St. Mihiel Offensive permitted a day-by-day brief examination of the observation activities of the American squadrons during a set military operation. The Meuse-Argonne Offensive lasted for approximately seven weeks. The missions of the observation squadrons in the latter offensive mirrored the missions during the St. Mihiel salient push. Again the observation crews performed visual reconnaissance, photography, infantry contact and liaison, and artillery observation duties. The United States Center for Military History views the Meuse-Argonne Offensive as a series of phases. This chapter will briefly cover each phase and the highlights of some observation missions during each of them.[54]

Meuse-Argonne Offensive

Initial Phase of the Battle: September 26–October 4, 1918

The first week of the offensive demonstrated the weaknesses in the American forces. While some more veteran divisions performed well in the short St. Mihiel Offensive, there were many untested divisions and an entirely new Army level formation (Second Army) in the field. Many units stumbled in their first combat experience—logistics proved challenging, and overall coordination of units at the army and corps levels were not as effective as required for a major military operation. The AES was not an exception to these issues. There were many new observation squadrons without prolonged combat experience, and coordination with the infantry divisions could be difficult. Some infantry units did not receive instruction in communication with the infantry liaison aircraft assigned to provide their reconnaissance and support. At the opening of the offensive on September 26, the veteran 90th Aero Squadron performed reconnaissance duties for two divisions of the American III Corps' 80th Division (until October 11) and the 33rd Division (until October 22). Based on the shifting of the infantry divisions from forward to rear (for reorganization), the observation squadrons were assigned to different units for the duration of the offensive. This could be problematic since, once the squadron had developed a good working relationship related to air-to-ground communication, it could find itself with a totally new division, and the process would begin again. Over the course of these seven weeks, the 90th Aero Squadron switched to support the 50th, 90th, and 79th American Divisions as well as the 17th French Corps. Rarely did the 90th Aero Squadron support the same division for more than two weeks before being assigned to another division or two. To compensate, the 90th Aero Squadron established a liaison school system:

> During this time the closest possible relations were maintained between the Squadron and the Divisions with which it was working, by the Squadron's liaison officers maintained at Divisional Headquarters. This was an experiment never tried before September 12, and was to improve the understanding between the Aviation and the Line. It had been found that line officers did not understand the nature of aerial work, and that communication between Divisions and their supporting Squadrons was often too slow. Lieutenant Frances and Lieutenant Vinson eventually became our liaison officers. They remained constantly at the Headquarters of the Divisions with which we were working, reporting daily to the Squadron Operations Officer by telephone, and rendered invaluable aid in maintaining close relations between the units. The 3rd Corps Group at the same time established a Liaison School for the officers of the Divisions with which it was working. Detachments from the 5th, 33rd, and 90th Divisions, each of about two hundred men and several officers, spent in turn several days with the group, the officers being entertained by the 90th Squadron during their stay. The training was doubtless of value and the intimacy which grew up between the men on the ground and the men in the air certainly increased the interest each took in the work of the other.[55]

The 50th Aero Squadron experienced similar coordination problems with the 77th Infantry Division. Lieutenants McCook (pilot) and Lockwood (observer) encountered stiff German machine gun fire on September 28. They were hit along the front lines, but both men survived the crash landing. The pair evaded German soldiers attempting to apprehend them and eventually encountered a French officer, who turned them over to a group of American soldiers. As the officer escorted the air crew to their headquarters, a conversation ensued about air to ground communication. The air crew were shocked to learn that these soldiers had not received any instruction in the recognition and use of the basic signals (panels and flares) to communicate their positions to American observation aircraft.[56]

George Kenney wrote about these coordination issues at the end of the war:

> The record point of note is one recognized as a constant difficulty—the matter of receiving proper panels or flares from the infantry front lines in reply to the observer's request by rocket. The repeated failure of the infantry to cooperate cannot always be visited upon them, because of their many and more immediate "troubles" during a hard attack, but it is to be pointed out that when reading a summary of "successful" or "unsuccessful" missions due allowance should be made for this difficulty when judging infantry contact work. Directly from this consideration the third point of note logically follows—that is, the altitudes at which the missions were flown. Repeated attempts to locate our front

line by means of flares or panels—attempts during which, for example, Lieutenant Bird, pilot, with Rogers, observer, flew their entire mission at under 900 feet—necessitated, later in the day, a sortie by Lieutenant Graham, pilot, and Lieutenant McCurdy, observer, with the particular determination to find the line by some other means. This mission they accomplished at considerable risk by flying under 500 feet, often at treetop level, and actually identifying various points and position by seeing the uniforms of the infantry—thus establishing an approximation of a continuous line.[57]

91st Aero Squadron Salmson 2A2

Reorganizing While in Contact: October 1–4, 1918

Gen. Pershing utilized this four-day period to reorganize his forces and shift the more experienced divisions that were still recovering from the St. Mihiel Offensive forward. The AEF missed their projected objective timeline with many of the divisions bogged down in the advance. The 77th Division was not an exception. The Division slogged its way slowly through the Argonne Forest during the first week of the offensive. It was during this period that one of the most well-known AEF incidents from the war occurred.

The 77th Division's Maj. Charles Whittlesey's reinforced battalion followed the division commander's orders and pushed forward into the German lines deep in the Argonne Forest with little concern for his flanks. However, the units watching his flanks did not make it as far as Whittlesey before halting from resistance. The Germans surrounded the unit on October 2, and they later became known by the term "the Lost Battalion." Although the unit dispatched a pigeon with its approximate map coordinates, Whittlesey presented the wrong location, preventing anyone from being able to find them. They remained surrounded for days as they awaited relief that was not coming. At times, American artillery dropped on their positions not knowing a friendly unit lay at those particular coordinates. They were short of food, water, and ammunition. Then the AES arrived.

The 77th Division requested aircraft to search for the missing unit on October 4. Aircraft were not able to spot the Americans based on the last reported coordinates of the battalion. On October 6, the 50th Aero Squadron attempted a new strategy. They would carry supplies in the aircraft and drop them along a ravine that ran through the incorrectly reported area:

Consequently, at slightly before noon, Lieutenant Pickrell, pilot, with Lieutenant George, observer, left the field to drop supplies. These supplies consisted, in each case of ammunition, food and medical supplies, together with what chocolate we could find. From noon on a continuous series of flights was kept in progress until dark, dropping considerable quantities of these supplies, and in addition two baskets of carrier pigeons. To insure a fairly "soft landing" for the imprisoned birds, a number of parachutes taken from parachute flares were fastened to each basket—about eight to each—and were seen to open up and act with surprising efficiency.[58]

Lt. Harold Goettler of the 50th Aero Squadron. Goettler and his observer, Lt. Erwin Bleckley, received Medals of Honor for their efforts to aid the "Lost Battalion" of the 77th Division.

Once, the unit had been located via the release of more carrier pigeons. The 50th Aero Squadron planned more deliveries of supplies to the new area that was indicated by the pigeons' messages. Three aircraft were shot down in their attempts to actually spot the Americans and deliver supplies. During these actions, a crew perished and received the only Medals of Honor awarded to AES observation crews during World War I. Their citations speak for the action themselves:

Citation: 1st. Lt. Goettler, with his observer, 2d Lt. Erwin R. Bleckley, 130th Field Artillery, left the airdrome late in the afternoon on their second trip to drop supplies to a battalion of the 77th Division which had been cut off by the enemy in the Argonne Forest. Having been subjected on the first trip to violent fire from the enemy, they attempted on the second trip to come still lower in order to get the packages even more precisely on the designated spot. In the course of this mission the plane was brought down by enemy rifle and machine gun fire from the ground, resulting in the instant death of 1st. Lt. Goettler. In attempting and performing this mission 1st. Lt. Goettler showed the highest possible contempt of personal danger, devotion to duty, courage and valor.

Citation: 2d Lt. Bleckley, with his pilot, 1st Lt. Harold E. Goettler, Air Service, left the airdrome late in the afternoon on their second trip to drop supplies to a battalion of the 77th Division, which had been cut off by the enemy in the Argonne Forest.

Having been subjected on the first trip to violent fire from the enemy, they attempted on the second trip to come still lower in order to get the packages even more precisely on the designated spot. In the course of his mission the plane was brought down by enemy rifle and machine gun fire from the ground, resulting in fatal wounds to 2d Lt. Bleckley, who died before he could be taken to a hospital. In attempting and performing this mission 2d Lt. Bleckley showed the highest possible contempt of personal danger, devotion to duty, courage, and valor.[59]

The Attack Resumes: October 4–16, 1918

Gen. Pershing renewed the attack on October 4, under considerable pressure from the French. Sgt. Alvin York of the 82nd Division achieved his Medal of Honor during this phase by capturing 132 German soldiers and neutralizing thirty-five German machine guns holding the advance of his division. After a week the offensive stalled again. A French Corps attacked on the east side of the Meuse River to provide some relief to American units. This time, Pershing reorganized the structure of First Army and established two smaller Army-sized units under his overall command of the AEF. This resulted in the shifting of some observation squadrons between corps-level units. Pershing also relieved a couple of his division commanders whom he determined were not aggressive enough or up to the position. Various problems still plagued the American logistical system, and the lack of training of many soldiers was evident. Despite this, the newly reorganized American forces slogged their way forward until First Army punched a hole in the German Hindenburg Line defensive system during the next phase.

It was in this period that a 50th Aero Squadron pilot performed an act of considerable heroism following an airborne accident:

On October 16, lieutenants Frayne and French had a narrow escape when a Very pistol went off accidentally in the observers' cockpit. This set fire to the gasoline tank. By utmost cool-headedness, Lieutenant Frayne side-slipped, thus keeping the fire from Lieutenant French, from 2,000 feet, and made a perfect landing in a small and strange field. Both jumped before the machine came to a stop and no sooner had they done so than the tank exploded. Lieutenant Frayne was recommended by Captain Morse for a decoration in view of his excellent judgment at such a critical time, and saving the life of Lieutenant French, but as it was not in the face of the enemy, it was disapproved at Headquarters.[60]

Breaking the Hindenburg Line and Pursuit: October 16–November 11, 1918

The 135th Aero Squadron's Lt. Lawrence Smart (pilot) and Lt. Henry Sheets (observer) conducted an artillery observation mission on November 1. The pair turned for their base after strafing a group of German soldiers and overseeing several artillery adjustments in poor weather conditions. Unexpectedly, a red-nosed German Fokker D.VII flew out of the clouds and directly at them. Five other Fokkers with yellow and orange noses emerged from the clouds and followed their leader on a course toward Smart and Sheets. Smart yanked his aircraft into an Immelman turn to avoid a collision, and the lead German pilot made a similar move as the two planes passed each other without firing. Smart was convinced the German was just as surprised and startled by the encounter as he was. Smart wrote the following about the encounter:

I have often wondered how close our wheels and under bellies came to each other during this sudden maneuver. Henry went into action—I dove for the ground which wasn't too far away. The whole gang came in on single file, each keeping his nose pointed straight at us with tracers and incendiaries flying past, but not registering any vital hits. They would get uncomfortably close and then turn and fall away, and then the next one would take a shot at us. [The fog] had helped us to get out of that scrap. By now we were over the tree tops and they gave up the chase.[61]

Four days later Smart and Sheets conducted another artillery observation mission. Upon completion of the work, they departed for their base and spotted four Fokker D.VII planes attacking two other 135th Aero Squadron aircraft on a photographic mission. One of the American planes dove toward the ground, and a single Fokker followed him while the other three German aircraft pursued the second American. The first observation plane landed just behind the American lines. Smart circled the downed American while Sheets fired upon the German fighter. The latter opted to withdraw from the engagement. Smart related what happened to his squadron mates, lieutenants Leland Schock (pilot) Otto Benell (observer), after the landing:

During their encounter they had shot down one Fokker. When they landed, just south of Bois de Beney, Schock found his throttle-rod connection had broken at the point where it was attached to the carburetor, preventing him from opening the throttle. He borrowed a pair of pliers from one of the doughboys who had come over to see the plane. He then cut some safety wire from one of the turnbuckles, fixed up the connection, and flew his plane out for home. I followed him in and we all made it without further incident.[62]

The morning of November 11 meant another day for a reconnaissance mission. Smart and Sheets walked to their plane for a flight in what seemed to be a morning for good flying weather. Smart started the engine and sat in the cockpit:

Henry [Sheets] was starting to climb into the rear cockpit when an orderly came running out, shouting something that I didn't hear with the engine running. He grabbed Henry who, in turn, jumped on the wing, reached into my cockpit, cut the ignition switch and yelled, "Shut the damn thing off, the war's over!"[63]

Lt. Percival Hart, the operations officer of the 135th Aero Squadron, offered what is perhaps the best conclusion to the American observation missions in World War I when he wrote:

Immediate plans were made to go to the Liegeois Cafe that evening; and there in the hilarious and brilliantly lighted city of Nancy we celebrated the end of an era in our lives, an era of adventure and romance such as in our younger days we had never dreamed could come to pass—filled with memories and friendships which only death itself can take from us.[64]

Just as pilot [Lieutenant French] was over Orte, he was hopped by three Me 109s and three Fw 190s.

—5th PRS operations report on a April 13, 1944 reconnaissance mission

Introduction

Prior to World War II, tactical reconnaissance faced the same issues as the other Army Air Forces (formed in June 1941 from the Army Air Corps) units—too few aircraft; even fewer up-to-date aircraft prepared to meet the needs of air warfare in 1941; and not enough trained personnel and equipment. As American involvement in World War II seemed more inevitable, the United States placed more emphasis on war preparation. The Japanese attack at Pearl Harbor on December 7, 1941; the American declaration of war against Japan; and subsequent declarations of war on the United States by Germany and Italy placed the country into a full war footing.

7th PRG F-5 (P-38 Lightning) in the UK, circa 1944

F-5 Aleutian Islands, May 1942

The Lockheed P-38 Lightning served as the primary combat-ready tactical reconnaissance asset as the United States entered the war. Designated as the F-4, the early reconnaissance version of the P-38E carried two K-17 vertical cameras. Lockheed built ninety-nine F-4s based on the P-38E and twenty of the F-4As based on the P-38F with cameras in the nose gun compartment. The two-engine plane offered additional speed and range compared to many other fighters. Maj. Richard Bong, America's highest-scoring ace in World War II, flew the P-38 Lightning. By 1944, The F-5 (P-38G and P-38J aircraft modified for reconnaissance duties with cameras mounted in the forward nose gun compartment) entered service and began replacing the war-weary F-4s.

The pilots, often known affectionately as "Photo Joes," also flew the F-6 (a reconnaissance variant of the P-51 Mustang fighter). Other tactical aircraft, including British Supermarine Spitfires, served American tactical reconnaissance squadrons and will

111th TRS F-6 (P-51 Mustang)

12th TRS F-6, 1944

be introduced in this chapter. Most flew unarmed, but some reconnaissance aircraft did carry weapons during the last two years of the war. Attempting to cover all of the American tactical reconnaissance units and/or the reconnaissance support for all of the campaigns and battles of World War II simply would not fit into a narrative here. Therefore, this chapter will examine the European theater (western Europe), the Mediterranean theater (North Africa, Sicily, and Italy) and two command areas in the Pacific theater (Southwest Pacific, and China, Burma, and India commands) and follow one or two reconnaissance units through the campaigns in their geographical areas. This provides an examination of how tactical reconnaissance aircraft supported the ground forces and of the bomber campaigns across four areas of the European and Pacific theaters of World War II.

European Theater of Operations

The two major Air Force–level organizations, which were based in England and supported American operations, were the 8th Air Force (strategic bomber mission) and the 9th Air Force (tactical ground support mission). Air units assigned to each Air Force provided support for its specific mission. Thus, reconnaissance missions of the 8th Air Force primarily provided pre- and postbomb target assessments, which could involve air fields, industry, dockyards and submarine pens, bridges, rail marshalling yards, and military bases and supply dumps. The aircraft also performed other reconnaissance missions as assigned. The reconnaissance mission of units assigned to the 9th Air Force primarily supported the tactical troops on the ground by meeting these requirements. These sorties included intelligence on enemy defenses and troop movement; observation of friendly force movements; pre- and postbomb target assessments of medium and light bomber units, which were targeting tactical targets at the behest of the ground commanders; weather intelligence; and other duties as assigned. The 9th Air Force shifted from the Mediterranean theater of operations in November 1943 in order to reorganize and provide support for ground troops prior to, during, and after the Allied landings in France in June 1944.

31st PRS photograph of a French beach prior to D-day. Note the German soldiers running as the aircraft makes the photographic run along the beach.

American ground units joined some small Allied commando raids in occupied Europe. However, the main ground efforts in northern and central Europe began with the landing of an Allied Army in Normandy, France, on June 6, 1944. Up to this point, many missions of the reconnaissance groups of the 9th Air Force included intelligence gathering, visual observation, photographic assessment, mapping photography, and weather information gathering along the coast and in the immediate inland areas of German-occupied territory opposite England in preparation for the Allied invasion.

By June 1944, the 9th Air Force included the 10th Photographic Reconnaissance Group (PRG) and the 69th Tactical Reconnaissance Group (TRG), and the 8th Air Force

Aerial photograph of bomb damage within the Paris marshalling yard prior to D-day

included the 7th PRG and 67th PRG. The 25th Bombardment Group (Reconnaissance) was formed under the 8th Air Force in July 1944, and there were reconnaissance adjustments within each Air Force until the end of the war in Europe. Squadrons of the 10th PRG flew the F-3 (reconnaissance version of the A-20 Havoc medium bomber), F-4, F-5, and F-6. The 67th PRG's squadrons included the F-5 and F-6.

The 7th PRG flew the Spitfire PR-XI and, later, the P-51 Mustang as a reconnaissance escort fighter. The 25th Bombardment Group (Reconnaissance) included the F-8 Mosquito, Mosquito PR-XVI, F-5, F-7 (reconnaissance version of the B-24 Liberator bomber), F-9 (reconnaissance version of the B-17 bomber), F-10 (reconnaissance version of the B-25 Mitchell bomber), and the B-26 Marauder bomber. The 69th TRG included the Mosquito PR-XVI, F-3, F-5, F-6, and F10 aircraft. The A-20 was a two-engine medium bomber utilized in the F-3 configuration for night photography and reconnaissance. The P-38 Lighting was a two-engine single-seat fighter and the P-51 Mustang was a single-engine fighter. All three of these aircraft included the addition of cameras for photographic reconnaissance duties in all later variants. The Spitfire PR-XI was the reconnaissance version of the Supermarine Spitfire single-engine fighter of the Royal Air Force. The Mosquito was a two-engine fighter-bomber primarily flown by the Royal Air Force. The B-17 and B-24 four-engine bombers were modified for reconnaissance work. The B-25 and B-26 were two-engine medium bombers.

The 67th PRG arrived in Europe in June 1942 as a unit of the 8th Air Force and shifted to the 9th Air Force in November 1943. Squadrons were either formed or deactivated, or had their assignments changed, within and between the PRGs throughout World War II. Tracing these many movements and changes is beyond the scope of this chapter, which will concentrate on particular units at specific points of time in the war in order to relate the American tactical air reconnaissance efforts of World War II. The squadron swap between two groups after D-day is briefly examined because the lessons learned from Normandy prompted a reorganization of reconnaissance assets.

The 7th PRG launched reconnaissance planes the morning of the D-day landings in France on June 6, 1944. The landing of American, British, Canadian, and smaller elements of troops from other countries on D-day represented a return of the Allied forces to Western Europe north of the Mediterranean Sea. The first 7th PRG pilots to return to base were Group commander Col. C. A. Shoop and Lt. Col. N. E. Hartwell. Upon debriefing by the group intelligence officers, fifteen war correspondents awaited their statements on what they had viewed of the landings from the air. The group recorded Col. Shoop's report:

> Colonel Harwell and I flew together over the landing beachhead. The first thing we noticed were the boats. The channel was packed with them—of all descriptions and sizes. Then we noticed the fighters—our fighters. There were hundreds of them. Dozens of small French villages were ablaze and all appeared to be deserted. We could see our troops splashing ashore from the landing craft. All seemed to know what to do and where to go. Some tanks and transport vehicles had been landed.[1]

Lt. Col. Hartwell added:

> The landing appeared to be well established. Some troops were a considerable distance inland. The beaches were pitted with bomb craters and I observed a number of gliders along the coast and a lot of parachutes. Smoke was beginning to obscure the beaches.[2]

Aerial photograph of equipment moving ashore after the initial D-day landings

Lt. John Cameron and Capt. Jack Campbell covered the beach areas together. Upon their return, Cameron added more regarding what he had seen over the invasion area:

At one point I observed a United States flag on the beach. Off shore our fleet was firing toward land and our troops appeared to be unopposed near the coast. Large numbers of parachutes could be seen on the ground and tanks were being unloaded. There were no enemy aircraft. I observed marshalling yards in one town on fire and there was a train burning at Vire.[3]

Later Maj. Robert Smith made a statement after being debriefed by intelligence personnel:

It surely was quiet over there. I saw an awful lot of tanks, trucks, and half-tracks on the beach. Boy, the string of boats. I never saw so many, and the sky was full of airplanes. All were ours. I didn't see a single enemy plane. Our troops were moving around on the beaches. One place looked like a crap game was in session.[4]

While these pilots and others photographed the beach areas, additional 7th PRG pilots flew sorties over airfields, rail lines, highways and other locations for reconnaissance photos that might indicate the movement of German forces facing the Allies moving inland from the beach areas.

The reconnaissance squadrons of the 67th Tactical Reconnaissance Group (TRG) were over the beaches of Normandy on June 6, 1944 as well. The Group's final preinvasion mission occurred the night before D-day, when Lt. Edwin Rackham of the 9th Weather Reconnaissance Squadron (Provisional) flew a weather reconnaissance mission over the Cherbourg peninsula to gather data for the Troop Carrier Command as the invasion fleet made its final preparations. Aircraft of the 67th TRG provided weather and general reconnaissance duties along the French coast for months prior to the D-day landings in June. As noted by the 67th TRG:

> Examples of the important role played by this group in setting the stage for the invasion were the tide-level "recce" flown in the Gulf de la Seine area, low-level missions spotting beach defenses, and reports on enemy troop dispositions. The 67th Group not only helped to provide our commanders with complete and accurate information on the enemy's defenses, but also participated in crippling those defenses. The German army's inability to get badly needed supplies and reinforcements to the front because of damaged bridges, wrecked marshalling yards, etc., was traceable to the previous work of this organization in conjunction with the Ninth Air Force's fighter-bombers and [B-26] Marauders. In the weeks immediately preceding the invasion pilots of this group helped to hamstring the enemy by spotting targets for the bombers and assessing the damage they had done.[5]

Prior to the Allied invasion at Normandy, the 67th TRG also conducted an important photographic reconnaissance mission for American artillery units. Group aircraft made a complete set of Merton oblique photographs for the entire Normandy peninsula to a depth of 20 miles inland. Although naval gun support is not mentioned in the unit records, one could assume the photographs aided them, as well. The group records note the photographs were also critical for artillery in "clearing the beachhead." However, details to verify this assumption are lacking in the records. Lt. Gen. Lewis Brereton (9th Air Force commander and the commander of the 12th Aero Group, a Salmson-equipped reconnaissance unit in World War I) commended the group for this work, which was accomplished ahead of schedule. Later, the group received high praise, according to reports from units on the front. They noted that the photographs had been instrumental for American artillery in the breakout from the beachhead in the days following the initial invasion.[6] Gen. Brereton's commendation for the 67th TRG reads in part:

> For outstanding and meritorious achievement in the performance of duty in action against the enemy in the European Theater of Operations from 15 February 1944 to 20 March 1944 . . . the 67th Tactical Reconnaissance Group was charged with heavy responsibility of executing one of the most extensive low altitude oblique photographic assignments ever undertaken over enemy territory. The magnitude of the task, the character of the heavily-defended terrain to be photographed and the exacting nature of the undertaking demanded that the utmost diligence be exercised in the preparation and execution of the assignment.[7]

67th TRG aircraft were continuously in the air over the invasion beaches, providing intelligence related to the movement of American forces and their German opposition on D-day:

> "Tac/R" [tactical reconnaissance] pilots [of the 67th TRG] were over the beachhead at H-Hour and, from that time, served as the "eyes" of the armies that landed there at every possible opportunity, though weather conditions were often unfavorable for such a task.

These pilots often returned from missions merely to eat, sleep a few hours, and go back up with another assignment. Personnel in all sections worked longer hours than before; those sections directly connected with operations were manned around the clock.[8]

Three F-6 (P-51) pilots of the 15th TRS of the 67th TRG [the squadron later transferred to the 10th PRG] each shot down a German Focke-Wulf 190 (Fw 190) fighter on the first day of the invasion. That had not been their primary mission, but the 15th TRS aircraft were armed in order to defend themselves. The three pilots were lieutenants Joseph Conkin, Ernest Schonard (who also received credit for damaging another Fw 190), and Clyde East. The latter pilot ended World War II as the highest-scoring American reconnaissance pilot in air victories, who later flew two reconnaissance tours of duty in the Korean War; served as the squadron commander of the author's father during the Cuban Missile Crisis; and retired in 1965 after leading an RF-101C reconnaissance detachment to Southeast Asia immediately following the Tonkin Gulf Incident. Naturally, Clyde East will continue to appear throughout this volume.

Lt. Clyde East (thirteen victories) is America's highest-scoring reconnaissance pilot ace.

East informed the author that he had not seen a German plane in the air until encountering the Fw 190s over France on D-day. As a visual reconnaissance pilot that day, his engagement rules for June 6 were to aggressively attack any German plane he encountered. By the afternoon of D-day, the visual reconnaissance pilots served as the eyes of the Army moving inland from the beaches. Each lead pilot and his wingman covered specific road or rail lines to spot German reinforcements heading toward the beaches. Flying without cameras, they radioed the size, type, location, and movement of German forces. This information would then be transmitted to fighter bomber units for interdiction missions. Lt. Conklin's Fw 190 kill is recorded in chapter

1 of this book. 67th TRG records document the first mission of East and his wingman, Lt. E. M. Schonard, over France on D-day. The narrative turns to the official records on the engagements made by East and Schonard during their visual reconnaissance of rail lines in France:

Lt. Clyde B. East, pilot in lead ship, took off at 1720 hours for visual reconnaissance over route Dinan-Rennes-Laval- Fougardes-Pontorson in France. Departed English coast in the vicinity of Portland Bill and entered French coast near C. Frehel . . . Marshalling yards at Rennes empty. Rennes to Laval NMS. At Y 5321, train of 80 goods wagons, one engine, stationary on siding. Laval to Pontorson to St. Lo NMS. At 1930 hrs at T 4462, ten MET moving north, regular interval. Near Laval, sighted four FW 190 preparing to land. #2 man [Schonard] attacked the last E/A [enemy aircraft] with a long burst. The E/A started smoking and as it crashed into the ground, burst into flames. In the meantime, #1 man [East] attacked the third FW with a 2 sec. burst and it crashed, spreading flames over an area of 50 yards. By this time, the second of the string of FWs was on the tail of the #1 man so the #2 pilot made a head-on attack on this E/A. Observed tracers going into the front of his engine nacelle. The E/A finally broke off to the right and the #2 pilot joined his leader and continued on their mission. Encountered intense accurate light flak at Laval Airdrome. Returned to base and landed at 2020 hours.[9]

As the invasion force moved inland from the beaches over the next few days, the mission of the 67th TRG altered along with them:

The advance of the Allied armies provided the first opportunity for this group to fly true tactical reconnaissance missions, i.e., missions at the request and in direct support of an army in the field. This type of support was typified in the first days of the offensive when a five-mile long column of horse-drawn artillery was sighted moving up behind the enemy's lines. [While a 5-mile-long horse-drawn artillery column seems implausible, this is naturally a direct quote from the unit records. It is more likely the artillery sections were scattered along a 5-mile stretch of road during their movement rather than being 5 miles long.] A report, radioed back to group headquarters from the scout plane and immediately relayed to First Army Headquarters through its Army liaison section attached to the group. Brought an attack by our fighter-bombers. The column was destroyed before it reached the front, in fact, within a few hours after it had been discovered.[10]

Following the D-day landings and as the tactical situation warranted, the 67th TRG and the 10th TRG exchanged half of the squadrons assigned to each group in order to balance the capabilities of each major unit. Each tactical reconnaissance group now included two tactical reconnaissance squadrons that provided visual observation of the battlefield as a primary mission; one photo reconnaissance squadron for photographic imagery; and one weather reconnaissance squadron for meteorology support missions. Each group also included mobile communications, meteorology, photo interpretation, photo intelligence, and photo technical units.

Lt. J. B. Matthews of the 22nd PRS was the first 7th PRG pilot to spot a German V-1 rocket ("Buzz Bomb" or "doodlebug") in flight. The Germans developed the unguided rocket as a vengeance weapon to terrorize the British population. The rocket flew with a sputtering sound until expending its fuel supply and then dropping silently to the ground where it exploded upon impact. The Allies granted an aerial kill to pilots who downed a V-1 while in flight. In this case, the surprised 22nd PRS pilots were more concerned with photographing the new weapon:

10th PRG photographic lab

Photographic interpretation

On 22nd June 1944, Lt. Matthews and Lt. M. P. Allway flew alongside one of the pilotless planes over the channel in the vicinity of Hastings. The target was flying a course of about 280 at an altitude of 3,000 feet. By indicating 400 miles per hour the target was passed up. While photographing the one target another larger one passed over the first target at considerably greater speed and the pilot was unable to overtake it. Lt. Allway did not get photographs but one oblique was secured by Lt. Matthews. Other unsuccessful attempts were made to get photographs by other pilots during the few weeks following the launching of the pilotless plane.[11]

Pilots of the 67th TRG flew numerous missions to discover V-1 rocket launching sites in the Pas-de-Calais. Unit documents record:

Before their [V-1] existence was a public fact, this group was systematically hunting the rocket "lairs," cooperating with our bombers in attempts to eradicate the threat. This work was successful in materially lessening the severity of the rocket attacks when the Nazis finally utilized their vaunted secret weapon to bombard London. These attacks were undoubtedly delayed several weeks by the Allied bombings of the Pas-de-Calais, a fact substantiated by estimates that 90 percent of the original launching sites were put out of commission before the first flying bomb was launched and by indications that the Germans were forced to use elaborate concealment of the sites they did manage to put into operation.[12]

Two 7th PRG pilots made the first shuttle reconnaissance flight from the edge of western Europe to Russia and back on June 15. Maj. John Hoover and Lt. Ralph Kendall flew eastward and photographed objectives in Berlin, Warsaw, Lodz, and other locations including the rail marshalling yards at Lom. They also photographed shipping on the Danube River before landing at Rechitsa, Russia. From there, they proceeded to the Russian airfield at Poltava, which hosted American shuttle bombers a couple of times during the war. From Poltava, Hoover flew to San Severo, Italy, and then back to his home base on June 19. Lt. Kendall did not return at the same time as Hoover due to damage to his aircraft.[13]

As the war in Europe approached its last month, little changed in the reconnaissance missions—but what they found became more interesting. In April and the first days of May 1945, reconnaissance units spotted horse-drawn vehicles moving to and from the front as well as military personnel heading toward areas they considered safer as the war drew to a conclusion. German pilots still offered a defense against bombers and fighters. The unit records of the 111st PRS offer insight into the reconnaissance situation and fighter hazards faced by American pilots in the last month of the war. The 111st PRS supported the Mediterranean Theater of Operations and entered southern France following Operation Dragoon (the invasion of southern France on August 15, 1944). At this point, the squadron provided reconnaissance support for the American 7th Army as it moved from the Mediterranean coast and into southwest Germany. The visual reconnaissance section of the unit records notes:

7 April 45: 1 truck towing armored force vehicle on trailer moving east and 1 truck towing trailer moved west at S-3603. 3 MT stationary facing northwest at S-3503. At 1710 hrs, 8 ME-109s flying west toward Stuttgart at 6000 feet. ME-109s jumped our mission. Mission got into Luftberry [a circular defensive formation where each plane guards the rear of the plane in front of it] with one ME-109. ME-109s broke formation. Leader fired at ME-109, saw strikes on wing root, cockpit and fuselage. Saw cowling

F-5 31st PRS, France 1944

Photograph taken along the Saar River by Capt. Holbury of the 10th PRG, on January 5, 1945. Holbury received a commendation from Gen. George Patton for this reconnaissance mission, conducted at very low altitude in the narrow valley during poor weather conditions.

come off and flames come from engine. Plane rolled over on its back and plane was at 1000 ft when last seen, in a straight dive. Weaver got on tail of one ME-109. Gave him a long burst and plane exploded and disintegrated in air at 5000'. Leader saw one ME-109 on Weaver's tail. Leader got on ME-109's tail and fired a long burst and saw strikes on him on the wings. ME-109 broke away and went into the clouds. No further contact with that plane. Our mission then pursued 6 ME-109s who were flying east. Weaver saw ME-109 firing at him from 45 degree angle to the left. Weaver broke into him, went into Luftberry and went down to 2500'. ME-109 broke off to the right, Weaver chased him to 4500 feet and attacked head-on. Weaver fired from slightly below and shot his tail off. ME-109 began smoking, split 8 and crashed into ground and exploded. Mission joined up and headed east to Goppingen, then turned west and headed west. At Neilingen A/D, saw ME-110 take off from field to the east. Leader went down and fired, getting only a few strikes. Our mission circled, and saw an ME-110 flying west on the deck. Leader attacked again, and made two passes, firing at ME-110. Killed rear gunner and saw right engine start smoking. Leader ran out of ammo but forced him to crash-land. Mission then returned to the base because of engine trouble. CLAIMS: 3 ME-109s destroyed, 1 ME-110 destroyed, and 1 ME-109 damaged.[14]

21 April 1945: 500 plus [sic] horse drawn vehicles and motor transports moving northeast from S2008 to X-2793. Mostly horse drawn vehicles on highways and motor transports are parked in the towns along the way. Called controller and 4 flights sent to attack, while mission was in area. Fighter-bombers hit concentrations in town at X-2196. Staffed concentration of approximately 200 horse drawn vehicles at X-2395. Also made road out at X-233948 at suggestion of Leader.[15]

World War II in the European theater officially ended on May 7, 1945, with the unconditional surrender of Germany. Capt. Clyde East of the 15th TRS departed the theater as the American reconnaissance "ace of aces" with a total of thirteen German planes to his credit. Attention is now turned to North Africa and the Mediterranean.

Mediterranean Theater of Operations

Sections of the 5th Photographic Reconnaissance Squadron (PRS) arrived in Great Britain beginning in late June 1942 with North Africa as its eventual—and surprise—final destination. The sections were reintegrated into a squadron that established itself at a new airfield. It received its F-4 aircraft as the depot assembled them from the crates in which they arrived. Plans called for the 5th PRS to provide tactical reconnaissance support for the American troops destined for the November 1942 landings in North Africa. At the end of

Offloading a camera from the nose of an F-5

F-5. Note the camera portals on the nose.

Camera bay of an F-5

October, squadron personnel boarded two ocean liners, with the unit divided by military occupation specialty between the two vessels. So, if something happened to one liner, the other half of the unit could arrive at their destination and function as a unit, even if it were half its original size. Squadron personnel learned of their destination after the convoy sailed from England. For the next three years, the 5th PRS conducted reconnaissance missions with the F-4 (P-38 Lightning) and the Spitfire PR-XII, later exchanging these for the upgraded F-5 (P-38 Lightning) and the Spitfire PR-IX. In late 1944, the squadron received the F-10 (B-25 Mitchell bomber) for long-range missions. The latter were operated by a pilot and an observer.

When one thinks of North Africa, "winter rain and mud" might not be included in that

F-5 with an open camera bay

image. Yet the 5th PRS quickly added this concept to their routine as they moved toward Algiers. Stress seized the day as the personnel faced an unfamiliar situation in poor weather conditions:

> Then the rains came. The squadron had struck camp to go on to Algiers. The order didn't come through. Delay. Worry. The men became cross, irritable. Buddies snapped at each other, nerves were taut . . . The rains came stealthily—just a mist at first, in a few hours, a torrent. By morning the mud was about six inches deep. It stuck to the boots, six inches of it, leaving dry dusty tracks behind the men as they walked. Rations floated away unseen and personal possessions were forgotten while men retrieved their equipment.[16]

In Algeria, a new Allied Reconnaissance Wing absorbed the 5th PRS along with other Royal Air Force reconnaissance detachments and units. The organization set the stage for future establishment of the Mediterranean Allied Air Force elements, such as the Mediterranean Allied Tactical Air Force, based on, for example, tactical and strategic orientations missions. On June 10, 1943, the 5th PRS departed Algiers and moved to a new base near La Marsa, Tunisia. As winter introduced weather miseries to the personnel, the summer proved to be just as challenging:

> As the summer wore on, heat, flies, and mosquitos became worse. Dysentery was experienced by many officers and enlisted men, with a few contracting malaria. In spite of the discomforts of heat and the handicap of sickness, the squadron not only maintained its capacity for work, but increased it. And by the end of the summer, it was averaging double the daily sorties of June.[17]

Throughout July and August 1943, the 5th PRS mapped over five-sixths of the Italian peninsula and a 50-mile-deep strip of French coast between Italy and Spain. It also performed its assigned reconnaissance duties that were associated with supporting American ground operations. The unit lost its first pilot during a mission on June 26, when Lt. Russell Crane did not return from a mission to photograph the Mediterranean coast of France.

The pilots of the 5th PRS proved adept at photographic mapping and demonstrated great skill in the face of adversity. Lt. Mills encountered four German Me 109 fighters while on a mapping run. Mills increased his altitude and enacted a series of evasive tactics to successfully dodge the four enemy fighters. He continued the mapping run until the four Me 109s found him again and attacked. For a second time, Mills successfully evaded the enemy aircraft, completed his photographic mission, and returned to Tunisia.[18]

In July, the squadron split into two sections in preparation for the invasion of Italy. As on the vessels sailing to North Africa, each section represented a miniature image of the entire squadron having the assets they needed to conduct complete reconnaissance operations, although on a smaller scale. The forward section departed Tunisia on September 19 and established operations at Pomigliano Airfield, near Naples. The rear section continued reconnaissance support for the Army during the move.

In November, the 5th PRS Advance Detachment in Italy faced an interesting problem that also plagued other Allied units flying over Italy:

A rather amusing incident called out to our attention the present inadequacy of our aircraft insignia of the plain white star. It so happened an enemy P-38 with markings identical with ours had been making trouble in the 5th Army Region. Consequently all planes of like markings were under suspicion. By chance today two cautious Spitfires spying Captain [Thomas] Barfoot's [commander of the 5th PRS] plane carefully escorted him clear back to the parking area where the Captain gave vent to his sentiments in a manner that was not complementary to the Spitfire pilots of the cautious brand.[19]

Air raids were not uncommon against the airfield from which the 5th PRS Advance Detachment operated. On November 10, a captured A-36 Apache flown by an enemy pilot buzzed the airfield and dropped a single bomb near the fuel dump without causing any major damage. Two days later, between 8 to 12 German Me 109 fighters strafed and dropped fragmentation bombs on the field. Two American fighters received direct hits from the fragmentation bombs, but all of the 5th PRS aircraft escaped damage.

The 5th PRS flew a hectic schedule of sorties in support of 5th Army troops on November 13. The squadron flew nine morning reconnaissance missions and, by that afternoon, was ordered to remove all aircraft from the area in response to enemy pressure. 5th Army countermanded the last order as the military situation stabilized. On November 26, the rear detachment of the squadron began arriving in Italy by way of Naples.

Col. Karl Polifka, commander of the 6th PRG, and who is covered again in this chapter as the commander of the 8th PRS in 1942, visited the 5th PRS in December 1943 and flew several missions with its pilots. Col. Polifka is one of the better-known pilots who flew reconnaissance missions in multiple conflicts and is discussed again in the chapter on the Korean War. Both elements of the 5th PRS reunited again in Italy by the end of December.

The 5th PRS lost a pilot on December 27. Lt. Ecklund survived when hit by high-altitude (25,000 feet) antiaircraft fire during a photographic mission. Allied artillery personnel reported seeing Ecklund crash-land approximately 0.5 mile behind German lines, near Cassino. German soldiers removed the pilot, who survived the crash, and escorted him to a nearby shelter. The plane exploded and burned following Ecklund's departure.[20]

The unit historical records for January 1944 provide insight into the evolving relationship between the 5th PRS and its support for Fifth Army:

F-5 of 3rd PRG, Algeria, December 1942

Our relationship in this field have been expanded and have grown more complex primarily in consequence of the establishment of the new bridgehead at Anzio. Covering these new and more distant battle sectors has meant using more auxiliary gas tanks on our aircraft. Also it has presented added problems of liaison and print delivery. Prints have been flown to Nettuno by C-78 (Cessna) very successfully. In general it can be said that the experience and ability of all concerned have been more than equal to the test of recent changes and developments the various departments.[21]

The 5th PRS and its sister squadrons of the 3rd PRG continued to support 5th Army movement in Italy, including the temporarily stalled invasion force at Anzio, which landed on January 22, 1944. The Allies intended for the Anzio landings to be a means of placing forces behind the existing German lines, which could then cut them off and take Rome. However, the landing forces met stiff resistance and made very slow progress inland. Lieutenant French flew a harrowing mission on April 13, 1944:

Lt. French received inaccurate flak which followed him from Orvieto to Orte. Just as pilot was over Orte, he was hopped by 3 ME-109s and 3 FW-190's [both were German fighters]. ME-109's were outdistanced as Lt. French dropped his tanks and put plane into straight dive. FW-190's followed for 100 miles (40 miles out to sea). They were gaining on pilot when they were lost in cloud (500' to 1,000').[22]

The month of May offers a good time to pause in this narrative and examine the state of 5th PRS reconnaissance support for Allied forces in the theater. One small detachment re-located to San Severo to provide Allied reconnaissance coverage of Albania, Yugoslavia, Bulgaria, and Romania. It rejoined the main body on May 5. During the month, the 5th PRS flew 157 sorties (133 successful) from its main base at Pomigliano and twelve sorties (eleven successful) from the detached location at San Severo. The squadron also flew fifteen courier missions to the beachhead at Anzio. Thirty enemy aircraft attempted interceptions of 5th PRS planes, and enemy antiaircraft guns engaged thirteen squadron planes. The squadron lost one pilot on May 10. He flew a mission to cover targets in central Italy and did not return. Unit records outline the squadron's mission at this point:

The bulk of our coverage continues to be for MATAF although we still cover routine and special targets . . . so that it might be said that 90–95% of our work is for MATAF. During the month [of May] our work and the work of TAF took on special significance in view of the awaited drive at Cassino & the beachhead at Anzio. TAF's job was to keep all rail lines to the south broken. Our job was to supply them with information regarding daily results and the condition of the rail lines at all times. Weather permitting, our daily coverage included most of the RR lines from Florence down to Rome for activity and serviceability—including the Bomb Damage Assessment. The results of TAF's effective bombing and our coverage is in a large measure reflected in the 5th and 8th Army's [British] successful advance towards Rome.[23]

Rome fell to the Allies moving north from the Anzio beachhead and up the Italian boot. With the Axis defenses south of Rome collapsing, the Italian capital fell on June 5. Seven Allied divisions departed Italy to participate in the southern invasion of France known as Operation Dragoon. The remaining Allied forces pushed northward from Rome against the German Gothic Line defenses. The 3rd PRG and its squadrons continued to support the northward advance of the Allies with photographic reconnaissance support. Unit records of the 5th PRS of the 3rd PRG illustrate the type of missions flown by reconnaissance pilots and the types of problems, especially mechanical, they faced. Two days of unit notes beginning with the day Rome fell are illustrative of the squadron daily operations:

5 June 1944: Lt. Hintze off [took off] at 0850 down [landed] 1045. 14 pinpoints [specific-location documented objectives] covered, after which pilot was forced to return to base when both turbo-regulators went out & manifold pressure would not go above 34. Lt. Wold off at 0845, down 1245. 100% coverage on 19 pinpoints & RR [railroad] in Florence-Leghorn area. Lt. French down at 1130 with all targets covered in area of NE Rome in spite of the fact that his radio & compass went out on take-off. Lt. Hoppe down at 1350 with pictures of 23 pinpoints, half of which were Bomb Damage Assessment Targets. Lt Caddell down at 1430 with 15 pinpoints covered.

12 June 1944: Lt. French down at 1350 with 70% coverage—5 targets obscured by clouds. Accurate flak encountered over Leghorn. Jumped by 2 E/AC [enemy aircraft] N. of Spezia. Lt. French evaded A/C before right engine froze. Retuned to base at low altitude over water & made single engine landing. Remainder of missions cancelled due to weather.[24]

At this time, the 5th PRS (through its higher headquarters, the 3rd PRG) supported the Mediterranean Allied Tactical Air Force (MATAF). The tactical assets of the American 12th Air Force were attached to the MATAF. As an MATAF asset, the 5th PRS provided the following reconnaissance support in May and June 1944:

Practically 98% of our work is still supplying intelligence for TAF. During May, TF had succeeded in cutting every rail line south of the Pisa-Rimini line . . . Our pilots aided TAF immeasurably in this success. During the month of June, our coverage has been concentrated in a new area—north of 44 degrees and bounded on the north by a line running from Venice to Milan to Turin & south to the coast. We have covered all of the A/Ds [airdromes] in this area, which has given TAF an exact disposition of the GAF [German air force]. We continue to follow bombers for BDA [bomb damage

5th PRG photographic battle damage assessment of a bridge near Verona, Italy

5th PRG photographic battle damage assessment of an oil refinery

assessment] photos, but most of our coverage is reconnaissance of new targets—namely bridges, M/Ys [rail marshalling yards], A/Ds, and Dump areas. Routine coverage of west coast and east coast ports continue.[25]

After being stationed at Pomigliano airfield since November 1943, the 5th PRS moved to Nettuno airfield and then Viterbo airfield (near Rome) in June 1944. By July, most of the reconnaissance objectives for the 5th PRS lay in the Po River valley. TAF planned a fighter bomber campaign against small bridges and railroad lines in the valley and required prestrike photographs of the potential targets. After the raids, the reconnaissance pilots made poststrike photographs for battle damage assessment. Similar missions continued into August. Capt. Dodson (pilot) and Maj. Elliott (observer) came close to disaster on an August 20 sortie in an F-10 (B-25 Mitchell bomber converted for reconnaissance):

Mission was to follow dive bombers along road and RR running from Turin. Made two runs following both flights of bombers into targets. While pulling up on second run, noticed tracers going by ship. No hits apparently. After proceeding south and cruising coast approx near Sevone, compass went out and on switching gas tanks noticed that left tank was mostly empty due to apparent flak hits. Proceeded to vicinity of Pisa and attempted to land at strip approx 8 miles S. of Pisa. Smoke pots and clouds obscured this strip, so due to shortage of gas, crash-landed at Postedera. German gun position was less than 300 yards away and started firing at plane. Pilot and observer ran to safety [at] southern portion of A/D and into a British artillery CP [command post], who said they would destroy plane with their guns.[26]

In September 1944, the squadron shifted operations to Malignano airfield in Tuscany as the front lines moved northward. The Po River area continued to be the primary reconnaissance area of interest for the squadron through October. Squadron aircraft photographed bridges, river crossings, marshalling yards, and ferry sites as well as shipping in the Gulf of Genoa. The poor fall weather hampered many missions. Within the last nine days of October, the squadron canceled all flights for six days due to the weather.

In January 1945, the 5th PRS moved to Pisa airfield from which it operated until the end of the war in May. The war continued to shift northward in Italy, and as late as April 1945, the reconnaissance missions of the squadron focused on the following:

Bridges, M/Ys, airfields, road and river strips, and pinpoints bombed by both medium and fighter bombers. All roads leading from the front lines into enemy territory was [sic] covered for bridge serviceability prior to the spring push by ground troops. By doing this, higher headquarters were able to determine the necessary bombing of bridges which might afford easy escape routes for the enemy. Consequently, many early morning and late afternoon sorties were flowing covering pinpoints after the bombing attack to determine whether turn about bombing was necessary. . . . The Po River was covered twice daily. This was done to locate possible enemy troop concentrations where crossings might be attempted.[27]

The 5th PRS experimented with night reconnaissance missions in March 1945, and by April, these had expanded to one-fourth (59 of 239) of the successful missions for the month. The night operations, under the nickname "Midnight Rover," involved reconnaissance patrols along the Po River:

5th PRG photographic battle damage assessment of the Landshut marshalling yard in Germany

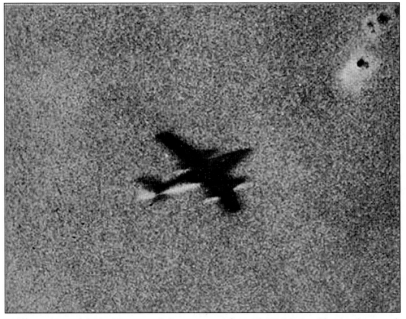

A German Messerschmitt Me 262 jet fighter passes under a 5th PRG F-5 and has its photograph taken in the process.

All observations were radioed into the controllers when spotted and later confirmed by photographs which were taken. On the night of 15th and 16th of April, several pontoon bridges and ferry sites were found to be very active. Night intruders were vectored to these areas where strikes were made with good results.[28]

The Germans officially surrendered on May 7, 1945. The 5th PRS flew nine reconnaissance missions for TAF during the first seven days of the month. Missions scheduled over Austria and Yugoslavia were canceled due to poor weather. Following the German surrender, the squadron flew a few missions to monitor areas where German troops were surrendering in northern Italy. The two F-10s were reassigned for courier duties; the other aircraft were flown for thirty minutes every three days for maintenance purposes. The personnel settled into sporting tournaments until they returned to the United States.[29]

Pacific Theater of Operations–Southwest Pacific Areas Command

Japanese forces drove Allied forces south-eastward toward Australia and westward toward India after the war commenced in December 1941. American and Filipino forces held out for four months in the Philippines but eventually surrendered. Japanese forces overran the meager American forces on Wake Island. The British lost Malaya, Singapore, and Hong Kong. The Dutch East Indies (modern Indonesia) fell, and Japanese forces invaded Burma and began chasing British and Indian troops to India. Allied forces lost several major vessels in naval engagements with Japan. The situation in Asia and the Pacific did not look healthy for the Allies.

The United States commenced dispatching troops and equipment to Australia in early 1942 in preparation for a possible defense of the country but primarily to form a force with its allies to halt the Japanese advance into the Southwest and central Pacific regions. The Navy and Marines assumed the lead in planning for a central Pacific campaign toward Japan and the Army, under Gen. Douglas MacArthur, aimed to erase the Japanese gains in the Solomon Islands and New Guinea with an intermediate goal to recover the Philippine Islands. British and Indian forces established primary responsibility, with support from American and Chinese troops, for the Burma Campaign.

The 8th PRS, the first tactical reconnaissance unit to deploy with F-4 aircraft, arrived in Australia on April 7, 1942, two days prior to the American and Filipino surrender in the Bataan Peninsula in the Philippines. Capt. Karl Polifka commanded the 8th PRS, and his name will appear again throughout this book. Polifka was one of the many well-known pilots who flew reconnaissance missions in multiple wars and rose to command reconnaissance units including a reconnaissance group in Italy during World War II and the only reconnaissance wing in the Korean War. The squadron flew its first combat reconnaissance mission (over New Guinea) on April 16, with F-4s. At this time, their only reconnaissance aircraft were four F-4s. Later in April, Polifka acquired a B-24 Liberator bomber and crew for long-range missions. This aircraft provided reconnaissance of the Japanese naval vessels gathering off Rabaul and destined for the Battle of the Coral Sea in the first week of May.

Personnel, equipment, and aircraft continued to arrive at the unit, which then increased in size during the summer of 1942. The 8th PRS flew reconnaissance missions to Buka Island (near Bougainville Island in the northern Solomons), Buna (on the southeast coast of New Guinea), and Rabaul (the main Japanese base in the area and located on New Britain). Many missions were staged through Port Moresby because of their distance from Australia. The addition of a couple of B-17 bombers permitted the squadron to begin long-distance mapping missions. In September, the B-17s were transferred to a bomber unit, and the 8th PRS moved operations forward to Port Moresby in New Guinea. From this location, the squadron maintained regular reconnaissance of the Japanese at Buka in addition to Buna, Lae, and Salmauna. This regularity paid off on September 11:

> Eighth Photo's Buna reconnaissance paid real dividends today. Lt. Savage . . . spotted two Zekes [Japanese Zero fighters] flying toward Buna. Following them in, he spotted 30 more aircraft on the drome. This he radioed to 4th Fighter Section and an afternoon striking force claimed destruction of eighteen.[30]

A newly promoted Maj. Karl Polifka returned to the United States in November 1942, where his experience in the Southwest Pacific resulted in his being awarded command of the 6th Reconnaissance Group bound for the Mediterranean theater. Reconnaissance collected by the 8th PRS, while it operated from Port Moresby, supported Allied operations during the Buna campaign along the Kokoda Trail in New Guinea (November 1942–January 1943); the landings in the Trobriand Islands off the southeast coast of New Guinea (June 1943); the Woodlark Islands near southeast New Guinea (June 1943); the Cape Gloucester landings on the island of New Britain (December 1943); and at the Battle of Arawe on New Britain (December 1943–February 1944).

Lt. Marvin Gardner prepared comments on one of his missions for the 8th PRS records. He wrote the following:

> We had arrived at Port Moresby early in September [1942] and as the months rolled by, our missions kept getting longer and longer. Finally we were asked to get photos of Buka Passage in the Solomons. Several pilots had attempted the mission, but on each occasion they had been forced to return because of severe tropical fronts. On the night of June 4th, I was briefed and at 0715 the following morning, I was on my way. About 100 miles off the east coast of New Guinea, I watched the Trobriand Islands pass beneath my wing—my first check point before the target—some 400 miles away over unbroken water. Directly ahead of me was a front so I detoured to the north and went through a break in it. Shortly afterwards, I began my climb to 30,000 feet and in about an hour I could see my objective. As I made my run I could see clouds of dust on the Buka runway which usually marked enemy fighters taking off for interception. There were a few cargo ships at anchorage just off the passage which I included in my run. Because of my altitude and speed I wasn't in any real danger from the planes that had just taken off and I headed home. The break I had skirted through the front had closed up on me as I entered the front on instruments and began a let down. At 14,000 feet I broke out from under the overcast, but I was also over an undercast. I leveled off and began to fly time and distance. Several times I passed over breaks in the undercast but the haze was actually so thick I was unable to see the water below. Just before my ETA [estimated time of arrival] was up, I saw another break and began a let down, circling so as to stay in the break. Under the impression I was still over water, I was quite surprised to discover I was over land after I had descended to 4,000 feet. I finally broke through completely at 500 feet and saw that I was only five miles from the coast. Because of the weather and a low fuel supply I made an auxiliary landing at Buna to refuel before going over the Owen-Stanleys [mountain range] to Moresby. After landing I sweated out the pictures at the lab and was quite pleased to learn that I had 100% coverage.[31]

Lt. Frederic Hargesheimer experienced more than one terrifying experience while flying missions from Port Moresby. The Japanese shot the pilot down on June 5, 1943, while he searched for barge traffic along the western coastline of New Britain. The submarine USS *Gato* (first of the Gato class of American long-range submarines) rescued him. Following the incident, Hargesheimer returned to duty with the 8th PRS. Five months later on November 1, Hargesheimer aborted a mission and flew back to his base after a double mechanical error that left him flying upside down in an area of "no visibility" outside his cockpit:

Hargesheimer took the dawn flight to Lae this morn and on the way out had a pessel of trouble. The report obtained from him while still excited is somewhat confusing but the following approximates the truth. Hargey was skillfully flying instruments when suddenly one supercharger cut out and at the same time the other engine ran away. This placed the excited one on his back and after losing seven thousand feet, he righted the aircraft. Since the weather was bad he returned to base.[32]

Two weeks after the Japanese shot down Hargesheimer over New Britain, the 8th PRS lost its commander at that time, Major Arthur Post. Japanese aircraft shot down Post during a reconnaissance mission over Rabaul on June 20, 1943. He safely bailed out of his aircraft along the southern coast of New Britain, where local inhabitants found and escorted him to a coast watcher. Post remained with the coast watcher until he was retrieved by the submarine USS *Grouper*. He spent a total of 101 days on New Britain. Post died on August 25, 1944, in an F-5 accident on Biak. He received a Distinguished Service Cross for this operation, and the citation for the medal reads in part:

While serving as a pilot with the 6th Reconnaissance Group, Fifth Air Force, in action against enemy forces on 28 September 1943, near Rabaul, New Britain. Major Post, in an unarmed and unescorted aircraft, voluntarily undertook a photographic mission over Rabaul. Although attacked by enemy planes, he completed his photographic run and, sighting an enemy convoy, photographed it also. After he had evaded the attacking planes with great skill for some time, and had sheared off the wing top of one of them, both his engines were finally shot out. He jumped from the crashing plane, and, to avoid being strafed, pulled the rip cord of his parachute at only 500 feet. Landing severely burned, with an injured leg, and in close proximity to the powerful enemy base, he contrived to find native assistance, and eluded enemy patrols. During a hundred days of hazardous jungle life, he assembled intelligence information which has proven invaluable in the assessment of enemy strength and in assisting the survival of Allied pilots in enemy controlled territory. Captain Post's unquestionable valor in aerial combat is in keeping with the highest traditions of the military service and reflects great credit upon himself and the United States Army Air Forces.[33]

The 8th PRS departed its station at Port Moresby on March 16, 1944, and arrived at Nadzab, New Guinea, the same day. From Nadzab, the squadron moved to Biak Island in August 1944. The 8th PRS of the 6th PRG departed Biak Island and arrived on Leyte on November 3, 1944. Operations for the 8th PRS in the Philippines commenced on November 26. During this last five-day period of November, the squadron flew reconnaissance missions with fighter cover. 8th PRS unit records highlight the transition and provide a view of the type of reconnaissance missions required in the Philippines at this time period:

US reconnaissance photo of a Japanese seaplane base, New Guinea, circa 1942–1943. Note the Mitsubishi F1M2 floatplanes.

Many excellent reconnaissance and mapping photographs were obtained of the Lingayen Gulf and Manila areas of Luzon, and of enemy [air] drones and installations on Bohol, Cebu, Negros, and Panay Islands in the Visayan group. At the same time much ground support work was carried out by the squadron in conjunction with the ground forces operating on Leyte Island. The amount of work done and the great need for photographs reminded the old timers of the days in Port Moresby when the 8th Photo Rcn Squadron was the only organization of its kind operating in this theater.[34]

During the same five days, the 8th PRS lost two aircraft. On November 24, Lt. R. Erickson departed on a mission to the west coast of Leyte Island. The unit heard nothing further of him. The second aircraft loss occurred during a Japanese air raid on the field at Tacloban, from which the unit operated.

8th PRS historical records allow for an examination of the incredible amount of photographic intelligence gathered by American tactical reconnaissance squadrons during World War II. In the month of December 1944, when the unit was fully operational in the Philippines following its move from Biak Island, the squadron pilots photographed objectives resulting in 8,223 negatives, which were then processed into 112,627 prints by the technicians in the unit. The number of prints represented a squadron record, and it is worth noting, since the official maximum potential capability of the unit was 105,000 prints. To produce the 8,223 negatives, the unit expended 9,925 feet of film in the aircraft cameras. That equates to 1.88 miles or 3.03 kilometers of film that month.[35]

The first full month of operations for the 8th PRS in the Philippines occurred in December 1944, during which the squadron pilots flew 168 sorties. Half of these missions covered the island of Luzon. Unit records note the primary objectives of the reconnaissance operations that month:

8th PRS F-5 in the Philippines

A majority of these missions were concerned with completing a top priority mapping project in the Lingayen Gulf area. The reconnaissance missions were flown to secure damage assessment photographs of the Clark and Manila air centers, both of which were under continual battering by daily strikes. Approximately 30 sorties were flown in direct support of ground operations on Leyte I. Coastline oblique photographs taken from minimum altitude by Lt. T. Daochowski were used by members of the 77th Division in their amphibious landing below Ormoc Bay, Leyte I., on 7 December 1944.[36]

Flight Officer Clyde McConnell went down during a mission on December 13. McConnell and Capt. K. Klages departed the squadron area on a reconnaissance mission over Japanese territory. After nearly two hours, McConnell radioed Klages to report he did not have sufficient oxygen to complete their mission. Capt. Klages ordered him to return to the airfield and continued on his own to complete the mission. McConnell disappeared after last being reported over Balayan Bay, Luzon. The 8th PRS declared him missing in action and did not hear anything further on the pilot until December 30, when word arrived he had been forced to bail out of his aircraft. Upon reaching the ground, Filipino guerrilla forces found him and assisted in his return to American forces.[37]

In 1945, the 8th PRS continued to support Army operations in the Philippines with photographic reconnaissance and dispatched pilots to assist other 6th PRG squadrons in their missions. What is probably the most tragic accident of the 8th PRS during World War II occurred on June 7, 1945. Capt. Lewis Gillespie took off from Clark Air Field in the Philippines and conducted a low pass alongside the aircraft carrier USS *Randolph*. Gillespie pulled his plane into a climb, and then it flipped to one side and dove toward the carrier. The F-5 struck the forward flight deck of the carrier and exploded. The explosion and resulting fire killed Gillespie and fourteen sailors on the vessel and destroyed eleven aircraft. The Navy could not locate Gillespie's body in what was left of the wreckage and shoved the debris overboard. The military declared Gillespie "missing in action" and then changed that designation to "Deceased."

The aircraft carrier USS *Randolph* burning in the background after being accidentally struck by an 8th PRS F-5 in the Philippines

On July 28, the squadron moved from the Philippines to the island of Okinawa, closer to Japan, in preparation for supporting the planned invasions of the Japanese home islands. American forces invaded Okinawa on March 26 and finally defeated Japanese troops on the island on July 2—just over two weeks prior to the arrival of the 8th PRS. The squadron remained on the island for two months and then moved operations to mainland Japan following the signing of the surrender documents.

China, Burma, and India (CBI)

The Japanese invaded Burma in January 1942 in support of their operations in Malaysia and the drive to seize Singapore from the British. The Burmese administrative capital of Rangoon, its port facility, and its oil refinery lay as the initial Japanese objective. Chinese troops entered northern Burma in February 1942 to assist the Allies in halting the Japanese advance. They engaged the Japanese but found themselves overmatched and overwhelmed. British and Indian troops resisted the main Japanese thrusts to Rangoon and also found themselves overwhelmed. The Allies ordered a general retreat to India following the fall of Rangoon in March, the Japanese advance to the Burma Road (a supply line to China), the loss of Lashio, and the defeat at Yenangyaung (where the oil fields were located).

The monsoon rains arrived in Burma in May 1942, hampering logistics and troop movements in the country. With the main Allied forces now in India, or having retreated to China, the campaign settled into a near-stalemate as both sides reorganized. Along with the rainy season, both sides contended with thick jungles, poor transportation networks, and the general difficulty of fighting far from main logistical support bases. To make matters worse, both sides viewed Burma as a back-burner issue for the allocation of soldiers, aircraft, and military equipment. This did not mean Burma was not important—the British viewed it as the Japanese pathway to India, and the Japanese considered Burma to be the far-left flank of their empire and a potential pathway to Singapore. As the dry season returned, the British launched two small offensives with limited objectives into Burma, with the larger offensive known as the Arakan Campaign, from December 1942 to May 1943. The United States dispatched a small number of units, including aircraft, to India before the end of 1942 to support the Allies in the Burma campaign and, more importantly, provide assistance to China. The American military referred to the general area as the China Burma India theater (CBI).

The 9th PRS arrived in October 1942 to support the Allied efforts in both Burma and China. The 9th PRS essentially operated in CBI as a number of detachments rather than one consolidated squadron. The unit split upon arrival in October 1942 when the first group of personnel departed India to establish a separate detachment of the squadron in China. In November, three P-3 and P-4 aircraft flew from India to join the new detachment that was forming in China. The main body of the 9th PRS traveled across India to the airfield at Chakulia at the end of the month. A 9th PRS mission statement was not articulated early after arrival but emerged later. The following mission statement provides a good summary of the purpose and operations of the 9th PRS in support of 10th Air Force and the Allied commanders in the CBI. The 9th PRS furnished information for Strategic Air Force Headquarters concerning the strength of enemy airfields, serviceability of important bridges and roads, checks on river transportation and shipping, and the movement around railway centers throughout Burma. Our photographs were used to a great extent in determining bomb assessment on various bridges, important links in the Japanese supply lines to their troops at the front.[38]

Two months after arriving in India, the 9th PRS found itself supporting the limited Allied offensives into Burma. Operations over enemy territory commenced with two sorties on December 13, 1942, and by the end of December, the 9th PRS had flown nineteen missions over Burma. On December 15, the squadron lost its first plane to Japanese antiaircraft. The Japanese defensive fire cut a coolant line, forcing the shutdown of an engine. The pilot attempted a return to the Allied forward airfield at Dum Dum but crashed during the landing approach. Although the plane was lost, the pilot escaped with only minor injuries.[39]

Lt. James Pelphrey successfully bailed out of his aircraft on January 12, 1943, following the loss of an engine within an area of poor weather. Pelphrey flew a reconnaissance mission over Burma and was returning to India when he entered the weather system. One of the engines shut down for unknown mechanical reasons, leaving the pilot to battle violent weather with only one engine. The crash resulted in the second total loss of a 9th PRS aircraft in less than thirty days. Counting this sortie, the squadron flew twenty combat missions during the month of January and was balanced the next month by the arrival of three new P-38 aircraft.[40] In February, Maj. Dale Swartz led the first squadron photographic reconnaissance mission over Rangoon, Burma. The following February, in which the 9th PRS flew thirty combat missions over Burma, the squadron lost its first pilot killed in an accident. Indian forces with the Arakan Campaign stalled in March 1943, and the Japanese counterattacked in April. By May, Indian forces withdrew to India. The 9th PRS reconnaissance missions over Burma continued.

Two additional B-25 bombers arrived at the 9th PRS in early June, bringing the final total to three long-range reconnaissance assets. The squadron flew its first B-25 combat reconnaissance patrol on June 10, and by the end of the month, the unit added seventeen more B-25 missions to its tally. The 9th PRS moved one B-25 with air and ground crew to the airfield

At Dinjan, India, for operations from that location, three new F-5s joined the unit, which amassed a total of thirteen F-4 and F-5 reconnaissance missions, in June. The last mission included the first F-5 photo sortie flown by Lt. Melvin Bates to Burma. He photographed Japanese installations near Pakkoku and Chauk, Burma. During the months of January through May, the forward deployed squadron detachment in China flew a total of forty-two reconnaissance missions.[41]

In June, the 9th PRS altered its operational pattern for covering reconnaissance targets in Burma:

Until [June], pilots had been instructed to take photographs of specific Japanese targets in Burma. Now they turned to picture hunting. A plane was sent out to cover a large area with instructions to shoot pictures of as many objectives as the weather permitted. On many occasions a plane arrived over a target area only to find that cloud cover or local rains made picture taking impossible. Despite these handicaps, photographs were secured on thirteen (13) missions out of twenty-eight (28) undertaken.[42]

The reconnaissance targets for these first six months of 1943 lay in Japanese-held Burma and were adjusted based on the weather and combat operations:

During the month of June, the main effort of the Squadron was directed at targets in the so-called dry area of Burma. Photographs were obtained of the railroad and Irrawaddy River lines of communications, Mandalay, Myitnge, Sagaing, Ywataung, Monywa, Katha, Nabe, Shawabo, Meiktila, Thajaw, Thazi, Myingyan, Pyawbwe, Chauk, Pakkokku, Agwe, Allanymo and the Yennangyaung oil fields. Other areas were not neglected. Four (4) efforts to photograph Rangoon were rendered abortive because of weather. A plane on detached service at Dinjan made two (2) flights over Northern Burma covering objectives in the Sumprabum, Myitkyina, Mogaung, Indaw, Katha, and Bhaso area. During the month planes of the Squadron made four (4) flights to photograph friendly installations.[43]

The Japanese continued to offer resistance to the intrusion of 9th PRS reconnaissance aircraft in June as in previous months of the year:

The operations of the Squadron in June were not without opposition from the Japanese, whose anti-aircraft batteries attempted to shoot down or drive away our planes. The Squadron's B-25s were fired upon over Sagaing on the 13th over Mandalay and Myitnge on the 15th and 20th and over Myingyan on the 17th. No damage was suffered and pictures were obtained on all occasions despite the efforts of the Japanese.[44]

The 21st PRS arrived in India in July 1943 to join the 9th PRS. Personnel in the forward detachment in China were swapped for personnel who were newly arrived with the 21st PRS. The 9th PRS lost a pilot on July 17:

Tragedy again struck the Squadron on the 17th when Second Lieutenant Chancey L. Preece left the Squadron and was not heard of for three days, at which time the Squadron was notified that a crashed airplane had been found in the vicinity of Nanur, India. A searching party was immediately dispatched to the scene and found very little left from the crash. The remains of Lieutenant Preece were buried at the scene by the party and later they were brought to Asansol, India, for burial. On the 28th the funeral was held for Lieutenant Preece in Asansol, the officers and part of the enlisted men attending … The cause of the crash will probably never be known.[45]

Flight Officer Jack Beardon suffered a fatal crash in August. Beardon took off on a local mission on August 4, and is believed to have experienced mechanical difficulty. The plane crashed near the airfield, and Beardon died on impact. The next day, a B-25 of the 9th PRS went down during an attempt to return the plane to the other detachment in India following maintenance work. The two pilots and three enlisted crew members survived, but some suffered serious injuries in the crash.[46] Two more P-38 aircraft of the 9th PRS were lost in September 1943. Both fell to Japanese antiaircraft fire in the vicinity of Rangoon, Burma. The Squadron listed Capt. Don Webster and Lt. Frank Tilcock as "missing in action."[47]

Lt. Philip Robertson flew a reconnaissance mission on September 5, for which he received the Distinguished Flying Cross the following month. His citation for the medal reads in part:

On September 5, 1943, Lieutenant Robertson flew one of the longest photographic reconnaissance missions on record. From its origin at an Indian base, this exceptional flight, lasting eight hours and fifty-five minutes, produced photographs of great importance to the Allied effort. Lieutenant Robertson flew his unarmed single seater aircraft over some of the most heavily defended objectives in enemy held territory as well as executing a 180[-]mile sea search over the Gulf of Martaban. This flight was executed in the face of difficult weather conditions which forced Lieutenant Robertson to perform his photography at altitudes much below those considered reasonably safe from enemy fire. The airline distance covered was almost two thousand miles, not including the mileage covered in evasive action nor the maneuvering required to procure the photographs of objectives. Without protection or the means to fight he returned to base with photographic proof that he had executed in an efficient and precise manner one of the most difficult navigational flights ever performed in this Theater.[48]

Two accidents on the same day in October 1943 resulted in the complete loss of both P-38 aircraft and the life of one pilot. Lt. Melvin Bates died during a take-off accident on October 5. As Bates climbed from the runway, his engine stalled and the aircraft crashed 2 miles from the airfield. The second accident occurred later that same day when Lt. Robert Martin was returning from a mission over Burma. His right engine caught fire, forcing him to bail out of the plane. He landed in the jungle and was missing for the three days it took to walk toward his home base.[49]

The 9th PRS flew 103 combat missions over Burma in November and December 1943. At the end of December, an evaluation of the squadron's first twelve complete months of combat reconnaissance operations became possible. From December 1942 through December 1943, the 9th PRS lost seven aircraft to accidents and/or mechanical issues, one plane to combat, and five pilots, including Lt. John Dunlap, who died in a crash while returning from a mission on December 2.[50]

Refueling an F-5 in Burma

Many of the reconnaissance missions flown in January 1944 targeted Japanese airfields in central Burma:

> The photographs revealed the strength, disposition, and type of aircraft presently employed by the Japanese in that area, and an up to date account of conditions existing at the airdromes themselves. In connection with the Allied bombing efforts, many varied and scattered targets were covered by our planes. The transportation conditions in and about Prome were photographed on several occasions to determine the objectives most vital to the Japanese in their attempt to supply the Akyab front via the Prome-Taungup Road. Other rail centers such as Mandalay, Sagaing and Rangoon were also visited. Photographic cover of the oil fields at Yenangyaung, Chauk, and Lanywa was necessary to assess the bomb damage inflicted on those targets during the month. Among the missions flown to fulfill the needs of the Allied ground forces were those over Kyaukohaw, the Maungdaw-Buthidaung area, and other sections of Burma which are less conspicuously important. In these efforts the Ninth Photographic Reconn Squadron Detachment, which is stationed at Dinjan, also contributed by obtaining photographs of the Northern Section of Burma.[51]

The weather conditions over Burma added to the challenges of Japanese air and ground defenses as the pilots of the 9th PRS flew photographic reconnaissance missions. Clouds frequently blanketed objectives and the wind often proved to be strong. The 9th PRS reported these conditions, which often taxed the most qualified and experienced pilots. The pilots often flew for hours over enemy territory without ever seeing the ground and without the advantage of navigational checkpoints below them. Winds could push an aircraft in any direction, leading the pilot to carefully monitor instruments and mentally determine the approximate location of the plane. In January, Lt. Warren Craig surpassed the flight time of Lt. Robertson in September while attempting to find a break in the clouds to photograph Japanese airfields in Burma:

He continued on, searching for an opening in the clouds until he reached an unknown landing ground in the vicinity of Khunyuam, Thailand, another at Na Soh, Thailand, and a third, also previously unreported one, at Luang Prabang, French-Indo China, over seven hundred miles on a direct flight line from the advance base at Chittagong. The entire flight time amounted to 10 hours and 5 minutes and the distance covered approximately 2,800 miles. The photographs of these airfields which he obtained contained much valuable information on a relatively unfamiliar territory.[52]

The unit documents for January 1944 offer the first glimpse of an attempt to intercept a 9th PRS aircraft by Japanese planes:

Only one case of fighter interception was reported. 1st. Lt. Harold Williams on January 14th, while making his run over Meiktila Airdrome, observed an enemy fighter plane a thousand yards away and above him, slightly behind and to the left. Our plane went into a dive, lost about 2,000 feet and made a slow turn to the left which put him over Kangaung Landing Ground, the last objective of the mission. He managed to take one exposure of Kangaung before the enemy plane again appeared, this time directly ahead and above and going into a medium dive. Lt. Williams headed into a steep dive for a thousand feet, leveled off and returned home without further incident.[53]

In the unit documents for February 1944, the commander's report better placed the mission of the 9th PRS into the context of Allied air operations in Burma at that time. During the month, Allied air assets were primarily directed at interdicting Japanese land communications and airdromes. The 9th PRS, in turn, provided the photography for 10th Air Force and Allied ground commanders to determine the order and type of strikes based on the current situation as recorded by the reconnaissance pilots. Then the 9th PRS pilots would return to the objectives and secure photographs for bomb damage assessment. The most common objectives assigned for photography in February included Japanese supply dumps and supply installations, airfields, and bridges. A good example of how this reconnaissance system worked can be seen in the Allied attacks on the Japanese Prome supply installations in Burma. Once selected as a potential target based on earlier photographic reconnaissance, Lt. Malin Francis flew a mission to Prome and secured fresh photographs for analysis. An Allied bombing raid occurred a few days later based on the photography. Following the attack, Lt. Samuel Roth of the 9th PRS flew a mission to Prome to record the bomb damage to the Japanese supply facilities. Upon Roth's return, technicians processed and interpreted the film that was removed from the aircraft. Apparently, Allied planners did not believe sufficient damage had resulted from the first attack and ordered three more waves of bombers to strike the supply installations.

The Allied bombing of a bridge at Budalin on February 7, in Burma, offers another glimpse into the role of the 9th PRS in Allied air operations. Capt. John Buffin made a reconnaissance flight over the bridge on February 7 and returned with photographs. After developing and processing, Allied commanders, including those at 10th Air Force, ordered a B-25 raid on the bridge in order to cut the transportation line and disrupt Japanese supplies and troops. Lt. Brown flew a bomb damage assessment photographic mission to the bridge after the raid. Technicians analyzing the photographs determined that the southern approaches onto the bridge were demolished, rendering the bridge unusable for military traffic. On February 22, Lt. Tucker received an assignment to return to the bridge for more photographs. Analysis of his photographs indicated that the Japanese had repaired the bridge and was again serviceable.[54]

In April 1944, the primary emphasis for 9th PRS reconnaissance was on the oil fields in Burma, although railway communications, airfields, and supply facilities remained important. The oil fields of Burma were (and are today) small by comparison to major fields across the world including those in Indonesia. However, all sources of oil were important for the Japanese war effort at this point in the conflict. Pilots of the 9th PRS also aided the American ground forces of Gen. Joseph "Vinegar Joe" Stillwell in northern Burma in this month by providing tactical reconnaissance in support of their operations.

On April 2, Lt. Arthur Schaaf found himself ambushed by a Japanese pilot during a reconnaissance mission:

About 15 miles west of Monywa an enemy aircraft dived out of the sun and attempted to attack him. Lt. Schaaf immediately put his P-38 into a steep dive and bank, reaching an indicated air speed of 300 miles per hour and lost the enemy, momentarily. He continued on his easterly course but the Japanese pilot followed him and once again tried to get close enough to attack, but Lt. Schaaf outmaneuvered him. Being so close to his objective, it would have been impossible to get any pictures, so Lt. Schaaf was forced to return to Chittagong.[55]

Lt. Clair Sauter found himself on the receiving end of tracers fired by a Japanese fighter on May 5:

Sauter, completing his run over Hmawbi airfield at 30,000 feet noticed red tracers passing over his plane. The source of these tracers, probably a Tojo [Japanese Nakajima Ki-44 fighter], appeared flying out of the sun at 10 o'clock and above Lt. Sauter's aircraft. After pressing his attack, the enemy passed 200 feet above. Using evasive tactics, Lt Sauter banked to the right and toward the enemy. It seems likely the enemy pilot was unaware that our plane was not armed. At any rate, he executed a split S maneuver and was not seen again by Lt. Sauter who photographed his final objective and returned to base with the mark of a Japanese bullet in his right aileron. He himself was uninjured.[56]

By July 1944, the primary missions of the 9th PRS centered on monitoring the number and types of aircraft at Japanese airfields and tracking traffic on the Irrawaddy River in Burma. The squadron lost a pilot, who crashed while conducting a P-38 altitude test.

In September, progress in the Allied offensive in Burma resulted in the first 9th PRS personnel moving from India to Tinghawk Sakan, Burma, to establish a forward detachment of the unit. The primary operational focus of the new detachment entailed providing reconnaissance support for Allied forces in northern Burma. The majority of missions for the squadron continued to focus on Japanese airfields and aircraft counts. Cloudy weather over Burma throughout the month contributed to the welcome relief that not a single 9th PRS aircraft reported receiving any antiaircraft fire or interception attempts by Japanese fighters.

Throughout October and into November, photographic reconnaissance of Japanese airfields continued to be the primary mission of the 9th PRS. The squadron did photograph other sites and installations as requested. For example, 224 Group of the Royal Air Force requested the 9th PRS to conduct a series of mosaic photography sweeps of terrain to assist ground operations of the British Army in Burma. American authorities asked for reconnaissance assistance along the coast of Burma in a search for a missing B-29.

40th PRS F-5 in Burma, 1945

Another pilot died in a P-38 test flight in December 1944. A noticeable shift in missions' emphasis from airfields and aircraft counts to photographic reconnaissance of Japanese lines of communication occurred in December. Roads, trails, and waterways were the focus of the missions. This mission emphasis continued into 1945—but, by February, the 9th PRS found itself photographing lines of communication into Thailand as the Allied offensive progressed. That month, other requests to the unit included mosaic photographic missions into southwestern China and northwestern French Indo-China (modern Laos). The Squadron flew fewer missions than normal in April after receiving orders to depart Burma and move westward back to India as combat in the CBI theater declined. From May until the end of World War II in September, the 9th PRS ceased flying combat missions as the war waned in the CBI.

Conclusion of World War II

The best way to close this chapter on American tactical air reconnaissance in World War II is to examine its conclusion through the eyes of a reconnaissance unit. The 71st PRG operated from the American-occupied island of Ie Shima, near Okinawa, when two Japanese Mitsubishi G4M Betty bombers arrived on the island with peace delegates enroute to Manila to meet with Gen. Douglas MacArthur. At Ie Shima, the Japanese delegation boarded an American C-54 Skymaster transport plane for the final stage to Manila. The unit historical records open with the events leading up to the arrival of the delegation:

This month [August 1945] has been a historic month, for besides the Headquarters movement [to Ie Shima], many events took place, changing the course of world events. First, the atomic bomb was dropped on Hiroshima, Japan, beginning a new atomic age, then Russia entered the war against Japan, on the Allied side. Rumors were started throughout the world concerning peace feelers put out by the Japanese, and toward the middle of August, it was announced that the Japanese accepted the Potsdam Ultimatum without reserve.[57]

One of the two Japanese G4M "Betty" bombers carrying the delegation to meet American general Douglas MacArthur in the Philippines to discuss Japan's surrender. Personnel of the 71st PRG watched the arrival of the Japanese aircraft to Ie Shima island, where the delegates transferred to an American C-54 Skymaster transport plane for the final leg of their journey.

Group documents record the historic landing of the Japanese delegation on Ie Shima on August 19, 1945:

Circling the small island of Ie Shima, the two Japanese twin[-]engined bombers arrived here at 1233/I 19 August 1945. The planes were painted white, with dark green crosses on the tail, wings, and fuselage. The Betty bombers looked as though they were painted in haste, with one giving the appearance of a brush paint job, and the other a spray job. The green crosses were as dark, that from the air they appeared to be black. Four B-25s had been sent up to give the Nip planes instructions as they approached the island, while one B-25 was a photo ship. Approximately forty allied planes, including P-38s, B-25s, [US Navy] Corsairs, a B-17, and a PBY [amphibious aircraft], covered the Japanese as they approached the island. The planes circled at 2,000 feet, then landed on B strip and were taxied to the South and to a revetment area. The surrender Envoys were enroute to Manila, to confer with Representatives of the Supreme Allied Commander, Gen. Douglas MacArthur . . . The Japanese pilots were very young, and one of them was difficult to distinguish from an ordinary American. He wore boots, silken overalls, and a fleeced lined flying cap . . . In the revetment where the planes were kept, the M.Ps. [military police] stood in an open doorway in one of the Nip bombers, with big grins on their faces. In their hands were two bottles of Japanese saki.[58]

The Korean War

Tactical Reconnaissance is a tough, lonesome business, requiring a special brand of courage and self-reliance.

—*Capt. E. R. Harden, 15th TRS*

Introduction

Japan occupied Korea in 1910 after thirty-four years of overseeing the peninsula via a "sphere of influence" arrangement. The United States and the Soviet Union split the Korean peninsula into two occupation zones after World War II. Cold War political issues resulted in the two occupied zones of Korea emerging as separate independent states, which is similar to what occurred with the two Germanys in Europe. A political rivalry developed, with both of the new Korean states maintaining that it held legitimate claim over the entire peninsula. North Korea aided the Chinese Communists in their struggle to overthrow the Chinese Nationalist government. After their victory and the withdrawal of the Chinese Nationalists to Taiwan, the new Chinese government under Mao Zedong provided philosophical and material aid to North Korea. This included forming and aiding socialist-based guerrillas in South Korea. North Korean leader Kim Il-Sung secured the support of both the Soviet Union and People's Republic of China and then dispatched his army across the 38th parallel, dividing the two Koreas on June 25, 1950.

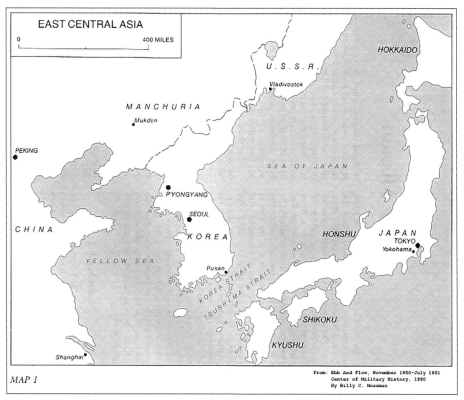

Map of northeast Asia and the Korean Peninsula

The United States was again not prepared for a conflict. Much of the American military had been demobilized after World War II, shrinking the total force to a size that could barely police the peace after the war, let alone fight a new one. In 1950, the United States Air Force maintained only three fully manned, tactical reconnaissance jet squadrons—two in the United States and one in Japan. The 8th Tactical Reconnaissance Squadron (TRS) unit represented the only available unit of its type that was ready for action in the western Pacific when North Korea crossed the 38th parallel. The squadron consisted of RF-80 aircraft, which were F-80 jet fighters modified to carry cameras for photographic reconnaissance work. The Lockheed F/RF-80 Shooting Star was the first operational jet fighter of the United States Air Force after World War II. While it was advanced technology when introduced in 1945, the plane was already becoming outdated in 1950 after the introduction of the American F-86 and Soviet MiG-15 fighters.

15th TRS RF-80

The Air Force converted sixty-six F-80A to RF-80A reconnaissance aircraft. Six of these were later modified again, along with seventy additional F-80A and F-80C to RF-80C reconnaissance planes at the end of the war. The F/RF-80s carried a crew of one and could attain a speed of 585 mph, an altitude of 46,800 feet, and a range of 824 miles. The RF-80 held cameras inside a translucent nose panel on a longer nose than the F-80. The extra length permitted the six machine guns to be replaced by the cameras, which meant these aircraft flew unarmed. However, many RF-80s retained their gun barrels in the nose despite not having the actual weapons as a hopeful deterrent.

1950

As of the first day of the attack, on June 25, Gen. Douglas MacArthur commanded the Far East Command from his headquarters in Japan. The Far East Command consisted of the Naval Forces, Far East, under VAdm. C. Turner Joy and the Far East Air Forces, commanded by Lt. Gen. George E. Stratemeyer. The latter's organization included 5th Air Force, based in Japan under Maj. Gen. Earle E. "Pat" Partridge. There were initial questions as to whether Korea fell under the command responsibility of MacArthur. President Harry Truman quickly cut this question off when he authorized MacArthur on June 25 to employ air and naval forces to halt North Korea. Two days later, the United Nations Security Council approved a resolution calling for collective United Nations action in Korea as a result of the Soviet representative's boycotting a meeting and not being able to cast his country's veto.[1]

Gen. MacArthur called for Gen. Partridge to hit the North Korean columns and logistics located south of the 38th parallel and establish an air cover over Japan in case the Soviet Union utilized the distractions in Korea to launch an attack on Japan. MacArthur firmly believed the Air Force could pound the North Koreans into halting the offensive. Partridge promised he would launch his first airstrike with B-26 medium bombers on June 27. However, before one can bomb, one needs reconnaissance to select the targets. Gen. Partridge turned to his only Air Force reconnaissance unit, the 8th Tactical Reconnaissance Squadron. The squadron moved some aircraft to Itazuke, Japan, for operations over the Korean peninsula.

1Lt. Bryce Poe of the 8th TRS flew a solo RF-80 mission to collect photos of potential targets south of the 38th parallel, resulting in a B-26 raid on June 28. Poe's flight was the first tactical combat jet reconnaissance mission for the US Air Force. Twelve B-26 bombers struck the Munsan railroad yard and then strafed North Korean trucks on a nearby highway. A flight of four B-29 bombers patrolled the four access routes of the North Korean advance and attacked targets of opportunity as they presented themselves on the roads. General Stratemeyer's diary briefly mentions Lt. Poe's flight, along with the other issues, on the twenty-seventh:

Airlift progressing; evacuees [US civilians departing South Korea] taken out by airplane and sea. Reconnaissance and actual combat proving that North Koreans supported by Yak–3s, Yak–5s, and some Il–10s. FEAF handicapped in this shooting war by not being permitted to cross the 38th Parallel to destroy enemy at its source of staging.[2]

Authorization from President Truman to strike targets north of the 38th parallel arrived on June 30—a day after MacArthur ordered a bombing attack on the airfield in the North Korean capital.[3]

A chapter on Air Force tactical reconnaissance during the Korean War would not be complete without a short narrative about Lt. Poe, future four-star general, who flew the first RF-80 reconnaissance mission. Poe piloted the first two jet reconnaissance overflights of the Soviet Union, completing both missions

Gen. Bryce Poe in a postwar photograph. As a lieutenant in the Korean War era, Poe flew several deep RF-80 reconnaissance missions over Chinese and Soviet territory.

in an RF-80 modified to carry larger wingtip fuel drop tanks. The reconnaissance targets of the first overflight in May 1949 (at the end of the Berlin Blockade) were the Kuril Islands; during the second mission, in March 1950, it overflew Vladivostok. It is interesting to note that American political authorities in Washington, DC, were not aware of these two overflights. The flights in the Far East Command were so secret at the time that Poe reported directly to generals MacArthur and Stratemeyer with his information and hand-carried the photographs of Soviet airfields. Poe also overflew Chinese coastal ports near Taiwan to ensure they were not being used to stage forces that might take advantage of the Korean War to land Chinese troops on the island. His combat record in the Korean war included over ninety missions over North Korea with an additional nineteen sensitive missions near airfields in China and to photograph the bridges over the Yalu River. Later, Poe flew 231 combat missions in the RF-4C during the Vietnam War.[4]

In August 1950, the Far East Command tapped Lieutenant Poe again to perform missions over the Soviet Union . . . this time with the knowledge and approval of Washington, DC. The overflight was to verify any changes in aircraft or possible alert status in preparation for any Soviet intervention in the Korean War or attack on Japan. He flew an RF-80 again and noted:

I was pulled again into Misawa to look at the Soviet airfields, and things got pretty hot. We'd have two or three missions to look at the Soviets, and then come back to Korea, and then have two or three more missions to look at the Soviets. I dropped fuel tanks there, too, but that was okay—because I had General MacArthur's permission to do so! Finally, things got so hot with the Soviets that I would take somebody to cover me, and we'd have the F–80s out. I was sure glad to see them! They never had to fight, but I was sure glad to see them. After this, General MacArthur called me for briefing, just one-on-one, and he knew all the targets and all the places.[5]

By July 7, the reconnaissance assets over Korea numbered at least eight RB-29s of the 31st Strategic Reconnaissance Squadron and twelve RF-80s of the 8th Tactical Reconnaissance Squadron. All of the RF-80s were now located at Itazuke, Japan. The North Koreans maintained a steady push southward along four axes of advance. The South Korean army melted to a fragment of its original size, and the United States was hard-pressed to place sufficient forces on the ground to stymie the offensive. United Nations troops from other states would need more time to join the effort. The 8th Tactical Reconnaissance Squadron scrambled to meet the reconnaissance requirements of the ground commanders. By August, the 162nd Tactical Reconnaissance Squadron (night photography) arrived from the United States. The unit flew RB-26 medium bombers, which now carried photoflash bombs rather than fragmentation bombs. The former are designed to produce a tremendous flash of light near the ground when dropped, permitting cameras to photograph the area. As during World War I and World War II, armies often move at night to avoid observation, and the job of night photography is to capture them in the act. A second reconnaissance technical squadron also arrived in Japan to assist with film processing and delivery.

The 162nd TRS RB-26s were in the air and providing night time reconnaissance very quickly. On September 4, one of the RB-26s reported evidence of large numbers of vehicles crossing the border from China into North Korea two months before the Chinese offensive. General Stratemeyer wrote the following in his diary entry for September 4:

Observation of 162d TAC Rcn Sq aircraft from 3,000 feet at 040030/K Sept 50: Scattered lights of estimated 200 vehicles going generally south from Yangsi (39°59′N–124°28′E). Numerous vehicles coming across Manchurian border above Yangsi into Korea. Other vehicular convoys observed on adjacent roads in general area between Yangsi and P'yongyang. Fifth AF reports missions have been laid on to attack these targets.[6]

162nd TRS RB-26 night-reconnaissance aircraft

12th TRS (redesignated from the 162nd TRS in 1952) RB-26 night-reconnaissance aircraft. Photo taken in Japan.

Gen. MacArthur's plan to break the North Korean push against the American and South Korean forces in the Pusan Perimeter involved a bold naval landing at the town of Inchon, which lay slightly southwest of the South Korean capital of Seoul. A quick advance could liberate Seoul and initiate an entrapment of the North Korean forces along the Pusan Perimeter. The move involved many risks due to the sharply rising and falling tides at Inchon, requiring the arrival of landing craft to be incredibly precise in their timing. The 8th TRS served as an important set of eyes for MacArthur and his naval commanders in planning the Inchon landings. The RF-80s flew numerous sorties across the area, photographing the planned landing areas at all times during the tidal cycle. At the same time, the squadron staff had to ensure the sorties were scattered in order to not alert the North Koreans to the American interest in Inchon. Lt. Poe commented that he personally flew many photographic missions over Inchon to gather the photographs needed by the naval commanders. Other RF-80 pilots continued supporting reconnaissance for Allied forces behind the Pusan Perimeter and scouting North Korean airfields and logistics sites.

Aerial reconnaissance photograph of Inchon prior to the United Nations amphibious operation of September 1950

Following the successful landings at Inchon on September 15 and the rapid movement of US troops from the coast, combined with a breakout from the Pusan Perimeter, the mission requirements for the reconnaissance pilots increased. Lt. Poe commented:

When the Inchon landings came at last, I had about seven times the work. The front split at Seoul, running west and east, and eventually joined together. We had tremendous recce demands, and the Marines and Navy sometimes covered our recce operations. It was a very pleasant thing when you had the Navy looking out for you with their blue airplanes.[7]

45th TRS RF-51

The 5th Air Force formed a new unit, the 45th Tactical Reconnaissance Squadron, on September 3, two weeks before the Inchon landings. Being a new unit, the squadron lacked everything and needed two months to receive its first aircraft. Plans called for the unit to operate with RF-51 aircraft. These were the P-51 Mustang fighters of World War II but modified for reconnaissance work. Mustangs held an advantage over the RF-80s when it came to maneuvering at lower speeds and altitude to locate North Korean troops and equipment in the hills of South Korea. The RF-51s could also fly for longer distances and loiter longer over the battlefield.

The 8th TRS lost two RF-80s in September. The first loss occurred on September 11, when Lt. Marshall Williams did not return from a reconnaissance mission. He was declared dead while missing in action. The second downed pilot, Lt. Donald Drama, departed the airfield at Itazuke, Japan, on September 16, for a reconnaissance mission over central Korea. All contact with Drama was lost as he approached the Korean coast. He is listed as missing in action and presumed dead. The precise circumstances behind the loss of both men behind North Korean lines in September is not known since they were flying without wingmen. Some sources indicate the 8th TRS lost a third RF-80 to small-arms fire on September 3, but corroborating information is lacking at this point, including the name of the pilot. It is possible that the plane had been damaged, returned, and was later misidentified.

American forces moved steadily toward the Yalu River border between North Korea and China. Since July, the Chinese government had been secretly discussing a possible intervention, which became probable after the Inchon landing. Chinese troops quietly crossed the Yalu River as early as October 19 and commenced limited operations on October 25. A month later, the Chinese were engaged in a full offensive.

Lt. Hamilton Shawe of the 8th TRS received a Silver Star medal for a mission he flew along the west coast of Korea on the first day of October. The award citation presents a good snapshot of a reconnaissance mission:

On 1 October 1950, while serving as a pilot of the 8th Tactical Reconnaissance Squadron, First Lieutenant Shawe displayed an exceptional degree of flying skill, courage and competence. Alone in an unarmed reconnaissance aircraft, he flew 425 miles to his target, the port of Wonsan in Korea. Upon reaching his objective he made repeated photographic runs at a dangerously low altitude over the strongly defended beach and port area. In spite of his aircraft being repeatedly hit by enemy ground fire, Lieutenant Shawe continued making passes until his mission of nine runs was completed. Information gained from the excellent photographs taken by Lieutenant Shawe proved invaluable to the United Nations forces in their subsequent planning for the landing at Wonsan. Lieutenant Shawe's conspicuous gallantry and outstanding skill were in keeping with the highest traditions of the military service and reflect great credit upon himself, the Far East Air Forces and the United States Air Force.[8]

The 8th TRS lost an RF-80 on October 20. The aircraft, piloted by Capt. Benjamin Rader, went down south of the North Korean capital of Pyongyang. He was listed as MIA and presumed dead. As can be seen so many times across the conflicts, a hazard of solo reconnaissance flights is the accumulation of MIA aircrews. When a lone reconnaissance plane goes down, there is not another person there who can pinpoint the location, verify a parachute or survivor on the ground, call for rescue, or even report what happened to the other aircraft and pilot.

November proved to be a tough month for the Air Force reconnaissance squadrons in Korea. Countering the Chinese offensive taxed their sortie capabilities (as well as those of all Air Force squadrons), and the 162nd Tactical Reconnaissance Squadron experienced a high number of "duds" among its flash bombs, preventing many attempts to conduct night photography of Chinese movements. Chinese intervention brought MiG-15 fighters into the fray, and they outclassed the unarmed RF-80 reconnaissance planes in speed, agility and, obviously, weaponry. Col. Sam Dickens, a reconnaissance lieutenant during the Korean War, spoke about this turn of events many years later:

Then along came the Chinese intervention in November. We recce'd [British slang for "reconnoitered"] targets at Anju and Sinuiju, in MiG Alley. One time, we had one RF–80 and two escort F–80s that tangled with three MiGs. I didn't tangle with them, but a classmate of mine did on another mission, to check on the location of enemy fighters. Somebody had said, "Well, you don't need any escort fighters," so my classmate had to fly his aircraft solo. He was jumped, and they tangled for a long time, but he was lucky and got back. We didn't fly any of those airplanes unescorted again.[9]

Gen. Stratemeyer dispatched a memorandum on November 5 to Gen. Partridge in reference to Gen. MacArthur's directives against the Chinese forces entering North Korea. A section related to tactical reconnaissance follows:

To: CG FAF (Stratline) CG FEAF BomCom (Courier) Info: CINCFE (Courier) COMNAVFE (Courier) CG TWENTIETH AF (Stratline) Personal Partridge and O'Donnell from Stratemeyer. This message in five parts . . . On 5 November 50, General MacArthur directed the following action:

It is essential that we obtain immediately photo reconnaissance of the Manchurian border area of North Korea, particularly of the international bridges. Your RF–80s should be put on this job at once. They must not violate the border in obtaining this reconnaissance. Advise me of any reconnaissance targets your RF–80s cannot photograph in accordance with this policy and I will assign those targets to the 31st Squadron [31st Strategic Reconnaissance Squadron with RB-29s].[10]

Despite the scarce number of tactical reconnaissance aircraft available for operations, politics diverted approximately 25 percent of the available aircraft flying for both the 8th TRS and 162nd TRS. A December Public Information Office project to "photographically display the ground support by the 5th Air Force" required the use of four RF-80 and four RB-26 aircraft . . . at a time when Chinese forces were moving down the Korean peninsula. General Stratemeyer directed Gen. Partridge to discontinue the use of these reconnaissance air assets to support the Public Information project. He added in his diary, "Every available recon airplane must work to determine where the Red Chinese armies are."[11]

The significance of his scarce tactical reconnaissance assets to overall battlefield planning and control can be seen in a Redline Message dispatched by Gen. Stratemeyer to Gen. Hoyt Vandenberg on December 21:

Recent successive rapid withdrawals of UN ground forces has resulted in almost complete lack of contact with Chinese Commies in Army Eight sectors. Field commanders have been directed by GHQ to conduct aggressive patrolling forward from defensive positions to locate enemy but best information in our opinion of pattern of enemy movement coming from air sighting and covert sources. Main supply routes in enemy rear areas are fairly well established by air reports and we are taking all possible action to interdict. Chinese advance combat elements displace forward by small elements over secondary roads and trails; are well dispersed over wide areas; apparently well trained in camouflage and concealment; and utilize very little motor transport or heavy equipment. Consequently photography furnished partial confirmation of visual sightings and is not conclusive in determining strength, dispositions, and movements. I consider situation most critical and have directed all out air reconnaissance, visual and photo, day and night, supplemented by combat crew reports to fill in picture of enemy ground dispositions.[12]

Gen. Stratemeyer added on December 26, that he could not rely on RB-29 aircraft for daily reconnaissance coverage of North Korean airfields due to their relatively slow speeds compared to the Chinese MiG fighters. He noted, "In my opinion, the RB–29s would not be able to live for visual or photo reconnaissance unless escorted by prohibitive numbers of fighters."[13] With the increasing losses of RB-29s, an unsuccessful test application of RB-45 jet aircraft, and the unavailability of the new RB-47 jet aircraft, the Air Force maintained an important reliance on its few RF-80, RB-26 (for night operations), and the newly arrived RF-51 aircraft.

The RB-45 was developed from the B-45 Tornado, the first jet-powered bomber of the United States. Only thirty-eight of the aircraft were built as the reconnaissance version or converted to that version, and they were not well-accepted during the Korean War. The RB-45's purpose involved strategic rather than tactical reconnaissance and is not a focal point of this book. But at the same time, the Air Force did experiment with it during the Korean War. The aircraft could attain a speed of 556 mph, a ceiling of 46,000 feet, and a range of 1,192 miles. The RF-80 could fly faster and higher than the RB-45. Its one advantage was a 50 percent greater combat range than the RF-80, making it a better choice for long-range strategic missions where fuel and distance were critical factors. The Air Force deployed three of the RB-45C aircraft to Japan for night operations during the Korean War. On December 4, 1950, A MiG-15 piloted by Aleksandr F. Andrianov shot down an RB-45 over China, demonstrating the vulnerability of the aircraft in an air-patrolled hostile environment. All four crew members died, although rumors persist that the pilot survived and "disappeared" following interrogations about the aircraft by Soviet personnel. One RB-45 reportedly flew tests with a special paint scheme designed to fool North Korean aircraft searchlights. In the end, the deployment of the RB-45 was more of an American test of the plane's capabilities and of being asset in overflying China and Vladivostok, Russia, than a tool in the holster for General Stratemeyer, who wrote on December 26:

> The lessons of this war so far have shown us that we need almost daily coverage of airfields if we are to successfully destroy the enemy's air capability. Since no additional RB–45s are to be deployed to this theater, I am worried as to just what we should do for this type of reconnaissance.[14]

RB-45C Tornado

45th TRS RF-51. Note the camera portal to the right of the star on the fuselage.

December showed at least one glimmer of hope when the 45th TRS received its first RF-51 aircraft. Much of the narrative of this chapter regarding 1951 will follow the 45th TRS via its own documents as the unit grew and developed into an experienced combat reconnaissance unit. The 45th TRS received ten RF-51 aircraft from December 3–4, and the remaining two RF-51s from December 6–7, providing the squadron with a full complement of twelve aircraft. Although the squadron now had operational aircraft, the pilots needed to undergo a reconnaissance training program. Those with reconnaissance experience from World War II trained the other pilots. Training included aerial gunnery, visual reconnaissance, and aerial photography techniques . . . with film that dated to World War II. Before the end of December, the squadron had certified nine of its twenty available pilots for reconnaissance missions. The 45th TRS lost one RF-51 on December 23, when Capt. Clyde East (the high-scoring reconnaissance pilot from World War II) experienced engine trouble during a training flight near Okayama, Japan. East bailed out at 2,500 feet and landed safely.[15]

Fifth Air Force ordered the 45th TRS to move from Japan to K-2 Airfield near Taegu, Korea. Ten RF-51s arrived in Korea on December 28, and two experienced pilots, including Capt. East, flew the squadron's first combat missions the next day. The squadron flew eight more combat missions on December 30–31. All of these were orientation flights to become acquainted with the terrain.[16]

The 15th TRS lost an RF-80 piloted by Lt. Hamilton Shawe, the pilot to whom the Silver Star was awarded after an October mission. Shawe was captured in December and held until the end of the war. Shawe's loss and the initial mystery surrounding it proved to be a major point in the argument for eliminating the requirement for reconnaissance aircraft to fly alone on missions. Fellow pilot Capt. J. B. Smith wrote:

Things were getting pretty tense and opinions were voiced that we should have a fighter escort or some similar protection. December rolled around with no operational changes. The old Recce motto, "Alone, Unarmed, and Unafraid" just didn't cut it anymore. I was devastated when Bruce [Hamilton Bruce Shawe] went down. The squadron did everything to discover some trace. We had a pretty good idea of the general area he should have been in. Eventually a pile of wreckage was located on the mud flats on the West Coast north of Seoul which we thought could be Bruce's RF-80. I and Stan Sebring stared at the photos with our stereoscopes for many hours but could not be sure.[17]

After Shawe's loss, the 15th TRS began assigning a second RF-80 on each mission to provide escort for the primary reconnaissance plane. As a reminder, an RF-80 was not armed; so, this escort plane could not defend its wingman but could provide another set of eyes and search for antiaircraft guns on the ground. Capt. Smith was shot down and captured one month after Shawe was lost.

1951

In January 1951, the Chinese offensive ground to a halt because of massive logistical issues. Chinese forces began to withdraw northward to reestablish their logistics lines before UN forces were aware of the shift. General Stratemeyer requested the assignment of Colonel Karl "Pop" Polifka in January. Some military personnel referred to him as "Photo Pop." Polifka, perhaps the most famous of the Air Force's reconnaissance officers in the twentieth

Col. Karl "Pop" Polifka, commander of the 67th TRW

century, established and assumed command of the 67th Tactical Reconnaissance Wing (TRW) in January. The 67th TRW was officially activated on February 25, 1951. This move provided the Air Force an opportunity to reorganize its reconnaissance assets, which originally had been assembled ad hoc. The newly formed 67th Tactical Reconnaissance Group (TRG) replaced the inactivated 543rd TSC. The 8th TRS received a new designation as the 15th TRS and continued to be the only tactical reconnaissance squadron flying jet aircraft. The 15th TRS, 45th TRS, and the 12th TRS evolved into the three operational squadrons of the 67th TRG. The 67th TRW under Polifka provided overall oversight of the 67th TRG. Colonel Dickens described the mission distribution among the squadrons of the 67th TRG in this way:

> Then there was the 45th Tac Recon Squadron, the "Polka Dots" squadron, which flew RF–51s. Then there was the 15th Tac Recon Squadron, which had been the 8th. The 15th was the only recce squadron that was equipped with jet aircraft, the RF–80s. Missions were divided between the RB–26 night photography; the RF–51s for close-in targets (closer to the friendly forces), visual reconnaissance, and photographic reconnaissance; and the RF–80s doing missions that were deeper.[18]

Throughout January 1951, the 45th TRS flew 236 operational sorties and logged 514 combat hours as a squadron. The RF–51s flew similar types of missions as the reconnaissance aircraft of World War II and even World War I. Ten missions involved photographic assignments, and the others were visual reconnaissance with photographic confirmation of anything deemed important. Fifth Air Force authorized the 45th TRS to add a ground

Photographic Interpretation Section

attack element to the missions on January 5, which was more in line with World War I than World War II. A pilot held the option to engage small targets while flying a visual reconnaissance mission. The shortage of tactical reconnaissance assets can be seen in the January 19 5th Air Force directive to assign single aircraft to each mission. Flying as pairs for protection was now a luxury in 1951.

The 45th TRS received its first battle damage to an RF-51 on January 26, when Capt. Warren Hawes returned with antiaircraft gun damage near the town of Chunchon. The next day, Capt. Lloyd Simpson received minor antiaircraft damage to his plane. Four days later, Lt. E. Carroll made a successful emergency landing due to an engine failure. While not stated in the maintenance and operational reports, the 45th TRS experienced two serious incidents of contaminated fuel, grounding all aircraft for three days while mechanics drained and flushed the RF-51s' fuel systems. The first, on January 14, resulted from dirt and foreign matter in the fuel tanks, necessitating a loss of two operational days, at a time when the Chinese forces were moving south and engaging UN forces. The second occurred one day before the emergency landing of Lt. Carroll:

On 29 January an alert crew chief discovered that a large amount of JP-1 fuel was present in the fuel within the tanks of his aircraft. An inspection of other aircraft on the line disclosed that all aircraft had fuel contaminated in the same manner. A full day's operational commitments had to be cancelled while the fuel systems on all aircraft were again drained and flushed. It is estimated that at least thirty (30) sorties were cancelled due to contaminated fuel in the month of January.[19]

The 45th TRS experienced other issues during its first full month of combat operations. Four flights were aborted due to radio difficulties and sixteen due to engine trouble. Another eight flights returned early as a result of engine trouble. Squadron personnel complained of receiving little support for these issues from any higher headquarters. Perhaps an even more important problem involved a shortage of aircraft. Demands for aerial reconnaissance meant the 45th TRS received a daily sortie rate of ten missions. Yet after the first crash in Japan, the squadron held only eleven RF-51s on its books, and maintenance requirements frequently prevented ten of these from flying on a given day. Each day that one or more aircraft could not be declared mission-capable meant ground troops went without aerial reconnaissance support during this crucial time in the Korean War.

From January 10 to 21, the squadron was assigned areas forward of US X Corps and Republic of Korea III Corps territories, which were not completely covered by friendly troops. The purpose of the reconnaissance in this area was to keep close coverage where only scattered friendly troops were placed, thereby permitting part of the X Corps and III ROK Corps to be deployed in other positions.[20]

The 8th TRS (soon to be 15th TRS) lost Lt. J. B. Smith in January. He received a special mission for a low and fast "all cameras" reconnaissance run over Pyongyang. Col. Polifka personally designed the mission and assigned it to Smith, who flew with a wingman, Lt. Stanley Sebring, to confirm intelligence reports of new gun emplacements. The pair conducted the overflight and returned, only to learn a camera had not functioned properly during the operation. Col. Polifka asked Smith whether he thought he could repeat the mission. Smith agreed, and Sebring later recorded what happened on both attempts:

> The mission went off as planned, but even with the element of surprise at 50 feet and .8 mach, he caught plenty of flak. Fortunately he didn't get hit. A couple of hours later in the photo lab it was Oh S**t Time! One of the side oblique cameras had malfunctioned. So, another meeting was called. This time Col. Polifka said, "JB, you did a fine job of flying that mission, but it needs to be flown again, and I know you can do it." So, JB tried it again. This time the North Koreans were not surprised and JB was shot down and became a POW. Of course at the time, we didn't know that. He was listed as missing in action. I packed up his personal effects and wrote a letter to his wife, Cherrie. It wasn't until the war was over that I learned that JB had survived.[21]

Fuel issues persisted for the 45th TRS into February when the unit lost another day of sorties due to contaminated fuel. Squadron pilots made four emergency landings as a direct result of enemy antiaircraft fire and one due to mechanical difficulty. Counting the four RF-51s making emergency landings due to hostile action, a total of ten squadron aircraft received antiaircraft damage that month. Eight involved minor damage; one plane received major damage, and one plane was shot down. The latter represents the first combat loss for the 45th TRS. The record of the loss follows:

> On 1 February Lt James L. Rice was forced to abandon RF-51 aircraft #44-84844 after it had received severe damage from three direct hits by 20 millimeter anti-aircraft fire. Lt Rice was able to fly his burning aircraft ten (10) miles to friendly territory before abandoning it. Lt Rice suffered a broken ankle as a result of a collision with the tail section of the aircraft. He was picked up by friendly forces, and has since been recuperating in a hospital in Japan.[22]

Capt. William Preston piloted an RF-51D that received severe damage during a mission. A 20 mm antiaircraft shell exploded in the aft section of the canopy. Shrapnel flying through the canopy and into the cockpit struck Preston's wrist. Fortunately, the injury did not prevent Preston from flying his damaged aircraft back and making a successful landing at Taegu. The high rate of aircraft being damaged in this way helped justify the assignment of ten additional RF-51s at the end of the month.[23]

Capt. Clyde East and Lt. James Dolan flew the longest 45th TRS reconnaissance mission of the Korean War on February 13. The five-and-one-half-hour mission involved a round trip flight of 1,400 miles to photograph a railroad running from Hoeryong on the Yalu River to Tanchon in northeast Korea. The author's father served as an RF-101 crew chief for (later colonel) East during the Cuban Missile Crisis, which opened a door in 2005 to chat with the retired pilot. When asked about this particular mission during the Korean War, Col. East gave a chuckle and a sly, personally satisfying hint that he had known what China looked like under his aircraft before turning southward to follow the railroad from the Yalu River border at Hoeryong to the coast at Tanchon.[24]

15th TRS pilot Capt. John Monaghan received the Silver Star for a mission he flew in an unescorted RF-80 over North Korea on February 3. Despite being trailed and attacked by a squadron-sized element of MiG-15 fighters, he managed to complete his photograph runs and escape to South Korea in his damaged aircraft:

The President of the United States of America, authorized by Act of Congress, July 9, 1918, takes pleasure in presenting the Silver Star to Captain John D. Monaghan, United States Air Force, for gallantry in action against an enemy as Pilot, 8th Tactical Reconnaissance Squadron Photo Jet (redesignated 15th Tactical Reconnaissance Squadron Photo Jet), FIFTH Air Force. On 3 February 1951, Captain Monaghan took off in an unarmed RF-80 type aircraft and flew unescorted to his assigned target area deep in enemy held territory. His mission required that he make nine photographic runs over targets in the immediate vicinity of two enemy jet fighter bases near the city of Sinuiju, North Korea. After completing several photographic runs, Captain Monaghan noticed approximately 15 enemy jet fighters circling above him. Fully aware that an attack was imminent, he skillfully maneuvered his aircraft to keep the enemy out of firing position while he completed the important photographic work. As Captain Monaghan broke away from his last target, several of the enemy aircraft started their attack. In the ensuing engagement, the enemy made numerous firing passes, inflicting major damage on Captain Monaghan's aircraft. One 37 mm shell struck a tip tank and another seriously damaged the left wing. Through his skill as a pilot and knowledge of enemy capabilities, Captain Monaghan evaded the enemy and returned his badly damaged aircraft to home base. The photographs obtained by Captain Monaghan proved to be of great value to the United Nations forces. Captain Monaghan's gallantry and devotion to duty reflected great credit upon himself, the Far East Air Forces, and the United States Air Force.[25]

45th TRS combat sorties reached 368 in March 1951, and three pilots did not return to Taegu, including Lt. Marshall Summerlin, Lt. James Dolan, and Capt. William Preston. On March 3, Summerlin radioed that his aircraft had a rough engine following a four-hour mission, and that he might have to bail out. Nothing further was heard from him, and he was declared killed in action in 1952. Dolan was the pilot who paired with Capt. East for the over 5 hour mission into northeast North Korea the previous month. On March 19, he departed Taegu on a visual reconnaissance mission to the Chorwon area. While diving on a troop position, his plane stalled and snapped on the pull out. Other aircraft reported Dolan crashed into a hillside and burned. They did not see any evidence of a parachute or personnel on the ground around the burning RF-51. His remains were later recovered. Preston's wrist had been wounded by shrapnel, but he managed to bring his damaged RF-51 home in February. On March 26, he conducted a visual reconnaissance mission in the Kaesong area. He did not return, and the squadron did not receive any reports. Preston was shot down over North Korea and held as a prisoner of war until repatriation in 1953.

A fourth 45th TRS aircraft went down on March 17, but the pilot, Capt. David Rust, survived and was rescued. The report reads:

> His aircraft was hit by enemy ground fire. The aircraft engine immediately ran rough and Captain Rust was forced to abandon it over the Imjin River, southeast of Kaesong. A flight of F-51s flew cover for him on bail out and alerted the Air Rescue Service. Captain Rust landed in the river and had to swim out. After reaching the bank, he hid in a fox hole until he was picked up by an Air Rescue helicopter about an hour later.[26]

Lt. Roger Wilkes managed to bring back a damaged RF-51 on March 12. Some 40 mm antiaircraft flak struck the tail assembly of the plane in the vicinity of Chorwon. The rudder and trim tabs for the elevator became inoperative. Rather than bail out, Wilkes returned for an emergency landing. Two pilots including Capt. East completed their combat tours in March. East reached 101 missions with thirty-nine of these flown with the 12th TRS and 15th TRS.[27]

Ground crew prepares to fit the RF-80 "Emma-Dee" with nose cameras while reconnaissance pilots watch the process.

Attempts to deceive tactical aerial reconnaissance began soon after aircraft began collecting photographic and visual information in warfare. The Korean War proved to not be an exception to the rule dating back to World War I. Deception by the North Koreans and Chinese took the form of hiding military assets, exaggerating the numbers of military equipment and troops, and even attempting to divert attacks to nonexistent targets. RF-80 reconnaissance aircraft located MiG fighters based in North Korea and provided information for attacks against them. Once the MiGs returned to China, the RF-80s spotted attempts to deceive them into believing the aircraft were still located at bases in North Korea. RF-80 reconnaissance photographs of an airfield near Pyongyang indicated the presence of Chinese MiG-15 fighter aircraft. Those who carefully interpreted the photos saw through the deception and identified the objects as dummy planes, which were made from straw and designed to draw Allied strike planes into wasting ordnance and possibly into flying into an antiaircraft gun trap. Another North Korean ruse involved placing straw over sections of recently attacked rail lines. From high altitude, the straw looked like cuts in the rail line. However, lower-level oblique (angled) photos demonstrated that the rails were still in operational order.

The reconnaissance squadrons countered deception attempts by taking photographs of target areas regularly (sometimes twice a day) in order to maintain constant observation of any changes in a target's status. Another tactic involved assigning some pilots to specific sectors rather than changing their reconnaissance targets each day. This was especially true for the RF-51 pilots, who could cover an area for a longer period at a slower speed. These pilots developed a keen visual understanding for their sectors and could spot changes more quickly than others who might fly the area two or three times a month.

The 45th TRS lost three pilots in April. Capt. McCollum went down near Hwachon Reservoir on April 10. McCollum's body was found the next day in the wreckage of his RF-51. Enemy ground fire struck 1Lt. Fogleson on April 14. His RF-51 caught fire and crashed, killing the pilot. Ground fire also brought Capt. Brown down on April 17. His RF-51 crashed and burned before he could get out. A total of thirteen RF-51s received battle damage from ground fire in April, demonstrating the greatest danger faced by these pilots during reconnaissance missions. Despite a shortage of aircraft and pilots in the 45th TRS, 5th Air Force approved a plan for all missions to be flown with two aircraft. Flying two planes allowed each to watch over the other, providing immediate visual observation if one aircraft is hit by enemy fire and/or the pilot bails out. It could also offer a second ship for photography.

The 15th TRS lost one pilot in June. Lt. Willis Thatcher's plane crashed and exploded after being hit while at low altitude. Lt. Umberto Stella, flying as Thatcher's wingman, witnessed the fatal incident. Two other 15th TRS pilots, captains Lloyd Simpson and Johnny Crowell, were both hit by ground fire, but they successfully bailed out and were recovered by friendly forces.

RF-80s over Korea participated in the first jet combat air-to-air refueling operation on July 6, 1951. Refueling probes were added to each of the fuel tanks of the RF-80, permitting refueling by a KB-29 (a modified B-29 bomber). The KB-29 released a fuel line with a basket-type device, into which the fuel probe would be inserted. This allowed the operator aboard the KB-29 to release fuel through the line and directly into the tank. The tanks and probes were assembled in Japan, and three 67th TRW pilots received temporary duty assignments to fly the RF-80s in the test. The pilots were Maj. Jean Woodyard, Maj. Clyde East, and Lt. Henry Ezell. The three RF-80s launched to complete three different reconnaissance missions. The planes flew together until reaching the RB-29 tanker, approximately 30 miles east of Wonsan. The RF-80s refueled and then departed to their individually assigned reconnaissance targets. Upon completing their missions, each pilot returned to Taegu with plenty of fuel after a total flight time of 4 hours and 45 minutes. The test proved successful, and 5th Air Force knew it could rely on tankers when dispatching RF-80s on long distance reconnaissance missions.

Chinese and Russian MiG fighters were things the unarmed reconnaissance pilots neither wanted to see nor become entangled with. The only means of escape involved either dropping the external fuel tanks and heading south while dodging them or being rescued by UN fighters that might be in the area. Lt. Stanley Sebring of the 15th TRS drew the mission to photograph the Chinese MiG base at Antung, using an oblique camera, from the south side of the Yalu River on June 24. While on the mission, Sebring spotted what appeared to be a group of MiGs attacking a formation of B-29 bombers. Since the MiGs were busy and far away, he figured they would not spot him. But he later noted:

I was wrong about that. Probably though, I just happened to be on their route back to Antung. Suddenly, a flight of MiG-15s flashed over me. I immediately jettisoned my external tip-tanks and headed south and down. The MIGs split into two elements and took turns diving on me. I'd turn as hard as I could into whichever element seemed to be attacking. Each time I could see a string of white tracer cannon shells flash past me. I kept twisting and turning and thinking that at any moment I was going to be blown out of the sky. But, just as quickly as they'd arrived they were gone.[28]

Sebring attributed his survival to the possibility that the MiGs were low on fuel and needed to return to Antung rather than to his flying skills.

July weather hampered the visual and photo reconnaissance missions over North Korea and the battle area. Cloud cover impacted low and high-altitude reconnaissance. The former could be even more disadvantaged by the mountainous terrain. A pilot attempting to get beneath the cloud cover had to contend with the terrain which could appear at any moment or never be spotted before the aircraft shattered into it. Five more 45th TRS RF-51s received battle damage from ground fire. The 67th TRW lost its commander, Col. Karl Polifka, on July 1. Enemy ground fire struck the RF-51 flown by Polifka. He bailed out from his stricken plane, but the parachute became entangled on his tail section. Tragically, as the plane dove to the ground, it dragged its pilot to his death. The 45th TRS lost Lt. Jackie Douglas on July 17, when ground fire downed the pilot's RF-51.

Capt. Joseph Daly of the 15th TRS tangled with two MiG fighters on August 9 while attempting to photograph a target along the Chinese border, resulting in his being awarded a Silver Star medal. This citation describes the action well and demonstrates his tenacity in returning with photographs despite the opposition:

The President of the United States of America, authorized by Act of Congress, July 9, 1918, takes pleasure in presenting the Silver Star to Captain Joseph F. Daly, United States Air Force, for gallantry in action against an enemy on 9 August 1951 as a Tactical Reconnaissance Pilot. Captain Daly volunteered to fly deep into enemy held territory, unescorted and unarmed in an RF-80 type aircraft to acquire much needed photographs of a communications line and other targets which were located only a few miles from a large enemy air base. Captain Daly flew to his targets and started his first photographic run over the communications line; several runs were necessary to complete coverage of all the targets. Another RF-80 type aircraft circling nearer the enemy base warned

Captain Daly that two enemy aircraft were taking off. With complete disregard for his own safety, Captain Daly elected to remain in the area and pursued his mission until the enemy jet aircraft made their attack. Captain Daly's aircraft was hit in the right wing by a 37 mm. shell, which completely destroyed one fuel tank. A 23 mm. shell hit the right side of the fuselage, and three fragments pierced the canopy. Violent evasive action followed, and through Captain Daly's skill in flying and his understanding of the enemy's capabilities, he was able to evade the enemy aircraft in the ensuing fight in which the enemy made at least five firing passes. He then flew his crippled aircraft twenty minutes under instrument conditions and returned to a friendly base two hundred and thirty miles away and with information needed on the enemy's activities. Captain Daly's gallantry, skill and devotion to duty reflected great credit upon himself, the Far East Air Forces, and the United States Air Force.[29]

Of the hazards of flying over North Korea, antiaircraft fire was the most deadly for reconnaissance pilots and included small arms and small to medium guns, such as manually aimed 20 mm cannons. It also included larger, radar-directed antiaircraft guns, many of which fired 37 mm shells. This can be seen in the large number of 45th TRS RF-51s hit by ground fire throughout the first half of 1951. The RF-80s of the 15th TRS carried an early warning system that provided an audio tone if radar "painted" the aircraft. This let the pilots know whether radar-directed guns were tracking them. Captain James Hanson recalled an August 18 mission over Pyongyang:

Oh, oh, there's a pulsing buzz in my earphones which means radar is tracking me and I can expect some flak as soon as the buzz becomes constant. There's the flak bursting back and to the side which means it isn't wind corrected. I'm at the point where I can cut the cameras off and get the heck out of here so I roll off to the south in a shallow diving turn and know that they can't get me now unless they put up barrage flak, which isn't likely against one lone plane.[30]

During the month of September, Capt. Hanson of the 15th TRS found himself cornered by a dozen MiG fighters while on a mission:

I take the mission today [September 22] and have an escort of eight F-84G's. Rendezvous is at 20,000 feet over Chinnampo, which is just short of the [MiG] Alley. We join up on schedule and head north to Sonchon where I start my photo run of the rail line up to Sinanju. Radar calls that many bandits are approaching and I soon see the twinkle of silver wings high above headed our way. The Escort Leader of the 84's knowing that they are no match for the MiGs calls for me to break off my run and advises me that I'm on my own. I cut the cameras off but continue the run as I watch 12 MiGs pass high overhead and start a turn. The leader and his wingman break out of formation so I know I'm spotted and am about to be attacked. I decide to let them think I haven't seen them and watch them continue with their pass. I wait up to the point where the leader starts pulling his lead on me. I watch over my shoulder until he should be getting ready to fire, then I pop my speed brakes open and break left into his turn. They overrun me, and as they pass to the outside of my turn I close my speed brakes and roll hard back towards them into a position where I'm looking right up the leader's tailpipe. If I only had guns it would be scratch one MiG. The pilot looks back at me and there is a puff of smoke out of his engine, I guess he firewalled the engine. Apparently he didn't know that I didn't have guns because the two of them pulled almost straight up and climbed out of sight heading back north. I decide to go back and start my run over and get the job done by myself. If the escort can't even take care of themselves we sure don't need them. They just alert the enemy radar where the F-80 might not. [31]

MiG fighters jumped Lt. James Nimmo of the 15th TRS on September 11 during one of the dreaded oblique photography missions to the Chinese airfield of Antung. He flew with fighter escort, but the planes were F-84s piloted by crews who lacked experience battling MiGs. Nimmo wrote of his experience:

"Break, Break" . . . Looking ahead, I saw nothing; looking off my left wing, there they were. Four flights of four each, with a flight of four MiGs already bending in to get on my tail. Another quick look around and no F-84s in sight but lots of orange balls from 37 mm MiG guns and they were close. Nothing left to do but evade and escape. MiGs closing on my left rear quarter so I broke hard left, power to idle thrust and popped speed brakes still holding full left aileron. It was the most violent spin maneuver I've ever been in. Besides the buffeting, the airspeed indicated well beyond the red line that indicated Maximum Safe Speed. The 37 mm orange tracers ceased as I passed through about 10,000 feet, and I leveled off at about wave top level crossing the shoreline headed back out over the Yellow Sea. I increased power back to normal and headed back to Kimpo. Leveling off just above wave tops and now headed for Kimpo, I called my escort and they replied, "We're heading back to base; we lost sight of you; are you OK?" You can imagine what I would like to have said at the moment but I talked myself out of it and decided to save it for the debriefing when I get back to base.[32]

The reconnaissance squadrons were not even safe at their airfield in South Korea. Capt. Hanson wrote of a theft and sabotage that occurred in September:

One morning we discover that the enemy has been in our midst. They have destroyed several thousand feet of film and stolen most of our airmens' [sic] rifles from the armament section. Then we find a loose cap on one of the F-80 wing tip tanks and a further check shows that dirt has been dropped in them and this would soon flame out an engine. Now they all have to be checked and a better security guard set up. The base doesn't even have a fence so that's now in the plans, and there will be one guard for each two planes with orders to shoot anyone approaching the planes at night without proper identification . . . so we now sleep with our 45's [.45-caliber pistols] under our pillows and each tent rigs up their own booby traps before hitting the sack. Even the fence doesn't fully do the job. Another morning, in dense fog conditions, I'm walking down the flight line to operations and see a Korean, dressed in white, dive under the fence. They had dug out a place where the ground drops away and he was gone before I could do anything. We found that they were carrying 50 gallon oil drums off on their backs on a wooden "A" frame. The amazing thing is that one of these full fifty gallon drums weigh about 300 pounds.[33]

The 15th TRS lost 1Lt. Bruce Sweeney on October 2 to a MiG-15 attack while flying over northern North Korea. Two MiG fighters jumped his RF-80, and the escorting F-84 pilots

Battle damage assessment photograph of the Wonsan oil refinery

declared that the American plane appeared to explode while at an altitude of 20,000 feet. They spotted an opening parachute and followed it to the ground. During a low-level pass, the F-84 pilots observed the parachute in a rice paddy and the RF-80 pilot lying facedown. They reported that the downed pilot did not show any signs of life. A fighter Combat Air Patrol returned to the area the next morning and noted that the parachute and pilot were not there.

The MiG threat continued to grow for the reconnaissance missions, particularly for the RF-80s. The aircraft lacked the speed and agility required to escape from attacking MiG fighters and often flew with escort fighters for protection. To give credit where credit is due, many skilled RF-80 pilots proved to be adept at maneuvering to avoid MiG attacks even though the plane lacked armament for defense. The best defense when flying alone involved withdrawing from the area as quickly as possible.

Capt. James Hanson managed to escape from a group of MiG fighters on October 30. Hanson recalled after the war:

The mission called for a photo run down the Yalu River to cover three airfields, two on the Korean side of the river, and an oblique of Antung, which is just across the river in Manchuria. There's no way to do this without getting into a hassle with the MiGs. So I was assigned an escort of eight F-86's from the 4th Fighter Group, and the rest of the Group would be in the area for their regular MiG fest. They were eager to do it because they were sure of a fight. As we near the target area, radar starts calling out "trains" leaving the station (MiGs taking off). They are all climbing and staying north of the Yalu River. I start my run to the southwest down the river with the F-86 escort to my left, on the Korean side, because American planes are not "permitted" to cross the border into Chinese territory. I complete the photo run on the first airfield when the escort leader calls out ten MiGs, line abreast, starting a run at us. They call for me to break left and under them but I call for them to break over top of me and into the

101

MiGs as I want to get the next airfield just ahead. There is no time to have a discussion, and when they see that I'm not changing course they break over top of me and meet the MiGs head on in their own territory. The MiG leader hadn't counted on that and they break off their attack and turn back north. I have to break off the run on the third airfield halfway through because I'm in the middle of a real dogfight between the 86's and MiGs. I get great cover and most of the job done so it is a "good show" all around.[34]

Although escorted by more-advanced F-86 fighters, 15th TRS RF-80s were jumped by MiGs eleven times in November 1951. Hanson and others discussed a possible solution after his September mission. Rather than fly with a large escort, which just seemed to attract the attention of the MiGs, the squadron could send a pair of RF-80s on a single mission. While one RF-80 flew the reconnaissance run, the other could provide watch and oversight in case MiG fighters arrived. The latter RF-80 would then radio a warning to the former along with an escape route.

Col. Sam Dickens explained that a more viable solution had been developed for the RF-80: convert a faster and more agile fighter to reconnaissance duties in areas where the chances of MiG interception are greater:

It didn't take too long for people to realize that the RF-80—which had a Mach limitation of 0.8—was not the aircraft to be operating in MiG Alley! But targets were up in the northern part of North Korea—so, despite escorts of F-86s or F-84s, RF-80s were flying very hazardous missions into MiG Alley and were being lost. A couple of the pilots in the 15th had flown F-86s in the United States. We were at Kimpo Air Base, K-14, near Seoul, and the 67th Tac Recon Wing was on one side of the base and on the other side was the 4th Fighter Wing. So these former Sabre pilots went over and looked at some of the F-86A aircraft that were in bad shape, that weren't being flown, that you couldn't even have called "hangar queens." They were trying to figure out how

RF-86 conversion from an F-86 Sabre

to rig some cameras on the F–86, and they came up with some ideas that were given approval. As a result, modifications were made in Japan, and the first RF–86As arrived in December 1951. The first missions were flown in 1952.[35]

These discussions resulted in a project known as "Honey Bucket" and "Ashtray." Six F-86 fighters at Tachikawa Air Base in Japan underwent a conversion to remove two of their six machine guns and the addition of reconnaissance cameras. While officially named "Ashtray," the aircrews dubbed the project "Honey Bucket"—an American nickname for the containers utilized by many Asians to gather animal and human feces for use as fertilizer or for disposal. Ruffin Gray, commander of the 15th TRS between October 1951 and May 1952, played a lead role in early work to convert an F-86 for reconnaissance photography:

We were urgently trying to find a better airplane, and everyone said that it was impractical to try to convert an F-86 to a camera role. But Joe Daly and I weren't convinced. We started spending hours on the 4th Fighter Wing side of the field in the nose of an F-86, and each time there was an accident, we were there trying to beg for the nose section. We finally figured out a way to mount a K-20 camera on its side by taking out the bottom gun and shooting vertical photos through a mirror mounted at a 45-degree angle. Col. Harry Thyng finally let us have two old war weary F-86A's and we worked a deal with the depot in Japan to mount the cameras, mirrors and camera windows. Joe Daly flew the first one in from Japan on its first mission. We left them painted in the exact same markings as the 4th Fighter Wing aircraft; kept them parked with the other F-86's and used them flying lead on one of the 4th Wing fighter sweeps so that the flight just happened to overfly the areas we needed to photograph. As soon as we began flying them, the experts from the states who had said it couldn't be done began coming out with all kinds of improvements. We had kept this all hush, hush under the code name "Honeybucket." We later had a flight of RF-86's and I believe that the squadron eventually was equipped with nothing but RF-86's that ultimately went to the ROKAF.[36]

Even flying a modified F-86 (to be designated the RF-86) did not guarantee a reconnaissance pilot's safety in MiG alley:

Lt. Jim "Fearless" Fosdick flew an RF-86 on a low level mission in MiG alley and picked up a lot of ground fire and aircraft strikes including a slug that came into the right console and knocked out the radio. When the slug came through, it hit a parachute harness buckle on Jim's hip; the slug split in half and half went into the instrument panel. The other half hit Jim in the side; hit a rib and slid around to his back. Jim flew back; landed and taxied in; made out the form 5; came down the ladder; pulled back the side of his backpack and asked the crew chief if he was bleeding back there. When the crew chief acknowledged that he was, Jim calmly asked that he call an ambulance since he had been shot.[37]

Although MiG fighters were a danger, the pilots still had to contend with antiaircraft fire, which was more likely to bring them down. On November 8, Capt. Dennis "Tex" Hill encountered accurate antiaircraft fire while flying an RF-80 mission over North Korea. Lt. Norman Duquette served in a mobile control radio shack at the end of the runway that day to oversee aircraft returning from missions. He observed Hill, his fellow 15th TRS pilot, arrive with battle damage:

Tex had received flak damage to his aircraft and wounds in his leg and was bleeding pretty badly for some time en route back to Kimpo from the far North. He radioed in regarding his difficulties. Tex was able to remove his belt and apply it to his leg to put pressure to control the bleeding. By the time he reached the Kimpo area his leg was numb and was of no assistance to him for controlling the aircraft for landing, nor the brakes after landing. He was told to make a straight in approach to Kimpo as soon as he had sighted the field. I monitored extensions of his landing gear, speed brakes and flaps, and his approach altitudes, aircraft attitudes and air speeds, and was in general "the friendly voice" of assistance. Tex made the landing, a little fast in air speed, but otherwise a good landing. At my suggestion, Tex shut down the engine after landing touchdown to enable the aircraft to come more quickly to a stop without having the assistance of braking action. The plane came slowly to a halt in the center of the runway about two thousand feet from the end. Good job by Tex. Ambulance etc. were immediately on hand to remove him from the plane and take him to the base hospital tents. His aerial photography films were immediately removed from the plane and taken to the photo labs for development and analysis. After initial treatments, he was flown over to Nagoya Hospital in Japan.[38]

United Nations forces conducted a series of counterattacks and offensives along the front lines at approximately the 38th parallel. These tended to be minor, although often bloody, operations to stabilize the front and secure better locations for defense and observation. These lasted from late January 1951 to June 1951, with interludes of Chinese and North Korean counterattacks, and then a Spring Offensive from April 22 to May 20. A successful offensive by United Nations forces following the defeat of the Communist Spring Offensive resulted in truce talks in July 1951. Both sides employed a military strategy of stabilizing their positions and avoiding major confrontations while the politicians argued off and on at the truce talks. During the summer and fall, the United Nations forces initiated a limited offensive to shorten its front and demonstrate resolve in the face of Chinese and North Korean walkouts from the truce talks. The offensive introduced geographical features, such as the Punch Bowl, Heartbreak Ridge, and Bloody Ridge, that later evolved into well-known names in American military culture. The year 1951 ended with a more-stabilized front and a military stalemate. Meanwhile . . . the air war continued.

1952

The military stalemate continued throughout 1952, and progress in the truce talks demonstrated that neither side would gain much from large offensives that would not erase territorial gains under discussion for the other side. The spring thaw bore witness to artillery duels, patrolling, and outpost attacks on both sides. These continued until the winter of 1952–1953. Meanwhile, the air war, including reconnaissance missions, continued.

The 15th TRS lost an RF-80, piloted by Norman Duquette, on January 26, 1952. Antiaircraft fire struck the engine of Duquette's RF-80 in the afternoon, northwest of the Hamhung railroad yards. Being an early jet fighter, the RF-80 did not have an ejection seat nor an ejection mechanism on the canopy. For this reason, the only way out of the aircraft in an emergency involved manually jettisoning the canopy and climbing out of the cockpit or possibly tipping the plane over and allowing gravity to help pull you out. The antiaircraft flak that struck the aircraft also resulted in wounds to Duquette's head:

It was probably a proximity-fused munition that exploded on the right side of the aircraft and sprayed shrapnel through the canopy and fuselage. I did not notice any damage to the wing though there could have been—all I knew was that I had been hit and was concentrating on the situation at hand . . . I felt like I had been hit on the helmet and head with a sledgehammer. A red fire warning light illuminated in the cockpit. I looked behind me and was trailing smoke. I immediately turned the airplane to a southerly direction with the intent of bailing out as close to the water as possible. I was aware of Navy ships operating in the vicinity of Wonson Harbor, so headed in that general direction.[39]

The pilot found himself injured and strapped inside a burning aircraft from which extraction was not easy at high speed . . . not to mention, he was flying over North Korea. The damaged plane was not going to make it to the sea and US naval forces. Duquette prepared to abandon his stricken bird over North Korea. Duquette remembered:

I unfastened my shoulder harness and safety belt, and stood up in the seat and attempted to abandon the aircraft but the aircraft canopy was jammed shut. I tried to force the canopy open with my shoulders while standing in the seat, but was unable to do so.[40]

Trapped inside the RF-80, Duquette dove his damaged aircraft into a break in the winter clouds and struck the ground at an estimated 200 mph. The pilot recalled hitting the ground with a "violent impact" and then the plane "bounced into the air, struck the ground violently again, and began to tumble as the wings dug into the snow."[41] Not being fastened into his cockpit, Duquette suffered violent tumbling of his own inside the cockpit and was unconscious by the time the plane came to a rest in an upward position. Duquette eventually regained consciousness and found himself upside down inside the cockpit. The canopy had broken off the plane, and Duquette managed to drag himself out and over the edge only to be immediately captured. The North Koreans, and later the Chinese, held Duquette in various POW facilities where he underwent beatings, mental torture, and hard labor with little food and no medical treatment for his injuries until released as part of the armistice on September 3, 1953.[42]

The introduction of the F-86 as the RF-86 to the reconnaissance world opened new opportunities for clandestine flights over Chinese and Soviet territory. While the RF-80 proved successful for earlier missions when flown as Lt. Poe had, increased Soviet and Chinese air defenses and more-advanced fighter assets necessitated a reconnaissance aircraft that could "get in and get out" with high-quality photographs faster. If these missions were successful, the world simply did not hear about them. The United States did not want to publicly brag that they had overflown Chinese and Soviet military facilities, and the People's Republic of China and the Soviet Union did not want to admit that the United States could successfully perform such missions.

Capt. Richard Chandler flew one of these missions on June 25, 1952. Earlier that day, F-86 pilots reported that they had spotted (or thought they had spotted) bombers sitting on three Chinese airfields on the north side of the Yalu River, which separates North Korea from the People's Republic of China. Naturally, the presence of bombers immediately concerned American and United Nations military personnel. Air bases and other locations were placed on alert, and Fifth Air Force ordered the 15th TRS to launch RF-86 aircraft to conduct a more definitive reconnaissance. Chandler and another pilot flew RF-86s in a formation with ten F-86s for cover. As the aircraft neared the Yalu River, Chandler dropped from formation and flew westward to photograph two of the Chinese airfields, and another 15th TRS pilot departed to photograph a third airfield on Chinese soil to the east. They would then gather with the other F-86s for protection and return to South Korea.

Chandler later wrote:

My first target was An-Tung Airfield which I photographed and visually checked the flight line and hangars, and saw no bomber aircraft. I then pulled up and made a dicing run on Ta-Tung-Kou Airfield with no unusual aircraft sighted. While in the vicinity and on my way home, I pulled up and turned right and made a similar photo run on Pak-a-Shan airfield on my return to the Yalu and back into North Korea where I had the protection of the fighters again. When high enough for radio contact, I relayed my visual sightings of no bombers on any of those airfields to the controlling agency. The trip back to K-14 was uneventful except for the being quite low on fuel. I climbed to 43,000 feet to conserve fuel and throttled back to idle when near enough and started my glide to make it to K-14. After I parked and shut down my plane the photo people immediately removed the film, told me that the cameras had worked, then rushed the film to the photo lab. I inquired about the pictures later after dinner and was told that they were good pictures but that I could not see them; they were classified beyond my clearance level![43]

Two days later, the 15th TRS lost Maj. Jack Williams (their newly arrived commander) on an RF-86 mission. Williams and Capt. Clyde Voss flew a pair of RF-86s on a reconnaissance mission to North Korea. Williams would conduct the photograph run, and Voss would provide cover and suppress any antiaircraft fire directed at the pair of RF-86s. Airborne cameras can function differently for each aircraft based on speed and movement or vibrations of the aircraft. In particular, with the RF-86, the 40 inch camera required a slower aircraft speed. Voss noted:

I briefed Jack Williams on the altitude to approach the target. . . , To get good photos at very low altitude with the 40" focal length camera it was necessary to slow the RF-86 to avoid motion in the lower one-third of the picture. The lens speed of this camera would not compensate for high-speed low altitude passes. In all the missions I flew with this camera I had to come in slow over the target. The 40" focal length camera did permit you to break off the target before passing over it, or you were in your break when the airplane went over the target. I also told him about the motion problem with a high speed pass and that he should consider a slower approach, but it was up to him.[44]

As the pair approached the valley for a photo run, Voss dropped behind Williams in order to provide overwatch:

We were flying at about 275 knots. I urged him to speed it up. He just once said, 'In a minute'. He sounded wide-awake . . . We had flown over the target hydroelectric facility without getting down to the low altitude we planned. Williams' plane began to stream what appeared to be fuel from the wing root trailing edges . . . I called Jack and told him he must have been hit and suggested he turn left [south] and start for home. There was no answer from him from that moment on, and no indications that any control inputs [to his aircraft] were made . . . I began taking pictures with my foreword oblique camera when I saw that he was losing fuel. I operated the camera manually when I actually had something to photograph. His airplane began a gradual climb and gentle turn away from home. His speed changed very little from that time on except for the normal slowing [that would occur] as the airplane began its very gentle climb—and very slight turn to the right [north]. We passed over the mountains that formed the northern part of the valley the river flowed through, and his airplane continued to turn until it was heading east, climbing gradually . . . I couldn't see in the cockpit it was so full of smoke. Fire was coming out of the fuselage behind the cockpit. I kept calling him and telling him to bail out. From the time I first saw the fuel streaming out around his wing roots, I couldn't raise him on the radio. At this point the plane rolled to the right and into me rather abruptly. I pushed over hard to avoid a collision as he passed over me and continued rolling. [This] caused him to get behind me. The last I saw him, his canopy was still on. I maneuvered hard to regain sight of him . . . and when I next saw him, his chute was deployed. I finally turned enough to get the scene in my windscreen and took a few pictures . . . After the airplane crashed and the chute was on the ground, I made calls for rescue and dived down around the scene. It was obvious that Jack was not moving about though I could not see enough to tell what his condition was. I was operating at very low-power to conserve fuel so I was neither very low nor very fast. It is safe to say that I was under 1,000 feet above ground level.[45]

Voss overflew the area multiple times, searching for any movement near the parachute on the ground, and placed a radio call for rescue assistance. Korean farmers approached the wreckage, prompting Voss to consider their intentions. He fired several machine gun bursts in front of the farmers, not to hurt them but to convey the message that they should not approach the wreckage or the parachute. Lt. Griffis, of the 45th TRS, launched from Kimpo Airfield in a ready F-80 fighter to assist with the Combat Air Patrol efforts to attempt to possibly rescue Williams. He was joined by Marine Corps F4-U aircraft and a Navy rescue helicopter. While the aircraft protected the helicopter, its crew retrieved Williams, who had died. Voss believed Williams's RF-86 had been hit by unseen antiaircraft fire as they entered the valley.

1953

The year 1953 brought another spring thaw and not only increased military activity along the front line but also great changes in the political arena. New geographical names, such as "Pork Chop Hill," entered American military culture. Dwight D. Eisenhower took the oath of office to replace Harry Truman as president of the United States. Meanwhile, Joseph Stalin of the Soviet Union died. President Eisenhower viewed continued American involvement in the Korean War as not being in line with United States strategic interests and sought a settlement to the conflict. The new Soviet leadership also sought a withdrawal of their military assets from the Korean War and an end to the conflict. Chinese forces relied as heavily upon Soviet military assistance as the Republic of Korea did upon that of the United States. American and Soviet desire for an end to the conflict prompted compliance from China and in turn from North Korea. The Republic of Korea's leader, Syngman Rhee, objected to many provisions of an armistice, but the United States refused to allow this opposition prolong the conflict any longer than necessary. Truce talks progressed despite South Korea's unsuccessful efforts to secure its demands, such as removing the Communist government from North Korea. The two sides signed a truce and established a Demarcation Line effective July 27, 1953. Until the date of the armistice, the air war continued.

In January 1953, the 45th TRS officially completed its transition from the RF-51 to the RF-80 aircraft by adding the suffix "Photographic, Jet" to its name. With this transition, both the 45th TRS and 15h TRS continued RF-80 (and RF-86 for the latter squadron) reconnaissance missions over North Korea and along the Chinese border.

For the 15th TRS, the month and year opened with an RF-86 mission flown by Capt. Mele Vojvodich Jr. on January 3. Following his return, Vojvodich received the Distinguished Service Cross (the second highest medal in the US military) for his highly successful completion of a critical mission, despite more than one hazard to the aircraft. His citation reads in part:

> Captain Vojvodich volunteered to fly an unarmed RF-86 type aircraft on an extremely hazardous mission of greatest importance to United Nations forces. Captain Vojvodich, exhibiting outstanding personal courage and skill, flew his unarmed aircraft deep into heavily defended enemy territory despite constant attacks from enemy aircraft. On his way to the target complex, he experienced a complete radio failure, and in addition, his drop tanks failed to jettison. Notwithstanding these obstacles, Captain Vojvodich, recognizing the vital importance of his assigned mission, elected to complete the photograph runs on his targets, exposing himself to firing passes from enemy aircraft. In order to insure complete coverage, Captain Vojvodich returned to re-photograph his first target, despite the presence of numerous enemy aircraft in the area. The intelligence data Captain Vojvodich obtained at great personal risk was of immeasurable value to subsequent United Nations operation in Korea.[46]

Years later and upon declassification, the military reported that Capt. Vojvodich flew approximately 300 miles across the People's Republic of China to determine whether Soviet bombers were located in the country along the border with North Korea. Later in his career, Vojvodich flew the Lockheed A-12 reconnaissance aircraft over North Vietnam for the Central Intelligence Agency.

Tactical jet reconnaissance missions continued over the front lines to observe combat emplacements and movement. Other missions flew deeper into North Korea to photograph important enemy assets, including airfields, hydroelectric plants, communications facilities, and logistics depots. While MiG fighters tended to operate closer to the Yalu River, there were times they roamed closer to the front lines to surprise United Nations Command aircraft that were unprepared for aerial combat. On March 27, MiG-15 fighters with external fuel tanks ambushed two RF-80s and their escorting Royal Australian Air Force Meteor fighters between Sairwon and Sinamk.

Although participating in armistice talks, the Chinese and North Koreans continued to plan and conduct limited military operations to strengthen their positions or force the United Nations Command to offer more concessions in negotiations. The 67th TRW provided valuable airborne reconnaissance to identify and report any movement that could indicate a pending attack. Two examples occurred in May and July. On May 27, reconnaissance aircraft collected information that indicated the Chinese and North Korean forces were preparing for a ground offensive. On July 12, RF-80 returned from a mission with photographs proving the emplacement of antiaircraft artillery opposite United States IX Corps and the South Korean II Corps. The movement and emplacement of heavy antiaircraft artillery on the front lines often indicated preparations for an offensive.

Officially, the last American to die in the Korean Conflict before the implementation of the cessation of fighting occurred on the day of the armistice itself. This American was a reconnaissance pilot with the 45th TRS. Capt. John Rhoads flew an RF-80 to photograph airfields in North Korea as the United States prepared to implement the terms of the armistice. Rhoads lost his life in the effort and posthumously received the Distinguished Service Cross for his efforts that day. His citation reads in part:

Captain Rhoads volunteered to fly over an extremely dangerous target to obtain photo intelligence of great importance to the United Nations. He was to photograph six airfields in the Sinuiju, Uiju, Sinanju triangle, one of the most heavily defended areas. After he had successfully photographed five of the assigned targets, his aircraft was struck by automatic weapons fire at an altitude of twelve thousand feet. Captain Rhoads' escort immediately warned him to bail out, since flames were trailing out two hundred feet behind his aircraft. Captain Rhoads ignored this imminent threat to his life, and after cutting off the fuel, attempted an air start. Again his escort warned him to bail out, but Captain Rhoads refused to abandon his aircraft, electing, at great risk to his life to attempt to return to base with the photographs he had taken. Captain Rhoads continued his efforts to start the engine until an explosion in the tail of the aircraft caused it to plummet to earth before he could bail out.[47]

The Korean War was unofficially concluded on July 27, 1953, with an armistice agreement that set a demarcation line roughly along the 38th parallel and was still patrolled by the military forces of North Korea, with South Korea and the United States as partners under the United Nations Command on the opposite side of a demilitarized zone. As of January 2021, thirteen 15th TRS and 45th TRS pilots are still listed as missing in action (presumed dead) from the Korean War. American tactical reconnaissance aircraft continued to fly clandestinely from Japan over Chinese and Soviet territory after July 1953 and provided a significant asset in the Cold War as it developed after the Korean armistice.

CHAPTER 5
The Cold War and the Cuban Missile Crisis

I guess they were debating whether to court-martial me or give me a medal.

—Capt. Tom Curtis, in support of the Cuban Missile Crisis

Lebanon 1958

By 1958, a politically delicate compromise between Lebanese Christians and Muslims was endangered by the calls among many of the latter to join a new Egyptian-Syrian federation. At the same time, the United States grew concerned about a possible shift of Lebanon toward the Communist bloc and increasing tensions surrounding elections that could replace the Christian government with a Muslim government. Lebanon's stability hung in the balance, and the country became a test case for the new Eisenhower Doctrine of the United States to protect states under threat of falling under Communist domination. President Dwight D. Eisenhower ordered the United States military to take over Beirut's airport and port to bolster the Christian government.

The United States Air Force deployed a composite unit of aircraft and support sections under a new concept known as the Composite Air Strike Force (CASF). The Air Force experimented earlier in the 1950s with a concept for assembling and moving tactical aircraft to meet the need for rapid deployment. The Korean War demonstrated that conflicts of all sizes could erupt anywhere around the globe, and small conflicts that seem to appear from more minor political crises presented a particular challenge. The Air Force would need a variety of aircraft capabilities in a small, rapid package. By 1955, the Air Force first experimented with the CASF concept. A political crisis in Lebanon and Jordan prompted the first deployment of a CASF in 1958.

Air Force Maj. Gen. Henry Viccellio explained the CASF concept. With the early 1950s development of the Soviets' capability to strike the United States with nuclear weapons, a concern emerged that the frequency of smaller wars might

1958 Lebanon Crisis

111

increase. The potential for nuclear counterstrikes checked the sole possession of nuclear weapons by the United States and potentially negated any veiled threat of their use if the Soviet Union or its satellites interfered in other states. Viccellio wrote in 1959:

> Economically and politically unstable areas throughout the world were reacting to various pressures which threatened to erupt into hostilities. As a counter to these threats to peace, the USAF directed Tactical Air Command to develop a force capable of deploying rapidly to any area of the world where outbreak of limited war was imminent. This force would free SAC and the theater forces from the necessity of opening gaps in their general war posture in the event of minor conflicts.[1]

The CASF concept included specific aircraft dedicated to the missions of tactical fighters, tactical bombers, day and night electronic countermeasures, transportation, fuel tankers, and all-weather reconnaissance. The number and mix of aircraft could be adjusted based upon need for the individual scenario. CASF Bravo deployed to Incirlik Air Base in Turkey between July and October 1958 to support American forces dispatched to Lebanon. The aircraft package assembled for CASF Bravo included the 363rd Composite Reconnaissance Squadron, comprising seven RF-101 Voodoo aircraft for photographic reconnaissance, seven RB-66 Destroyer aircraft, and three WB-66 aircraft for weather reconnaissance. The aircraft and personnel assembled into this temporary formation came from ten different permanent Air Force units.

The RF-101s departed Shaw Air Force Base, in South Carolina, and flew to Turkey via the Azores, France, and Libya. Three of the Voodoos aborted due to mechanical issues, and two more were dispatched from Shaw Air Force Base. By July 18, 1958, there were six RF-101s on the ground in Turkey. Six RB-66s and three WB-66s deployed from Shaw Air Force Base with one RB-66 needing to abort. The eight aircraft arrived in Turkey on July 19 and were joined by two additional RB-66s the next day.

Due to the nature of the military intervention in Lebanon and needs of the ground commanders, the reconnaissance assets were the most active aircraft employed by CASF Bravo. The missions included photographic, visual, and weather reconnaissance. Although the Air Force had originally planned to utilize the RB-66s for night photography, commanders halted their missions because of concerns that local inhabitants in the area of operations would misunderstand the illumination of flash cartridges being dropped by the planes.

The RB-66s proved to be questionable platforms for visual reconnaissance during the deployment of CASF Bravo. They needed to fly "low and slow" to conduct visual reconnaissance, and this set them up as profitable targets for ground fire. Small-arms fire struck four of the RB-66s. While less vulnerable due to speed, one RF-101 also returned with a bullet hole from ground fire. This immediately dispelled any myths that low- and fast-moving aircraft like the RF-101 could avoid being hit by small-arms fire. Within five years, ground fire in Laos would be striking the RF-101s deployed to Southeast Asia. In post-deployment reviews, the one reconnaissance requirement missed by commanders in CASF Bravo was the RB-66C electronic reconnaissance aircraft. Planners agreed that three RB-66C aircraft should be added to future CASF packages.[2]

Taiwan 1958

The Air Force deployed CASF Xray Tango to Taiwan between August and December 1958. The Taiwan Crisis of 1958, also known as the Second Taiwan Strait Crisis, involved the shelling

363rd TRW RF-101 Voodoo. Note the portal for the camera lens on the side of the aircraft's nose. Another can be found on the flat nose itself.

RB-66 Destroyer

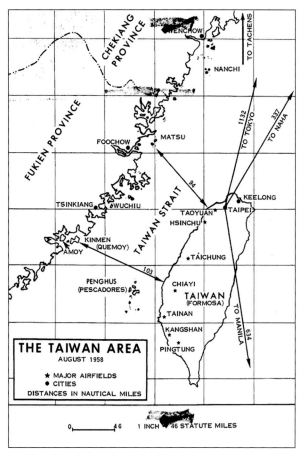

THE TAIWAN AREA
AUGUST 1958

★ MAJOR AIRFIELDS
● CITIES
DISTANCES IN NAUTICAL MILES

1958 Taiwan Crisis

of two Taiwanese islands by the People's Republic of China (PRC). The Taiwanese-held islands of Quemoy and Matsu, located adjacent to the coast of the PRC, were under artillery bombardment by the PRC on a semi-regular basis. In August 1958, the military forces of the two clashed when the PRC sent troops to land on the island of Dongding. President Eisenhower dispatched US troops, aircraft, and naval vessels to reinforce Taiwan and demonstrate American resolve to resist a PRC military takeover of Taiwan. The PRC eased tensions in the face of American reaction. There is also speculation that the Soviet Union helped persuade the PRC to reduce the tensions.

CASF Xray Tango deployed with a mix of aircraft assets similar to CASF Bravo's. Six RF-101s provided the photographic reconnaissance capability for the deployment. This crisis played out differently than the one in Lebanon. Taiwan operated its own air force, and CASF Xray Tango demonstrated American resolve in the crisis by providing a quick deployment and reinforcement air package to the area. Taiwanese fighters shot down eight aircraft flown by China while losing one plane in a midair collision. The reconnaissance capability of the Taiwanese air force during the crisis included seven RF-86Fs for reconnaissance, and they received four RF-101s in 1959 to enhance their capability after the crisis subsided. American RF-101s deployed under CASF Xray Tango departed the area after December 10, 1958.[3]

Dominican Republic 1965

The Air Force assembled an air package to support the deployment of American paratroopers to the Dominican Republic in April 1965. Earlier in the month, a group known as the Dominican Revolutionary Party seized the National Palace and deposed the government of the country. Troops loyal to the government resisted the coup, resulting in fighting within the capital area. The American ambassador informed American President Lyndon Johnson of the event and expressed concern for American lives. Officially, President Johnson ordered a military intervention to protect Americans but was primarily concerned the move was orchestrated by Fidel Castro of Cuba as an attempt to install a Communist government. In actuality, the issues behind the actions of the belligerents in the Dominican Republic were deeper than an attempted Communist coup and reflect issues dating back to a military coup in 1963. President Johnson opted to intervene, and the United States persuaded the Organization of American States to dispatch an international peacekeeping force to replace American troops and oversee new elections in 1966.

The declassified summary of American reconnaissance assets designated to support the deployment of American ground forces follows:

The tactical reconnaissance element of six RF-10l's and three RB-66's deployed to Ramey [Air Force base in Puerto Rico] on 2 May. Its activities were under the close scrutiny of the American ambassador to the Dominican Republic, W. Tapley Bennett, who vetoed any proposed flights that he considered unnecessarily dangerous or provocative. Frequent tropical showers interfered with scheduled missions, and the photo processing equipment deployed with the camera planes proved unable to turn out as many copies of photographs as desired.[4]

The aircraft deployed for this operation (known as Power Pack) were based outside the Dominican Republic, and most were in Puerto Rico. The primary mission of the reconnaissance aircraft involved monitoring routes from Cuba to ensure that it did not send military equipment to the Dominican Republic during the crisis. The air assets completed redeployment back to the continental United States by December 1965.

The Cuban Missile Crisis 1962

Four years after the Taiwan Crisis, Capt. George (Bill) Bernert maintained a steady eye on the terrain ahead of his speeding McDonnell Douglas RF-101 Voodoo photo reconnaissance aircraft as he passed over unfamiliar territory at only 100 feet above the ground on Monday, October 29, 1962. Any miscalculation at this altitude could end in disaster, with his aircraft spread across the Cuban countryside in small pieces. The "One-O-Wonder," as it was affectionately called by some pilots, flew at a maximum speed of 1,000 mph thanks to its two Pratt & Whitney J57-P-55 engines. When first produced in the 1950s, the F-101 series aircraft could fly faster than any opposition fighters. The RF-101, the reconnaissance version of the F-101 fighter, looked like the perfect photograph- gathering aircraft with a narrow nose that seemed to suggest that it was designed for speed and agility. Flying at low altitude permitted the reconnaissance aircraft to dash underneath radar coverage and photograph targets and be heading home before opponents realized they had just made the United States Air Force episode of Candid Camera. In this case, Bernert, flying wingman for Captain Art Beckstrom, planned to photograph a Soviet medium-range ballistic missile (MRBM) site in Cuba at the height of the Cuban Missile Crisis.

The two pilots roared across their target, shooting photographs, before the Cubans even knew they were in the area. Over forty years later, Bernert remarked to the author that he could see Cuban soldiers dashing across a field to reach their antiaircraft guns as he crossed the target. Almost as soon as he appeared over the MRBM site, Bernert completed his photo run and was heading north for the safety of the Cuban coast. Lights in the cockpit began to flash, and then—just as suddenly as they illuminated themselves—they died as the RF-101 approached the coast. The plane's entire electrical system failed along with the lights. At that point, the pilot did not know whether he had suffered a mechanical problem or been hit by the Cuban gunners he had spotted at the target. "If in trouble over Cuba, the first priority was to get 'feet wet' over water in any direction, preferably to the north for obvious reasons. The Navy presence around the island and availability of fighter cover made Search and Rescue pickup pretty certain. Key West Naval Air Station was the emergency divert for us on that mission," recalled Bernert. After they cleared the coast safely, Bernert made hand signals to catch the attention of Beckstrom, who already suspected something was amiss, since his wingman had not answered a radio call.

Cuban antiaircraft guns and support equipment. Photo made two days before Capt. Bill Bernert's RF-101 overflight across an antiaircraft gun site.

Bernert indicated that he had an electrical failure, but neither pilot knew the cause. Beckstrom maneuvered his RF-101 around his wingman and searched for battle damage. Seeing no obvious damage was a relief, and he signaled this to Bernhert, who commented later, "He asked by standard hand gestures if I wanted to go into our emergency base at Key West or continue to MacDill Air Force Base. I signaled to continue having satisfied myself it was a transformer rectifier failure that posed no immediate danger."

Approaching MacDill Air Force Base, near Tampa, Florida, Beckstrom radioed that his wingman was landing with an electrical system failure. At this point in the Cuban Missile Crisis, Gen. Walter Sweeney, the commanding general of the Tactical Air Command (TAC), was visiting MacDill, and he assumed that Bernert was arriving with battle damage. As soon as Bernert brought his RF-101 to a halt, ground crews placed a ladder on the side of the aircraft. Bernert turned toward whom he thought would be his crew chief and realized he was looking straight into the eyes of a general officer. "Where did they hit you?" were the first words out of Sweeney's mouth as he clung to the ladder. It took time for Bernert to explain that he was fairly certain that he had not been struck by Cuban gunners but had suffered a mechanical malfunction—a fact confirmed by the maintenance personnel who had swarmed around the aircraft to search for battle damage. In 2004, the pilot commented to the author, "Sweeney seemed genuinely disappointed."[5]

Most Americans realize that the United States and Soviet Union came close to war over the existence of nuclear missiles in Cuba. Yet few realize that several senior military officers wanted President John F. Kennedy to authorize an invasion of Cuba on the day of Bernert's overflight and were itching for an incident to justify an American "retaliatory" strike. Tensions were high that day, and the United States stood on the brink of war despite a preliminary agreement between President Kennedy and Soviet premier Nikita S. Khrushchev to solve the Cuban Missile Crisis.

Cuba and Florida during the Cuban Missile Crisis

American relations with Cuba deteriorated soon after Cuban revolutionaries, led by Fidel Castro, forced themselves into power during the first week of January 1959. The concerns about a pro-Soviet government lying 90 miles off American shores prompted President Eisenhower to approve an invasion of the island by Cuban exiles. President Kennedy inherited the plan and opted to implement it despite many misgivings. The failed 1961 invasion at the Bay of Pigs became an embarrassment for America and a prompt for Castro to develop even closer ties to the Soviet Union for the protection of his government. American high-altitude reconnaissance overflights of Cuba by Lockheed U-2 aircraft began to record an increase in the arrival of Soviet military equipment in August 1962.

The increase in Soviet military movements to Cuba concerned the United States military. Acting Central Intelligence Agency Director Carter responded to a military request for low-level Air Force and Navy reconnaissance overflights:

Washington, August 30, 1962.
Special Group Meeting—General Lemnitzer stated that Mr. McCone [*sic*] had called him and posed a possible requirement for low-level photography of critical Cuban targets. General Lemnitzer said that from the military point of view this was feasible, utilizing either RF 101 or F8U aircraft flown by US pilots from various bases or carriers in the Caribbean area . . . I pointed out that we are accused daily of overflights in any case and that the possibility of Cuban protests should not dissuade us from making these flights if they are necessary. It was pointed out that other types of photography, while useful in pinpointing critical targets, do not give sufficient detail for precise identification of certain types of

equipment. After some discussion, the Group agreed to take cognizance of this matter and requested that it be reopened at an appropriate time when specific targets and information needs could be identified. (Minutes of Meeting of the Special Group, 30 August 1962).[6]

After initial intelligence on the presence of Soviet missile systems in Cuba, United States government officials again discussed the need for low-level aerial reconnaissance (as in tactical reconnaissance aircraft rather than U2 or SR-71) to verify missile sites for proposed ground inspectors from the United Nations (UN). There was general debate on whether to use American tactical reconnaissance assets or those piloted by non-Americans; there was also debate on whether to fly low-level reconnaissance missions if UN officials were on the ground in Cuba. The following is the official Summary Record of the 11th Meeting of the Executive Committee of the National Security Council on this topic from October 29, 1962. Due to the link between tactical reconnaissance and the highest levels of the United States government on October 29, when Bernert flew his mission, the following document is worthy of examination in its complete format:

Washington, October 29, 1962, 10 a.m.
Director McCone [CIA director John McCone] summarized current intelligence, including evidence that all Cuban military forces have been ordered not to fire at US planes unless fired upon.

The President [President John F. Kennedy] read and approved the announcement of the creation of a Coordinating Committee which will handle all matters involved in the conclusion of the Cuban crisis.

Secretary Rusk [Secretary of State Dean Rusk] acknowledged that we need aerial reconnaissance missions today, but he recommended that none be flown until after the Russian negotiator Kuznetsov sees the UN Acting Secretary General in New York today.

The President agreed that we could wait today, but that we did face the longer range problem of how we continue surveillance of Cuba, recognizing that we cannot rely on the UN to undertake adequate surveillance.

Under Secretary of the Air Force Charyk reported on a conversation last night with UN officials. He said he had offered them RC-130 planes, [these are reconnaissance versions of the C-130 transport aircraft. The Soviets shot down one in 1958 when it crossed the Turkish border and into Armenia.] which they were prepared to use, but they did not want these planes flown by U.S. crews.

Mr. Charyk said the Canadians, South Africans and Indonesians have crews which could fly these planes.

Mr. Charyk said the UN official, Mr. Rikhye, who would be organizing the UN aerial reconnaissance, acknowledged that the UN could not make arrangements to fly reconnaissance missions today, but the UN observers could be on the ground in Cuba by Wednesday morning. The UN official said the UN did not want US reconnaissance planes overflying Cuba during the Secretary General's visit there on Tuesday and Wednesday. Mr. Charyk said that air reconnaissance could be very efficient. Pictures taken would reveal suspicious locations to which ground observers could be promptly dispatched. Mr. Charyk said there had been no discussion yesterday of US reconnaissance flights today, but UN officials had asked for our voluntary suspension of the blockade on Tuesday and Wednesday, leaving, however, the US ships on station. UN inspectors would be in all ports and would report to us on incoming and outgoing cargo. We would make available film to the UN reconnaissance missions if they would provide us with copies of the exposed films.

Secretary McNamara [Secretary of Defense Robert McNamara] recommended that we send reconnaissance missions this afternoon after notice is given to the Cubans and to Kuznetsov. The decision would be final unless new information came out of the U Thant/Kuznetsov discussions in New York. He recommended that US ships remain on station, challenge all ships entering the quarantine zone, and let such ships through because their cargo would be inspected by the UN observers in Cuban ports.

Secretary Rusk emphasized that we must maintain the quarantine until arrangements for UN inspection of offensive weapons in Cuba are completed.

The President made clear that we should have US observers on any planes flown by the UN. He agreed that the US ships should stay on station, but that we should leave ambiguous for the next twenty-four hours whether or not we will maintain the quarantine. He said we should not say that the quarantine was off pending installation of a UN inspection system. He agreed that the call up of the air reserves should not be reversed.

Secretary McNamara urged that the new Coordinating Committee work immediately on the question of Communist covert aggression in Latin America which would be based in Cuba.

The President said he had talked to Ambassador Stevenson yesterday[3] whose view was that the phrase "peace in the Caribbean" covers subversion. The President said Ambassador Stevenson had discussed this question with U Thant and would try to get back into the formulation of the settlement some specific reference to subversion.

General Taylor [General Maxwell Taylor, later chairman of the Joint Chiefs of Staff] urged that we be prepared to fly six to eight low-level missions today, but no high-level missions. He said we had seen nothing from Saturday[4] until now. He recommended that we announce in advance we were conducting low-level reconnaissance pending satisfactory and effective UN reconnaissance arrangements.

The President agreed to the low-level reconnaissance unless he directed otherwise before 2:00 p.m. He turned again to the question of what we would do on the surveillance problem for the long run.

Secretary Rusk noted that Khrushchev expressed his wish that reconnaissance cease, but he had not made it a condition to withdrawal of offensive weapons. U Thant will have to deal with this subject in the New York negotiations.

The President decided that no public announcement of the aerial reconnaissance would be made, but that if we decided to fly these missions, we will notify the Cubans and Kuznetsov immediately prior to the overflights.

General Taylor restated the requirement for the reconnaissance missions if we are to know whether the Soviets are actually dismantling the missile sites or whether they are continuing to work on the missile complexes.

Secretary McNamara noted that U Thant believes that the UN observers arriving in Cuba on Wednesday will see no missiles.

The President, saying that we would need aerial pictures on Wednesday, asked the group to consider how this should be done. Aerial missions today are not crucial, but this week we must have aerial pictures of the missile sites. Secretary McNamara expressed his doubt that we can get the UN to fly reconnaissance missions. Such missions must be flown to satisfy domestic opinion. He recommended that the flights be authorized today, subject to any developments taking place in New York.

Bromley Smith [executive secretary of National Security Council][7]

RF-101 Voodoo on display with aerial cameras prior to the Cuban Missile Crisis. *Mays family*

Photographic evidence of a Soviet nuclear missile site emerged after a mission on Sunday, October 14, 1962. Confirmed evidence was presented to President Kennedy on Tuesday, October 16, and the "thirteen days" of the Cuban Missile Crisis began its countdown. President Kennedy met with selected staff, cabinet members, and the Joint Chiefs of Staff on Saturday, October 20, to discuss American options. Although the military chiefs advocated an airstrike against Cuba, the President opted to implement a naval blockade, or "quarantine," as it was called, since General Sweeney noted that he could only guarantee a 90 percent success rate for finding and destroying all of the missiles in a single airstrike on Cuba. Kennedy expressed concern about the other 10 percent and decided that the naval quarantine could provide time while he sought a solution to the crisis.[8]

The United States Air Force, already flying the U-2 missions over Cuba after having relieved the Central Intelligence Agency (CIA) of the duty, entered the crisis at the tactical reconnaissance level on Sunday, October 21, with the alert and deployment of the 363rd Tactical Reconnaissance Wing (TRW) from Shaw Air Force Base, South Carolina, to MacDill Air Force Base, Florida. The wing established operations in Florida with four squadrons. The 20th and 29th Tactical Reconnaissance Squadrons (TRS) flew the RF-101 Voodoo. A third RF-101 squadron, the 4414th Combat Crew Training Squadron, a unit that trained RF-101 pilots, dispatched its aircraft piloted by instructors and the most advanced students at the time of the missile crisis. The 9th TRS and 16th TRS flew their Douglas RB-66 Destroyer aircraft to Florida. The RB-66, a reconnaissance version of the B-66 bomber, was powered by two Allison J71-A-11 turbojet engines that delivered a maximum speed of 585 mph. The RB-66 aircraft did not make any overflights of Cuba but were utilized for the speedy delivery of film to Langley Air Force Base, Virginia, or Andrews Air Force Base, Maryland. EB-66 aircraft did fly in international airspace near the island to gather intelligence from electronic emissions. The men of the 363rd TRW trained and waited for an order to launch their reconnaissance planes over Cuba.

On Monday, October 22, President Kennedy addressed the nation live on television and announced the presence of the Soviet nuclear missiles in Cuba. Although the president preferred a peaceful solution, he still authorized military preparations in case of the necessity for an armed strike. The next day, Tuesday, October 23, the Navy initiated the first

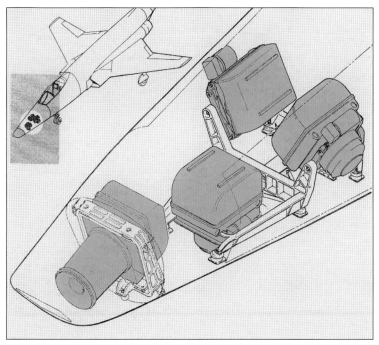

Placement of the four KA-45 cameras in the nose of an RF-101

low-level reconnaissance overflights of Cuba with Vought RF-8 Crusaders from Florida. The RF-8, a reconnaissance version of the F-8 fighter, was powered by a single Pratt & Whitney J57-P-20A jet engine, providing the plane with a maximum speed of 1,135 miles per hour and a basic combat radius of 1,425 miles.

The U-2s would continue to fly across Cuba, but in 1962, low-level missions offered advantages in photographic detail not always available from the high-altitude platforms. The Air Force grew restless with its reconnaissance resources sitting on alert in Florida while the Navy made all of the low-level overflights of Cuba. Gen. Curtis LeMay, the chief of staff of the Air Force and the father of the Strategic Air Command, complained vigorously about the all-Navy low-level reconnaissance show and demanded the participation of his branch of service. Three days later, LeMay's demands were met, and the Air Force received the nod to dispatch its reconnaissance aircraft. The Air Force ordered the 363rd TRW to launch its aircraft beginning at 10:30 a.m. on Friday, October 26. The first Air Force pilots to make low-level overflights of Cuba were captains Hallett Marston Jr., Carl Overstreet, Thomas Hennagan, Edwin Atterberry, James Payson, Bobby Martin, Jerry Rogers, Simon Moses, Gordon Palenius, and Byron Marvin. The Cuban Missile Crisis was moving closer to possible military confrontation, and no one knew whether the reconnaissance planes would meet a hostile reaction or be ignored over Cuban airspace.

Martin flew as the wingman for Payson to photograph two targets in southeastern Cuba near the United States Navy's base at Guantánamo Bay. Martin and Payson rendezvoused with two aerial tankers off Key West to top off their fuel before making the hazardous journey across hostile territory. The duo then dashed across Cuba at low altitude and reached their first target without incident. They photographed the site and then flew to a second target and captured it on film before turning and making their exit from Cuban airspace. Martin remarked to me, "My greatest surprise was that we did not encounter any MiGs [Soviet-built fighters] or AAA [antiaircraft artillery]." The mission lasted only ninety minutes.[9]

Installing a camera in an RF-101 during the Cuban Missile Crisis

Rogers, with Moses as his wingman, tackled a missile site west of the targets photographed by Martin and Payson. Again, the pilots did not know what to expect and were relieved to complete the mission without encountering Cuban or Soviet opposition. They topped off their fuel with the aerial tankers before commencing their approach to Cuba. Their first target was covered by clouds, so they flew on to their next location, a missile site. Rogers remembers seeing "lots of scurrying and activity" below him as the pair of pilots caught the site by surprise. Looking back in time, it certainly had to be a shock for Soviets and Cubans to suddenly see and hear two slender, silver aircraft zooming above their heads at an altitude of 100 feet before disappearing again as quickly as they had arrived. The pilots turned north to the safety of the open water with their film.

Rogers commented to the author that his film was blurry after developing due to the speed of his aircraft. The RF-101 carried a camera that necessitated a reduction in speed to around 500 knots over a target to prevent a blurred image. When asked at MacDill why he flew his aircraft across Cuba at close to 600 knots, Rogers replied, "It wouldn't go any faster."[10] This was certainly a logical comment when noting that these pilots flew under the understanding that they could be jumped by MiGs at any point in the overflight. The Air Force solved this problem by borrowing cameras from the Navy. The Navy RF-8 utilized a camera that operated well under faster speeds at low-level altitudes. Another modification involved the actual film carried

Vans of the 363rd TRW's Photographic Interpretation Section at MacDill Air Force Base, Florida, during the Cuban Missile Crisis

by the RF-101s. The film in the U-2 reconnaissance aircraft camera was half the thickness of the film utilized in the RF-101s. The U-2 film fit into the cameras mounted in the RF-101s, which meant the low level-planes could carry more film and take more photographs.[11]

The low-level American overflights and a Soviet refusal to engage the U-2s with their surface-to-air missiles (SAMs) infuriated Castro. He ordered Cuban antiaircraft gunners to fire upon any low-level American reconnaissance missions starting the next day, Saturday, October 27. President Kennedy and his advisors met that same day to review the situation in Cuba. During the meeting, the attendees were informed that a U-2 had been downed by a Soviet SAM over Cuba, a move that was unauthorized by the Soviet government.[12] The president, again, opted to show restraint because of concerns that the confrontation could escalate and result in Soviet nuclear weapons being launched against American targets. Attorney General Robert Kennedy, the brother of the president, noted the growing impatience of the Joint Chiefs of Staff at this conference. He wrote in his diary, "The Joint Chiefs of Staff joined the meeting and recommended their solution. It had the attraction of being a very simple next step—an airstrike on Monday [October 29], followed shortly afterward by an invasion. They pointed out to the President that they had always felt the blockade to be far too weak a course and that military steps were the only ones the Soviet Union would understand."[13] Robert Kennedy's diary was posthumously edited by presidential speech-writer Theodore Sorensen into book form as the classic, *Thirteen Days*.

That evening, Soviet Ambassador Anatoly Dobrynin met with Attorney General Kennedy and relayed the following observation in a diplomatic cable to Premier Khrushchev: "R[obert] Kennedy said . . . 'Because of the plane [U-2] that was shot down, there is now strong pressure on the president to give an order to respond with fire if fired upon when American reconnaissance planes are flying over Cuba. The USA can't stop these flights, because this is the only way we can quickly get information about the state of construction of the missile bases in Cuba . . . But if we start to fire in response, a chain reaction will quickly start that will be very hard to stop.'"

RF-101 shadow passing over a freighter in Cuba's Casilda Port

President Kennedy and Premier Khrushchev reached a compromise on Sunday, October 28, following an exchange of messages, diplomatic cables, and personal meetings between Soviet and American staff members. Khrushchev agreed to dismantle and remove the Soviet nuclear missiles in Cuba in exchange for an American pledge to not invade the island and to bring home the aging Jupiter nuclear missiles based in Turkey. Despite the compromise, some senior American military officers still pushed for the military option and argued that an attack on another reconnaissance plane should serve as a trigger for an attack on Cuba. Into this political fire flew the pilots of the 363rd TRW.

On Monday, October 29, the 363rd TRW launched another round of reconnaissance missions flown by lieutenant colonels Clyde East and Joe O'Grady and captains Thomas Estes, Jack Bowland, Arthur Beckstrom, and George (Bill) Bernert. The pilots did not know what type of response they would meet from the Cubans but expected the worst, based on Castro's October 26 declaration. Lt. Col. Clyde East, the commander of the 20th TRS and a reconnaissance pilot examined in the chapters on World War II and the Korean War in this book, mentioned that the overflights were "very intense operations" with everyone knowing that President Kennedy was observing. East targeted a military complex on his first mission over Cuba.[14] Bill Bernert and Art Beckstrom made their first overflight this day, with Bernert returning to MacDill Air Force Base with an electrical failure, as already related. However, it was Lt. Col. Joe O'Grady, the commander of the 29th TRS, who became the Air Force pilot most remembered after the Cuban Missile Crisis. O'Grady and his wingman Jack Bowland flew across the San Julián Air Base, at the western tip of Cuba, on October 29. Intelligence indicated that the Cubans and Soviets were assembling medium bombers at San Julián. O'Grady stated, "I flew right down the runway and they [the Cuban gunners] opened fire. When I landed in Florida, Gen. Sweeney said he didn't believe the Cubans shot at me. Well, the film developers found photos of the Cuban gunners shooting at my aircraft. Sweeney then changed his attitude."

Gen. Sweeney informed O'Grady that he was going straight to Washington, DC, to personally brief the Joint Chiefs of Staff. Sweeney also advised him to wear a dress uniform. Naturally, O'Grady had not brought a dress uniform to Florida. O'Grady was bundled onto an EB-66 that stopped at Shaw Air Force Base, South Carolina, so he could pick up his uniform. Then, he was whisked to Washington, DC, where he was debriefed.[15] Gen. LeMay and other officers were still itching to invade Cuba and hoped that O'Grady's story would prompt other senior officers and the president to support the plan of action based on this second attack of an American reconnaissance jet by the Cubans and Soviets. However, this last-minute effort failed because President Kennedy had already made the deal with Premier Khrushchev for the removal of the weapons. It would not make sense to risk a war, when the American government had obtained their objective by peaceful means.

SSgt. Edgar M. Mays, crew chief with the 20th TRS, stands with his RF-101 (#60168) in a photo taken just prior to the Cuban Missile Crisis. #60168 made several overflights of Cuba during the crisis with different pilots. *Mays family*

While the pilots flew the RF-101s over Cuba, the maintenance crews ensured that the RF-101s were in the air, making their contributions just as important. The maintenance crews of the 363rd TRW worked day and night to keep the wing's RF-101 and RB-66 aircraft operationally ready throughout the Cuban Missile Crisis and its aftermath. While most maintenance personnel develop an affection for their aircraft, RF-101 Voodoo crews often wore a unique, unofficial uniform patch that referred to them as "Voodoo Medicine Men" out of pride for servicing these planes. SSgt. Edgar M. Mays, the author's father, served as an RF-101 crew chief with the 20th TRS during the Cuban Missile Crisis and is best able to describe the procedures developed by the wing for launching and receiving the RF-101s designated for overflights of Cuba:

> We kept four to six RF-101s on the front line to fly the "hot" missions over Cuba each day. The others flew parts- and equipment-chasing missions, aircrew exchange missions, or rushed film to Langley Air Force Base, VA, or Washington, DC. When our "hot" birds returned from Cuba with "hot" film, the pilot would drop the canopy to the half-open position as he taxied to the fuel pit. There was an alert van with a full camera crew in position watching the incoming birds. Every time one taxied in with the canopy

in the half-open position, they scrambled to it. We would stop the bird, throw a chock under one wheel, and put the ladder onto the cockpit. Except for adding the ground wire in place, I then quickly got out of the way while the camera crew offloaded the "hot" film for processing. When the camera crew left, I would refuel the aircraft and tow it back to its designated spot.[16]

The Photo Interpretation Section was a group composed of men and equipment from the squadrons assigned to the 363rd TRW as well as a contingent from the Strategic Air Command. The section worked around the clock with the day shift evaluating and titling the film, preparing target materials, and writing evaluations. The night shift printed and enlarged the best negatives from each overflight mission. By the end of the wing's operations in mid-November, the section had processed 192,884 feet of film.[17] Lt. Col. Clyde East offered praise for the photographic section. He noted, "They worked hard and took lots of tongue lashings."[18]

The Cuban Missile Crisis cooled by November 1, when the Soviets agreed to remove the nuclear missiles from Cuba. The operations flown by the 363rd TRW on October 26 and 29 were to locate and document missile sites and other targets for a potential American invasion of Cuba. The overflights in November were developed to monitor the Soviet dismantling and withdrawal of their offensive weapons systems. Six RF-101 pilots flew missions on November 1 and became the first to officially monitor the withdrawal and test the pledges that they would not be fired upon while over Cuba. Capt. Doug Yates made his first overflight on this day with Capt. Bruce Keller. The pair targeted a row of missile sites west of Havana and a port facility. They flew the mission without incident, and upon returning to Florida, Yates discovered that Gen. LeMay was awaiting his arrival. "LeMay ordered me out of the cockpit for debriefing and said that my paperwork could wait, " Yates remembered. "On the way to the debriefing with LeMay, the flight surgeon gave me a cup of whiskey which was a standard practice for many units after air crews returned from a combat mission. I walked into the room to see Gen. LeMay while carrying my cup of whiskey. The next week, there was a new directive that the surgeon could not administer combat whiskey after a mission."[19]

Overflights of Cuba by the 363rd TRW continued until November 15 to monitor the withdrawal of Soviet weapons systems. While the published works on the Cuban Missile Crisis appropriately maintain a serious overtone about the entire event, one should note that Americans seem to find humor in any situation. The pilots of the 363rd TRW were not an exception to this point. Capt. Howard Davis flew two missions in November. After photographing his targets on one mission, he approached an airstrip as he flew toward the Cuban coast. Davis casually informed the author with a smile, "I lined up with the airstrip doing 500 knots. There was a Cuban L-20 plane at the end of the runway waiting to take off. I flew right over him at low altitude. That Cuban pilot probably had to change his underwear after I passed over him."[20] The de Havilland L-20, also known as the U-6, was powered by a single propeller engine and designed for light transport and courier duties.

Capt. Charles Lustig maintains fond memories of overflying Cuba in November. He had photographed the port of Mariel and two missile sites and was maneuvering to depart Cuban airspace, when he passed over a school at low altitude and a speed of 480 knots. "The kids were waving at us as we flew over their school," Lustig remembered with a chuckle.[21] John Leaphart informed me that his first overflight was "right fun." The pilot broke out of the cloud cover and swept down to photograph a missile site. As usual, the RF-101s caught the Cubans and Soviets off guard with the suddenness of their appearance. Leaphart noted that he "broke up a volleyball game" as he watched the players scatter upon the arrival of the American aircraft.[22]

President John F. Kennedy attaches the Outstanding Unit Award streamer on the unit flag of the 363rd TRW for outstanding service during the Cuban Missile Crisis.

President Kennedy traveled to Homestead Air Force Base, Florida, to meet and decorate the various Air Force units that had participated in the Cuban Missile Crisis. He personally attached an Outstanding Unit Award to the unit flag of the 363rd TRW. In a separate ceremony, the sixteen 363rd TRW pilots who flew the missions of October 26 and 29 received Distinguished Flying Crosses from General Sweeney and Admiral Robert Dennison, the commander in chief of all Atlantic Forces. Despite a grand finale awards ceremony, November 15 did not mark the end of Air Force low-level reconnaissance missions over Cuba. Few realize that four RF-101s were dispatched on a short-notice and hotly debated mission over Cuba in February 1963 after some doubts arose concerning a complete withdrawal of all Soviet personnel. One of these flights would be shadowed by a Soviet-built MiG fighter.

During the Cuban Missile Crisis, the RF-101 performed its reconnaissance missions as designed—with the speed necessary to surprise a target, take photographs, and escape before an opponent could react. The pilots demonstrated that years of flying low-level training missions had honed them into true masters of their aircraft—able to cross unfamiliar, hostile terrain at

Personnel and RF-101s of the 363rd TRW in formation for the awards ceremony conducted by Adm. Dennison and Gen. Sweeney

100 feet of altitude while flying at well over 500 knots. The skills of these pilots and the agility of their aircraft would be tested again in the skies over Laos, North Vietnam, and South Vietnam soon after the Cuban Missile Crisis. The daring of these pilots over Cuba produced the photographs that helped bring the Missile Crisis to a peaceful conclusion rather than a nuclear exchange. President Kennedy delivered what is perhaps the most fitting tribute to the pilots and ground crews of the 363rd TRW, when he personally told them at Homestead Air Force Base, "You men take damn good pictures."

The 1963 Overflights of Cuba and Regional Maritime Routes

Histories of the Cuban Missile Crisis that mention the low-level tactical reconnaissance missions over Cuba tend to end their story in late November 1962. The United States Air Force reconnaissance missions concluded on November 15, and most aircraft returned home by the end of the month although some remained on alert into December. Contrary to popular belief and the classic histories of the crisis, November was not the end of Air Force low–level reconnaissance overflights of Cuba. In fact, possibly the most dangerous mission of the Cuban Missile Crisis was flown in February 1963! President John F. Kennedy and his advisors grew increasingly concerned in early 1963 that high-altitude U-2 photos indicated that many of the Soviet military personnel in Cuba were not departing the island as expected after the Cuban Missile Crisis. Considerable debate and speculation dominated meetings about Cuba. Some advisors believed the Soviet soldiers were there to keep an eye on Castro, while others thought there could be other offensive weapons systems hidden on the island.

A declassified National Security Council meeting memorandum detailed the discussions with the president on whether and how to employ additional low-level tactical reconnaissance flights. These documents are added verbatim into the text due to their importance for understanding the issues of tactical reconnaissance at the highest levels of the United States government during the Cuban Missile Crisis:

Washington, January 12, 1963, 10:30 a.m.
SUBJECT
Meeting with the President—Cuba Aerial Reconnaissance
OTHERS PRESENT
Vice President, Secretary Rusk, Secretary McNamara, General Taylor, Director McCone, Assistant Secretary Nitze, Assistant Secretary Tyler, Mr. McGeorge Bundy, Mr. Jeffrey Kitchen, Mr. John McNaughton
Mr. Bundy said that we had evidence of greater participation of Cuban nationals in the air defense system of Cuba which raised the possibility of an attack on one of our reconnaissance planes. Although the President was not being asked to reach a decision today, the group did wish to discuss two questions:
In the event there is a radar lockon of one of our planes, does the plane complete its mission or abort?
Is our need for information about the cargo of a Soviet ship approaching Cuban waters sufficient to fly low-level reconnaissance, both day and night, including flights during the time the ship is being unloaded in port?
The President asked why a plane should abort in the event of a radar lock on.

The first four RF-101s arrive home to Shaw AFB after the Cuban Missile Crisis.

The first four RF-101 pilots to return home to Shaw AFB after the Cuban Missile Crisis. *Left to right*: Thomas Hennagan, Clyde East, Howard Davis, Tom Curtis. Each man made overflights across Cuba.

Mr. Bundy replied that if the plane continued on its flight, it is possible it would be shot down. Secretary McNamara said he did not think we should permit ourselves to get into a situation where we would have lost a plane and not yet have decided how we would respond to such hostile action. He suggested that there were three possible courses of action:

We could fly a reconnaissance mission, have a plane shot down, and then decide how we would react.

We could fly missions equipped with our most sophisticated electronic counter-measures equipment. The cost of using the ECM equipment would be the possibility of compromising highly advanced and highly classified instruments.

We could use alternative equipment such as drones.

In response to the President's question, Secretary McNamara said we did not have yet positive proof of a radar lockon on any of our planes although we had evidence indicating radar tracking.

The President said that he thought the Defense Department should decide whether or not to use our sophisticated ECM equipment. He said he intended to believe that if it appeared that the Cubans were taking actions with a view to shooting down one of our planes, the plane should abort the first time this happened and we could then prepare ourselves for prompt reprisals in the event the circumstances were repeated.

Mr. Bundy said that during this week there would be no change in the present rules regarding aborts by reconnaissance planes.

Director McCone said he favored using the U-2 in good weather, but if the weather were bad, he thought we should fly low-level missions.

Secretary McNamara said that he did not agree with low-level aerial reconnaissance in bad weather because the loss of a US plane or the controversy arising out of low-level flights would be all out of proportion to the value of the information obtained from pictures taken at a low-level. He said that the cargo of the Soviet ship[1] probably did not consist of missiles and that certain knowledge about it was not worth the complications arising out of low-level flights.

Director McCone said that CIA was trying to find out what was in the cargo and would continue to do so during the time the cargo was being unloaded, but he was not certain that they would be able to obtain the information we wanted. He expressed a view that the cargo might contain armaments dangerous to us.

Mr. Bundy said there were political problems immediately ahead of us, such as Donovan's proposed visit to Havana in connection with the remaining prisoners in Cuba and Kuznetsov's visit this week. He said the group would return to the President at a later time when more information was available.

Secretary McNamara said the Defense Department would be prepared to carry out low-level missions on very short notice if the President so decided.

Bromley Smith[23]

The matter rose to a crucial point during the first week of February 1963, with the arrival of intelligence data that a Soviet freighter was approaching Cuba with suspected military cargo. The exact contents carried by the freighter was a mystery but needed to be verified. Many advisors requested President Kennedy to authorize another series of fourteen low-level reconnaissance missions to photograph the ship offloading its cargo and shoot pictures of Soviet troop concentrations. A reluctant President Kennedy agreed to a compromise and ordered the Air Force to dispatch four reconnaissance aircraft if the freighter docked at Mariel and not Havana Harbor. At the same time, he sent a message to Soviet premier Nikita Khrushchev, asking for an explanation for the large number of soldiers still on the island. A section of the Summary Record of the meeting of the National Committee of National Security Council recorded the conversation related to this discussion:

Cuban Reconnaissance

The President called attention to reports that a Soviet incoming ship would arrive on February 8th loaded with what was suspected to be military equipment. He noted the request of KOMAR for low-level reconnaissance flights in order to be certain that we knew the exact nature of the cargo of this Soviet ship.[5] The President said he felt there are two limitations on our use now of low-level reconnaissance missions; (a) negotiations to obtain the release of US prisoners in Cuba, which he understood might be successfully concluded sometime in early March, and (b) possible withdrawal of Soviet military personnel. Low-level flights might influence a Soviet decision involving the removal of their troops from Cuba. The Russians might misread low-level reconnaissance flights as an indication of our preparing ourselves for military action in Cuba and decide that their forces must remain to counter anticipated US actions. He requested that a letter to Khrushchev be drafted raising again the question of when the Russians plan to pull back their troops.

Director McCone said he wished to reserve on the low-level recommendation until we knew whether the incoming Russian ship would dock at Havana or Mariel. If it came into Havana, the problem of knowing the nature of the cargo was much more difficult than if it docked at Mariel where facilities were such that its cargo would have to be displayed on the dock and thereby visible to high-level cameras.

Secretary McNamara said that the USIB had listed twenty-one targets in Cuba which they wish to cover with low-level reconnaissance missions involving fourteen sorties. He said the risk of the loss of a low-level US plane is very slight, but the risk of a strong Soviet and Cuban reaction is very high. In addition to the two limitations mentioned by the President, Secretary McNamara thought a low-level flight might initiate escalating actions which would place in jeopardy our current high-level reconnaissance flights. He said he saw no military need for the low-level flights but did recognize that there was a domestic political problem which had to be met. In his view, low-level flights are justified only under two circumstances; (a) when we have reason to suspect that offensive weapons are being reintroduced into Cuba, and (b) when we are preparing for an invasion and must have current information in order to do our military planning.

General Taylor acknowledged that there was a military need to know but not necessarily tomorrow. He agreed with Secretary McNamara that there was very little risk of one of our planes being shot down. He also referred to the requirement that our intelligence be kept up to date so that we could keep our invasion plans current. With respect to intelligence on incoming Soviet ships, he said the Chiefs felt less strongly about the need for intelligence and were prepared to recommend low-level flights on a case-by-case basis. He acknowledged that once a Soviet ship was in harbor we obtained a great deal of information from agents in Cuba.

The President decided that we should send a letter to Khrushchev on the Soviet troop withdrawal problem but not undertake low-level reconnaissance flights until we knew where the Soviet ship would dock.

Director McCone said that the intelligence community was very concerned about unexplained military activity taking place on Cape Francis, an island some ten miles offshore Cuba. He suggested that a low-level flight over this area would be highly useful but added that he shared the views expressed by Secretary McNamara and General Taylor as regards the US prisoners in Cuba. He said he suspected that Donovan would be concerned if he were asked what effect such flights would have on his negotiations.

The President said we would decide on the reconnaissance missions on Friday. His current view was that if the Soviet ship went to Mariel we should probably overfly it. If we carried out this mission, we should probably also overfly Cape Francis.[24]

The freighter arrived in Mariel Harbor on February 8, and the Air Force ordered a reconnaissance mission for the next day. Many of the pilots of the 363rd Tactical Reconnaissance Wing (TRW) were scattered at various locations after completing their missions in support of the Cuban Missile Crisis at the end of 1962. Several of the RF-101 reconnaissance aircraft were temporarily at Myrtle Beach Air Force Base, South Carolina. Four pilots (captains Tom Curtis, Ross Shaw, John Leaphart, and Bruce Matthews) were tapped to cease their activities and immediately fly to Cuba to conduct photographic overflights. The pilots split into two pairs over southern Florida. Leaphart and Matthews went after their targets, while Curtis and Shaw flew to the port Mariel to photograph the offloading of the Soviet freighter. Curtis related, "We dropped to just above the wave tops to avoid Cuban radar. Our first target was a large harbor. We popped up to 500 feet. However, the port was full of ships and equipment. It was impossible to get full coverage at 500 feet altitude." Curtis and Shaw moved on to their next target, a military staging area. After completing their ten-target mission, Curtis opted to break the first rule of reconnaissance—never go back to a target on the same mission. Several pilots were shot down later over Southeast Asia for violating this rule. Not only did Curtis return to Mariel but he also violated his altitude orders and climbed to 1,000 feet to ensure wider coverage for his photos.

The two pilots rendezvoused with a KC-135 tanker over Florida and then returned to Shaw Air Force Base, South Carolina, where the photos were processed and immediately dispatched to Washington, DC. Although Curtis and Shaw were not aware of it, they learned later that Soviet-built MiG fighters located and stalked them when they returned to Mariel. Curtis remembered, "We found out later that we were picked up by fighters on the way back to the port for more photos. The fighter pilots had requested permission to engage us. However, their ground control turned down the request." An American airborne control aircraft monitored the conversation between the MiG pilots and their ground controllers. Obviously, a serious international incident would have developed if the MiGs had shot down one of the RF-101 reconnaissance aircraft. Leaphart and Matthews landed without incident but were later accused by the Cubans of strafing their targets—a far-fetched claim, since RF-101s were unarmed.

Curtis faced an Air Force Board of Inquiry for violating the rules of the mission. He altered his altitude and returned to a target that he had already photographed. He remembered that there were a combined total of nine stars on the shoulders of the general officers sitting on the board. One general officer informed him, "It would be a shame to have an international incident because of an overly aggressive pilot." However, the exceptional photographs that he captured of Mariel during a time of heightened tensions helped his case. He was cleared and awarded a Distinguished Flying Cross for the mission. Curtis commented to me, "I guess they were debating whether to court-martial me or give me a medal!"[25]

CHAPTER 6
Southeast Asia and the Vietnam War

They really let us have it as I crossed the field at 480 knots!
—Capt. Burton Waltz, 15th TRS

Introduction

France returned to its Indo-China colony after World War II with the intent of holding it longer despite calls for independence by the Viet Minh, an armed nationalist group who renewed a low-level military campaign after the departure of Japanese forces. The conflict grew in intensity as France struggled to hold Indo-China within its colonial orbit. The United States viewed the conflict with the Viet Minh as representing the post–World War II spread of communism and similar to the conflict in Korea. Nationalists were also active in what is now Laos and Kampuchea, or Cambodia. Despite calls for more direct intervention as the situation worsened, the United States opted to avoid greater involvement and instead supported a process that might settle the question politically. The 1954 Geneva Conference partitioned Indo-China into four separate political areas—North Vietnam, South Vietnam, Laos, and Cambodia. The Geneva Accords that emerged from the Conference called for a referendum by July 1956, to determine the political direction of a unified Vietnam formed from North and South Vietnam.

South Vietnam held its referendum (actually an "election") in October 1955. The clearly fraudulent process ended with the American-backed candidate, Ngo Dinh Diem, declaring victory and announcing that the state would not participate in the national reunification referendum with North Vietnam.

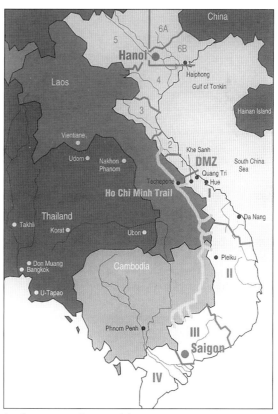

1961–March 1965

Laos devolved into civil war after 1959 with a North Vietnamese invasion of its territory and a coup against the government. The United States grew concerned about the North Vietnamese troops in Laos, the involvement of the Soviet Union in the civil strife, and the ramifications of the conflict on the other countries in the area. The Central Intelligence Agency established itself in Laos through the employment of pro-Western paramilitary and advisory groups to counter the communist attempt to overrun the country. America's efforts in Laos required intelligence—from aerial reconnaissance sources.

Southeast Asia at the time of the Vietnam War

American tactical aerial reconnaissance in Southeast Asia can be said to have its origins with the VC-47 (VIP transport version of the C-47 Skytrain aircraft) World War II–era transport of the United States Air Attaché in Saigon, Vietnam. The Air Attaché was accredited in both South Vietnam and Laos and traveled frequently between the capitals of the two new countries. Lacking independent American air reconnaissance assets, the Air Attaché employed a K-17C aerial camera mounted in his aircraft and a hand-held K-20 oblique camera. He ensured that his aircraft slightly modified its flight path between the two capitals to fly over important small airfields, roads, road junctions, and fords across rivers. He then delivered these photographs to the Royal Laotian government.[1]

Project Field Goal RT-33. This aircraft flew sixteen missions under this program.

Project Field Goal

The United States Air Force dispatched an RT-33, a camera-modified, T-33 jet-powered trainer, to Udorn Royal Air Force Base in Thailand on April 17, 1961, to provide aerial reconnaissance in support of the American air attachés and friendly governments in the area. The 15th Tactical Reconnaissance Squadron (TRS) at Kadena Air Base in Okinawa and the 45th TRS at Misawa, Japan, rotated the air crews that flew the RT-33 missions only eight years after the Korean War armistice. The missions continued until May 10, when the International Control Commission (ICC) halted the flights.[2]

Pipe Stem

South Vietnam officially requested that four RF-101C aircraft of the 15th TRS participate in an air show at Tan Son Nhut Air Base in October 1961. The invitation proved to be a means for the United States to send the aircraft and avoid any complications with the ICC. South Vietnam canceled the air show after the arrival of the American reconnaissance aircraft, which remained to officially photograph flooding along the Mekong River in support of South Vietnamese government relief efforts. Meanwhile, the aircraft flew sorties over Laos

RF-101 Voodoo

beginning on October 21 to monitor North Vietnamese personnel and logistics in that country and along what would become known as the Ho Chi Minh Trail to South Vietnam. On October 23, the aircraft successfully photographed the Tchepone Airfield in Laos, obtaining proof that Soviet IL-14 transport aircraft were parachuting supplies to anti-Laotian-government Pathet Lao and North Vietnamese forces. Two days later, a return mission resulted in the RF-101s' coming under their first-recorded antiaircraft fire in Southeast Asia. The ICC could not continue to ignore the prolonged presence of the aircraft and ordered them to depart on November 21. Pipe Stem resulted in sixty-seven successful reconnaissance missions in its thirty-one days on the ground.[3]

Able Mable

The success of the Pipe Stem missions prompted American military officials to examine how they could return Air Force reconnaissance jets to the area and avoid ICC opposition. This resulted in the temporary return of the Field Goal RT-33 to Thailand, but this time to Don Muang Airport, for missions destined to be in Laos. American ambassador Kenneth Young requested permission from the Royal Thai government to deploy four RF-101 aircraft to Don Muang in October 1961. With the 15th TRS flying the Pipe Stem missions, the 45th TRS dispatched personnel and aircraft to Thailand for what became known as the "Able Mable" mission for an initial thirty days. The United States Pacific Air Forces increased the available aircraft to seven.

Four RF-101s arrived in Thailand on November 7 and began operations the next day. Cloud cover in Laos frequently forced the pilots to fly at altitudes that were lower than desired. However, other than small arms, there were only two major concentrations of antiaircraft guns, with one being in the area known as the "Plain of Jars" and the other at

Tchepone Airfield at this time. Navigation could be challenging on account of a lack of navigation aids and maps that were so inaccurate that the pilots carried maps printed by the French Auto Club. Formal rescue assets were not available if the pilots crashed during a mission. The dense jungle of Southeast Asia added new problems for aerial reconnaissance, since the foliage often covered bomb damage, hid North Vietnamese and Pathet Lao equipment, and generally limited the assessment of the photographs.

The first Able Mable pilots in front of an RF-101C. *Front row L(eft to right)*: 1Lt. Fred Muesegaes, Maj. Ken Harbst, and 1Lt. Jack Weatherby; *back row (left to right)*: Capt. Ralph DeLucia, Capt. Bill Whitten, and 1Lt. John Linihan. Muesegaes, Weatherby, Linihan, and Whitten also flew RT-33A Project Field Goal missions.

As a result of fuel consumption and the need to process the film at Tan Son Nhut, high-priority missions often launched from Don Muang, overflew the photographic target area, and then landed in South Vietnam to deliver the film for developing. The pilot would have the plane refueled and then returned to Thailand. Small-arms fire struck four RF-101s in the initial weeks of operations over Laos. A1C Leland Olson served as a crew chief during this first rotation into Don Muang and remembered his pilot returning after being hit by small-arms fire:

> Major Harbst landed one day after a .50-cal. round shattered the canopy right behind his head. I saw some blood on his neck when I was unstrapping him from his ejection seat. A piece of the canopy hit his neck just below his helmet.[4]

Thirteenth Air Force, which provided oversight of missions, ordered the 45th TRS to dispatch two aircraft on each mission for the same safety and operational reasons as accomplished during the Korean War.

Aircraft continued to return with small-arms fire damage but usually just a hole or two from "lucky" hits. This changed on August 11, 1962, when a 37 mm or 57 mm round slammed into an RF-101 flying between 8,000 and 10,000 feet. The round entered the plane through the bottom of the fuselage and detonated under the pilot's seat. The uninjured pilot altered course for a return to Don Muang. Upon landing, the front nose gear collapsed, but the pilot had returned safely. Further RF-101 reconnaissance flights were halted at this point for an evaluation of the situation. The Pathlet Lao recovered the RF-101's right camera access door, which had been blown off the aircraft by the antiaircraft round. They presented this piece as evidence of American intrusions over Laos.

Able Mable flights commenced again on September 1 but with a minimum flight altitude of 35,000 feet and restrictions on where the aircraft could operate over Laos. The following week, a pilot reported observing between 100 and 200 rounds directed at his aircraft despite being above cloud cover, indicating they could have been radar-directed guns tracking him. On September 14, all flights were halted again until an intelligence review could determine the radar capability of the North Vietnamese. On November 15, 13th Air Force successfully requested the transfer of the Able Mable program from Thailand to South Vietnam where they would have shorter flying times. The Air Force would also have to frequently rotate the aircraft to avoid ICC complaints.

Following repeated calls for more aircraft, including a more desperate offer to accept the replacement of the four RF-101s with eight RF-84s, the Air Force agreed to increase Able Mable to six planes. The two additional aircraft arrived on April 1, 1963. On July 8, 1963, PACAF assigned Able Mable to the 33rd Tactical Group at Tan Son Nhut. The 15th TRS and 45th TRS continued to rotate aircraft and crews to provide the assets for this mission.[5]

On November 21, 1964, the Air Force lost its first jet-powered reconnaissance aircraft over Southeast Asia. In that November 21 incident, Capt. Burton L. Waltz, launching his RF-101 mission from Tan Son Nhut, flew into Laos with an escort of two F-105 strike aircraft to photograph a small grass airstrip. Waltz swept through the Mụ Giạ pass between Laos and Vietnam and attracted the attention of antiaircraft gunners, who fired a few ineffective bursts at the aircraft. Waltz violated an important rule among reconnaissance pilots—never return to a target for a second look. Thinking that after eight minutes the gunners had returned to a state of complacency, the pilot reversed course toward the airfield, flying within 20 degrees of his original course. Waltz recalled, "They really let us have it as I crossed the field at 480 knots!" The gunners "walked" their shells until they struck the RF-101. The pilot later estimated approximately six 37 mm shells hit the RF-101. Waltz ejected but was seriously injured when he fell from trees in which his parachute had become entangled. The escorting planes returned fire against the ground targets and established protective cover for a rescue. An Air America (CIA) helicopter diverted to the scene and rescued the pilot.[6]

The two F-105 Thunderchief pilots escorting Waltz were assigned to the 80th Tactical Fighter Squadron (TFS). The official squadron historical report includes details of the event:

> During a second pass over a known concentrated flak area, on 21 Nov., an RF-101 escorted by Capt. Charles W. McClarren and 1Lt. Murphy N. Jones was fired upon and hit. Capt. McClarren and 1Lt Jones were in position to deliver immediate retaliatory fire on the AAA site, each making one rocket pass. Capt. McClarren, then exhibiting excellent professionalism, kept the burning RF-101 in sight and advised the pilot of his situation and to bail out. With the pilot successfully bailed out, Capt. McClarren set up a momentary rescap [rescue combat air patrol] over the downed pilot long

enough to plot his position and direct rescue aircraft into the area. Realizing that there would not be enough time for both himself and his wingman to reach a tanker before both aircraft would be in a precarious position in regards to fuel, Capt. McClarren directed his wingman to return to Korat while he attempted to rendezvous with the tanker. Upon completing his refueling, he then returned to the location of the downed pilot and continued to provide cover for rescue aircraft and a helicopter until the pilot was successfully picked up.[7]

March 1965–November 1968: Operation Rolling Thunder

After 1955, the United States replaced France as the primary financial and political supporter in what was then known as South Vietnam. The latter represented a pro-Western government, while the communist states backed North Vietnam. The Viet Cong (pro-communist / pro-North Vietnamese supporters within South Vietnam) initiated an armed struggle against the government of South Vietnam with the assistance of North Vietnam. The United States poured money and advisors into South Vietnam to bolster the state. As the conflict grew, more Americans arrived to provide military assistance, and by 1964, 23,000 American advisors were on the ground in South Vietnam. Continued escalation led to the August 1964 Tonkin Gulf Incident and the American decision to deploy combat troops and aircraft to South Vietnam. Viet Cong attacks on American forces led to President Lyndon Johnson's decision to initiate Operation Rolling Thunder with the goals of responding to the attacks on American forces, warning North Vietnam to not interfere in South Vietnam, and restoring the morale of the South Vietnamese government and military. The military bombing campaign demanded support aircraft including protective fighters, fuel tankers, command and control aircraft and reconnaissance assets.

The Rolling Thunder campaign of 1965–1968 against North Vietnam placed greater demands on the USAF for tactical aerial reconnaissance assets. Between March and July 1965, the USAF dispatched four RB-66s, one RB-57, and three EC-121s to South Vietnam and twelve RF-101s and six RB-66s to Thailand. As the number and complexity of reconnaissance missions increased to support Rolling Thunder, RF-101s began falling from the sky. Eight RF-101s (three

Operation Rolling Thunder map showing airstrike (target Hanoi) support locations including SAR (search and rescue), CAP (combat air patrol, fighter coverage), ECM (electronic countermeasures aircraft, often EB-66s), and tankers (fuel)

RF-101 shadow captured in the battle damage assessment photograph of a North Vietnamese bridge.

based in South Vietnam and five from Thailand) fell to antiaircraft gunners between April and October 1965.[8] Considering that an RF-101 squadron generally consisted of twelve aircraft in 1965–1966, the USAF lost the equivalent of two-thirds of an entire RF-101 squadron in the first eight months of Rolling Thunder.

October 1965 marked a change in USAF tactical reconnaissance with the introduction of the RF-4C to South Vietnam. The 16th TRS arrived in Tan Son Nhut with nine RF-4Cs in October 1965 from Shaw AFB, South Carolina. An additional nine 16th TRS RF-4Cs arrived in December 1965. By the time Rolling Thunder ended in the fall of 1968, USAF tactical jet reconnaissance assets included one RF-101 and two RF-4C squadrons in South Vietnam along with one RF-101 and one RF-4C squadron in Thailand.

About 42 percent of all RF-101 combat losses between 1961 and 1970 in Southeast Asia occurred in the first twelve months of Operation Rolling Thunder and the associated missions that were technically under other operational names. It is worthwhile to review these losses in more detail to examine the types of situations in which these aircraft were downed.

The second RF-101 that failed to return from a mission since their introduction into Southeast Asia succumbed to enemy ground fire on April 3, 1965—the first full month of Rolling Thunder. The United States identified the North Vietnamese rail system located south of the 20th parallel to be one of the authorized targets for the Rolling Thunder campaign. A strike package prepared for a April 3 attempt to take out the Thanh Hoa Bridge as an element of the antirail plans. The force consisted of seventy-nine aircraft including forty-six F-105 Thunderchiefs, twenty-one F-100 Super Sabers, two RF-101s for postmission photography, and ten KC-135 tankers. North Vietnamese gunners hit one of the RF-101s flown by Capt. Herschel Morgan who fought to maintain control of his aircraft and extricate himself from not only the battle area but also North Vietnam. The plane went down 75 miles southwest of the bridge. The North Vietnamese captured an injured Morgan, who remained a prisoner of war (POW) until repatriation in February 1973.[9]

Three weeks later, the 15th TRS lost another RF-101 over Laos. On April 29, Capt. Charles Shelton departed Thailand for a mission over Laos with a wingman. The reconnaissance flight targeted the Pathet at Sam Neua near the Laotian border with North Vietnam. The American pair descended to 3,000 feet, and Shelton commenced his first camera run over the cave complex. An apparent antiaircraft round struck the centerline of the RF-101. Fire erupted on the aircraft, which was located at the Lao headquarters, and Shelton called his wingman asking if he had been hit. The wingman confirmed and watched as the canopy blew from the stricken aircraft and the pilot ejected. Rescue aircraft arrived upon being called and spotted Shelton and his parachute on a ridge near the target. One of the pilots reported talking to Shelton on his emergency radio. A rescue helicopter called off the retrieval attempt due to poor weather and promised to return the next day. Continued efforts, including a ground insertion, to rescue Shelton failed although they knew Shelton was still evading the Pathet Lao up to May 2. Rescue attempts continued for three more days before they were called off. A local villager later stated that he witnessed Shelton being captured, and the United States officially listed the pilot as a POW. Capt. Shelton did not return to American control after the war, and conflicting information emerged as to his situation, including how long he may have survived as a prisoner. Capt. Shelton received a Distinguished Flying Cross for this mission. The citation reads in part:

Captain Charles E. Shelton distinguished himself by heroism while participating in aerial flight as pilot of an unarmed RF-101 reconnaissance aircraft over hostile territory 29 April 1965. On that date, Captain Shelton volunteered to fly an important Bomb Damage Assessment mission known to be particularly hazardous because of large concentrations of hostile anti-aircraft positions in the area to be photographed. Penetrating at low altitude and high speed, with utter disregard for personal safety, he found the target heavily defended, but nevertheless, in order to gain badly needed photo-intelligence, he pressed his determined run, only to have his aircraft sustain a direct hit in the fuel tanks, forcing him to eject. The outstanding heroism and selfless devotion to duty displayed by Captain Shelton in the face of heavy odds reflect great credit upon himself and the United States Air Force.[10]

The 45th TRS lost its second RF-101 a week later on May 6. The aircraft, piloted by Capt. Robert Stubberfield, did not return from a mission to photograph bomb damage of the Vinh Linh barracks at Bến Hải, a complex located a few miles north of the demilitarized zone (DMZ). Investigators believe small-arms fire struck the RF-101. His rescue "beeper" did activate indicating a possible successful ejection from the damaged aircraft. However, rescue attempts could not locate the pilot. The remains of Capt. Stubberfield were returned by the North Vietnamese in 1989.[11]

The 20th TRS, operating from Udorn in Thailand, lost Maj. Marvin Lindsey during a Green Python mission over North Vietnam on June 29, 1965.[12] Evidence of a successful ejection did not emerge. His remains were never found, and as of 2021, Maj. Lindsey is listed as missing in action–presumed dead.

One month later, the 45th TRS lost Capt. Jack Wetherby on July 29, 1965. On this day, Capt. Wetherby flew wingman with Maj. Jerry Lents. The pair were returning from a mission over North Vietnam, when they received a message about a need for a photographic operation to a surface-to-air missile (SAM) site near Hanoi. Both reconnaissance pilots were experienced, and Wetherby had even flown over SAM sites earlier, so the pair volunteered. Wetherby lost his radio transmitter early in the mission, forcing the pilots to communicate through Lents. Lents would talk, and Wetherby would key his microphone to produce "clicks" in reply to questions. Yet the pilots refueled from a tanker and continued the mission as poor weather added more hazards. Nearing the location of the SAM site, the pair descended to 200 feet

RF-101

RF-101 landing with its chute engaged

and initiated an approach to the target from a distance of 40 miles. North Vietnamese ground fire commenced and grew in intensity as they neared the site. Immediately after Wetherby turned on his cameras, an antiaircraft round struck the RF-101 and passed through the plane, opening fuel cells, and then exiting without exploding. Lents called for Wetherby to eject. However, Wetherby continued the photographic run, ignoring the damage to his RF-101, which could explode at any time. Upon passing over the SAM site, the pair maneuvered into and through a narrow valley at extremely low altitude while unable to dodge the antiaircraft fire with Lents following Wetherby. Suddenly, Wetherby's aircraft exploded and crashed into the valley floor. Lents actually flew through the fireball of Wetherby's disintegrating plane. Although the crash destroyed the film, Lents was able to return to Tan Son Nhut and report the precise location of the SAM site, having followed Lents during the photographic run.[13]

The 363rd Tactical Reconnaissance Wing (TRW) lost Capt. Frederic Mellor on August 13, 1965. Mellor and his wingman were on a mission over Sơn La province when ground fire struck Mellor's RF-101. His wingman could not contact him by radio and witnessed a fire in the nose of Mellor's aircraft. Another RF-101 entered the area and established radio contact with Mellor, who ejected after his wingman assumed the lead on the photographic run. However, rescue helicopters could neither establish contact nor find Mellor. The United States declared Capt. Mellor MIA and in 1977 changed that to "presumed dead" after returning POWs could not verify ever seeing or hearing of him in the prison system. In 1991, an MIA investigation team located individuals claiming to be witnesses to the events surrounding Mellor's disappearance. They stated that Mellor evaded local militia for half a day and then engaged them with his pistol when discovered. The militia returned fire, critically wounding him, and he died from those injuries.[14]

The fourth 15th TRS aircraft combat loss of 1965 occurred on September 27, 1965, when Capt. George Hall did not return from an RF-101 Green Python mission into North Vietnam. The North Vietnamese learned quickly that major strikes against bridges were preceded by a single reconnaissance flight and trailed by a second reconnaissance aircraft in order to collect pre- and poststrike photos for bomb damage assessment. Capt. Hall flew the lead reconnaissance RF-101 on a strike set for September 27. As Hall flew across the targeted bridge, North Vietnamese antiaircraft fire peppered his aircraft, igniting the fuel tanks. The pilot turned his stricken RF-101 toward the coast to attempt to be rescued by the Navy. As the plane broke apart, he ejected; his next conscious memory was lying on a table, in pain from injuries resulting from his departure from his aircraft. He spent the next six years as a POW with Capt. Herschel Morgan of the 45th TRS, who had been shot down on April 3, 1965.

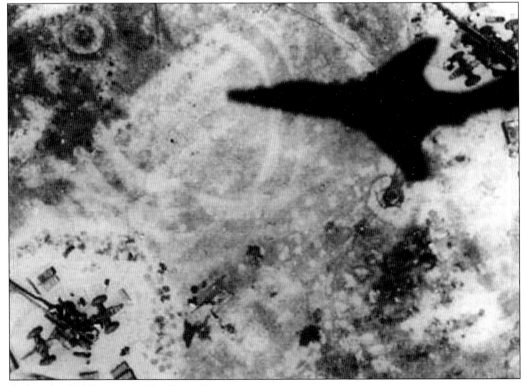

Shadow of an RF-101 over an antiaircraft gun site

RF-101. Location is probably Tan Son Nhut Air Base near Saigon, South Vietnam, on the basis of the presence of an RB-57 in the left background

Capt. Hall's Silver Star medal citation from the mission reads in part:

Captain Hall masterfully led a flight of two reconnaissance aircraft deep into hostile territory to secure Bomb Damage Assessment photography of vital bridge complexes which had just been struck by fighter aircraft. The locations of these targets necessitated separate passes through a veritable curtain of antiaircraft fire which guarded all approaches. After successfully leading his flight across the first target, Captain Hall was turning on the second complex when his aircraft was mortally damaged by ground fire. Not to be deterred from his mission, Captain Hall displayed a superior degree of airmanship and aggressiveness as he heroically, and with utter disregard for his own safety, pressed on with the photography run.[15]

One week later, on October 5, 1965, another 15th TRS pilot failed to return from a mission over North Vietnam. Capt. Robert Pitt and a wingman departed Thailand on a mission to conduct Battle Damage Assessment photography of the Lang Met ammunition depot and a bridge near Hanoi. Plans called for the RF-101 pilots to conduct their photographic runs fifteen minutes after American bombing raids on each target. Cloud cover kept the planes at a lower altitude where they could utilize their cameras but also where it would be more challenging to dodge antiaircraft fire and SAMs. Approaching the targets, both reconnaissance aircraft crossed a ridge and flew into a heavy concentration of antiaircraft fire. Both aircraft received hits as they passed through the barrage. Pitt's aircraft ignited with visible flames and the pilot shut off one of the engines, extinguishing the fire. As Pitt headed toward the ocean for a possible ejection where the Navy could rescue him, his wingman completed both photographic runs and then turned to follow and watch over Pitt. As the pair approached an area near Da Nang Airbase, Pitt opted to attempt a landing at the base. Low on fuel and not able to refuel from a tanker due to aircraft damage, Pitt lined up his approach with practically no fuel and lowered his landing gear. Capt. Pitt could not guide the roll of the plane on the runway due to the failure of the rudder controls. The damaged RF-101 rolled off the runway and into a small building before stopping. The pilot ended his wild ride with only minor injuries but with a heavily damaged aircraft.[16]

Capt. Norman Huggins of the 20th TRS went down on 1 November 1965 during a hunt for a SAM site in North Vietnam. Huggins nursed his RF-101 to the coast and ejected over the Tonkin Gulf. F-105 Thunderchiefs fired upon North Vietnamese boats dispatched to pick up the pilot who was rescued by the crew of a Grumman HU-16 Albatross amphibian aircraft.[17] On January 26, 1966, the North Vietnamese shot down another 20th TRS RF-101. Despite being seen in North Vietnamese propaganda in healthy condition as a POW, Capt. Wilmer Grubb was not repatriated in 1973 and was reported by his captors as having died in February 1966 while in captivity.[18] On March 7, 1966, two RF-101 pilots of the 15th TRS did not return from a mission over North Vietnam and were declared MIA until the North Vietnamese returned their remains in 1988. It is believed Capt. Gordon Page and Capt. Jerdy Wright were both shot down by SAMs. Capt. Arthur Burer was shot down on March 21, 1966, and held as a POW of the North Vietnamese. After his release in 1973, Burer very simply explained what happened to him:

On March 21, 1966, while on a reconnaissance mission deep in the heart of North Vietnam, my aircraft was struck by hostile fire and I was forced to abandon the aircraft over enemy territory. Within moments after reaching the ground I was captured and imprisoned in and around Hanoi, North Vietnam, until my release on February 12, 1973.[19]

The first RF-4C lost in combat failed to return from a mission on April 26, 1966. The 16th TRS crew of Warren Anderson and James Tucker were never found after radar units in South Vietnam lost contact with the plane as it crossed a mountain ridge north of Đồng Hới, North Vietnam. A visual search the next day failed to produce any evidence of the aircraft or its crew. Anderson and Tucker are still listed as "MIA–presumptive finding of death" by the US government as of 2021. There is some speculation the crew flew into the mountainous

16th TRS RF-4Cs preparing to depart Shaw Air Force Base, South Carolina, for the journey to South Vietnam in 1965

RF-4C of the 16th TRS. The aircraft began operations in this paint scheme and were repainted to camouflage in the Philippines.

terrain, while others consider it likely North Vietnamese antiaircraft fire struck the RF-4. The author's father, then staff sergeant Edgar Mays, once commented that many in the 16th TRS at the time believed the crew struck terrain accidentally, since it was a night mission, but this does not negate the possibility that they were trying to avoid hostile fire.[20]

The USAF maintained four types of manned aerial reconnaissance aircraft during this period. The first category provided *visual* reconnaissance and included the famous 0-1 Bird Dog. This particular plane was purposely slow (single propeller driven) and intended to provide real-time visual observation of a battlefield as a forward air controller (FAC). The Bird Dog worked directly with the Army, and its information could be immediately radioed to the commanders on the ground. *Electronic* reconnaissance represented the second category and included planes such as the EC-121 and EB-66. EC-121 planes were large, four-engine propeller aircraft that provided airborne radar support for airstrikes against North Vietnam. They also kept an eye on the borders of South Vietnam to ensure North Vietnamese aircraft remained on their own side. EB-66 aircraft were twin-engine, subsonic jet bombers modified to gather intelligence on the electronic emissions of North Vietnamese air defenses as well as provide countermeasure support for airstrikes. The third category involved *photographic* reconnaissance aircraft and included the RF-101, RF-4C, RB-66, and RB-57. The RF-101, a variant of the F-101 fighter, was the USAF's first supersonic jet reconnaissance aircraft. The McDonnell Aircraft Corporation constructed the twin-engine aircraft in the late 1950s. The one-seat plane boasted two Pratt & Whitney J57 turbojet engines with afterburners. The plane saw action over Lebanon, Cuba during the missile crisis, and Indochina.

RB-66 Destroyer at Tan Son Nhut Air Base near Saigon, South Vietnam

RB-57, South Vietnam, 1967

The RF-4C Phantom II, probably the best-known tactical reconnaissance jet during the Vietnam War, was modified from the McDonnell Douglas F-4 fighter. The two-seat aircraft boasted two General Electric J79-GE-15 turbojets, providing the plane with a maximum speed of over Mach 2. The RB-66 provided high- and low-altitude regular and infrared photographic capability, as did the RB-57, which was a twin-engine, two-seat, subsonic modification of the British-designed B-57 bomber. *Strategic* reconnaissance represented the fourth category and included the secret U-2, the single-engine high altitude "spy" plane made famous for its overflights of Cuba during the Missile Crisis; and, even more famous, the SR-71 Blackbird.

The North Vietnamese, as did other states in previous conflicts, attempted to camouflage the objectives of reconnaissance air missions. They also worked to deceive the reconnaissance pilots with false targets. One documented example involved an attempt to deceive and then trap American reconnaissance aircraft operating in North Vietnamese airspace. A two-ship RF-101 mission flown by Marvin Reed and his wingman Chuck Lustig chatted with the author in July 2004. The pair photographed a SAM site near Hanoi. When they returned, photographic interpreters determined that the site was not genuine but had been set up to lure American low-flying aircraft into a zone where they could be hit by hidden 57 mm antiaircraft guns.[21] Another attempt to deceive, and possibly attract American aircraft to a nonexistent target, involved a fake antiaircraft gun position:

At one time or another, the Communists used virtually every conceivable technique to hide their activities from aerial surveillance. The enemy also attempted on occasion to deceive aerial reconnaissance as to his strength and dispositions. A classic example of such deception occurred in December 1969, when an RF-4C of the 432 TRW photographed what appeared to be a four-position, heavy caliber, anti-aircraft artillery site. Closer examination by photo interpreters using stereo viewers revealed that the guns were actually logs.[22]

The Introduction of Drones to Tactical Reconnaissance

The year 1964 witnessed a new turn in tactical reconnaissance, when the Air Force deployed its first drone over North Vietnam, nicknamed the "Bumble Bug." The drone, built by Ryan Aeronautical Company as an updated version of the "Firebee," with a 32-foot wingspan, conducted high-altitude photographic missions over North Vietnam. Later versions with 12-foot wingspans arrived in 1965 and 1966 with modified equipment that allowed the drones to collect electronic signal data such as the emissions from radar and SAM sites. Aircraft, such as modified C-130 Hercules transport planes, carried the drones and released them near the North Vietnamese border.

Drones could carry a variety of camera types, including those designed for high-altitude, low-altitude, and panoramic photography. They were able to produce better reconnaissance work than manned missions in cloudy areas, such as during monsoon season. Two immediate advantages of a drone compared to a manned reconnaissance aircraft are cost and pilot safety. Production of a drone is less expensive than a manned aircraft, and a pilot is not onboard if it is lost during a mission.

Utilization of the drones increased after 1969 as Operation Rolling Thunder ended. The Air Force continued limited RF-4 missions over North Vietnam but tended to assign the most dangerous sites to drones. At the same time, drones proved fairly successful at surviving missions during this period in the war:

Overall, the "Bug" proved to be a difficult target for enemy air defenses. Its relatively small radar cross section made it an elusive target to acquire electronically. Of the 291 drones launched for over flight of the North in 1970, only three percent were known to have been lost to enemy action. SAMs knocked down five of the drones, MiGs shot down three and antiaircraft fire accounted for one. Another six percent were lost due to operational causes. Thus, of all the drones launched in 1970, approximately eight of every nine were successfully recovered. EB-66s of the 42 TEWS and EA-6As from the 1st Marine Air Wing played an important role in obtaining this high survivability rate by degrading enemy radars with electronic counter-measures.[23]

The Strategic Air Command (SAC) conducted drone reconnaissance in Southeast Asia, since the missions were oriented primarily towards fulfilling national reconnaissance objectives. A unit of the 100th Strategic Reconnaissance Wing at U-Tapao Royal Thai Air Force Base (RTAFB) conducted actual field operations under the nickname Buffalo Hunter (formerly Bumble Bug and Bumpy Action). Launch operations moved to U-Tapao RTAFB from Biên Hòa Air Base in South Vietnam in April 1970, when Vietnamese air force (VNAF) expansion reduced ramp space there.

The launch platform for the reconnaissance drones was a specially configured DC-130. Two of the DC-130s were configured to carry four drones externally, while the remainder carried two each. Spare drones were kept in varying stages of readiness at the launch site at U-Tapao. Drones were air-launched from the parent aircraft and normally flew along a preprogrammed track using only internal navigation systems. Controllers in the mother ship monitored the drone's guidance system in case the vehicle departed from the desired track. Flight profiles varied with the model of drone being used and the mission. In the low-altitude mode, the drone was air-launched and descended before beginning its target run. Usually, a drone would make runs over several target areas before turning toward the recovery area. The high-altitude drone climbed from its launch point to an over-50,000-foot cruising altitude, covered its target areas, and then proceeded to the recovery zone. The actual recovery of drones occurred near Da Nang Air Base. As the drone neared the designated recovery point, its engine shut down and a parachute system was deployed. Waiting at approximately 10,000 feet was a CH-3 helicopter equipped for midair recoveries. The CH-3 snagged the descending drone and ferried it to Da Nang for downloading of the film. In 1970, approximately 98 percent of all returning drones were successfully recovered in this manner, although surface retrieval was occasionally necessary.[24]

Drone use continued, along with RF-4 flights, into the last aerial phase in 1972. The Air Force slowly began replacing specifically designated manned aircraft for reconnaissance in the years after the Vietnam War.

November 1968–May 1972

Tactical reconnaissance missions continued over North Vietnam during the bombing halt between 1968 and 1972. Initially, these RF-4C missions, with armed escorts, proved to be just as dangerous as they had been during Rolling Thunder. Following the loss of an RF-4C in December 1968, American government officials complained to the Soviet embassy about North Vietnamese attacks on unarmed reconnaissance jets. The North Vietnamese greatly reduced their antiaircraft attacks against the RF-4Cs and did not shoot down another RF-4C until early 1970.[25]

Col. Don Dessert, the deputy J2 for intelligence at MACV headquarters, flew as the GIB (Guy in Back) on at least two RF-4C missions over North Vietnam in 1969. Dessert, a former P-61 Black Widow night fighter pilot in the South Pacific during World War II, flew on numerous USAF and Army air missions to better understand their intelligence-gathering capabilities. He noted to the author that in 1969, the RF-4Cs received very little antiaircraft fire or surface-to-air missile (SAM) attacks compared to the Rolling Thunder period.[26]

Vietnamization of the Conflict

As the aerial war in Vietnam moved into its post–Operation Rolling Thunder period, a military/political program known as "Vietnamization" emerged. In 1968, Americans elected a new president, Richard Nixon, who promised to bring United States troops home from

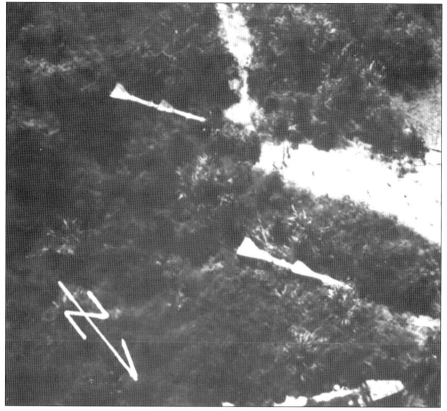

Aerial photograph of a North Vietnamese surface-to-air missile site

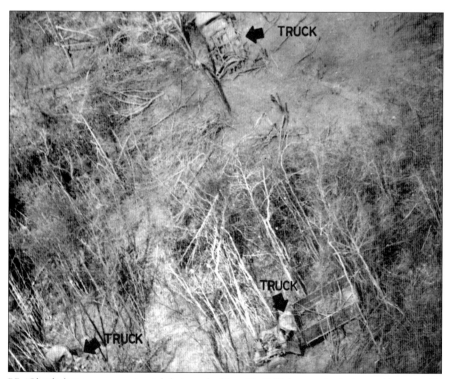

RF-4C battle damage assessment aerial photograph of three North Vietnamese trucks damaged in an airstrike on a supply route

Vietnam and prepare South Vietnam to assume a greater role in military operations, with the goal of standing on its own. This process would be neither easy nor short in duration. Vietnamization involved stabilizing the post–Tet Offensive situation in South Vietnam, training and equipping the South Vietnamese military, reducing the number of American troops, and arranging a political agreement with North Vietnam that would permit a full withdrawal and return of American POWs, among whom many were reconnaissance crews.

Vietnamization included the gradual withdrawal of Air Force manned reconnaissance assets, an increase in the number of South Vietnamese reconnaissance aircraft, and the equipment and training related to the technical skills of camera maintenance, film processing, and photographic interpretation. As of 1969, South Vietnamese forces included one tactical reconnaissance unit, the 716th Reconnaissance Squadron, consisting of nine U-6A de Havilland Beavers (a small propeller-based utility aircraft) primarily flown for Airborne Radar Detection Finding (ARDF) operations, one EC-47 for testing of navigation equipment at bases rather than ELINT, and three RC-47s for coastal reconnaissance. RC-47s were fitted with glass panels at the bottom of the aircraft for photography.

The primary mission for the glass-bottomed RC-47s was to perform daily coastal surveillance. The VNAF's 716 Reconnaissance Squadron furnished the flight crews, while Vietnamese Navy personnel performed the actual visual reconnaissance. The combination proved to be a happy one. The RC-47s flew at an altitude of 700 feet, allowing the Navy observers to inspect watercraft at close quarters. As one American advisor commented, "If there is one boat out of place they [the Vietnamese naval observers] can spot it immediately." Radio contact between the RC-47s and naval vessels permitted rapid reaction to inspect and, if necessary, board suspect craft.[27]

Vietnamization plans included the introduction of six RF-5A reconnaissance aircraft by December 1971, twenty additional EC-47s by October 1974, and nine more RC-47s, also by October 1974, to the existing inventory of aircraft as of 1969. These aircraft would be organized into two reconnaissance squadrons. The RF-5A is the reconnaissance variant of the Northrup F-5 Freedom fighter, a lower-cost fighter developed for multiple missions and a means to equip primarily Allied air forces. The numbers and types of South Vietnamese reconnaissance aircraft planned would cover only 10 percent of the missions flown by the United States over South Vietnam in 1969.

USAF tactical reconnaissance assets began withdrawing from South Vietnam and Thailand along with other American units in 1970. The 45th TRS, the last remaining RF-101 squadron in the area, was inactivated in November 1970. By the beginning of the 1972 Linebacker air offensive against North Vietnam, USAF tactical jet reconnaissance assets based in the area numbered only twenty RF-4Cs in a single squadron located in Thailand. Although combat air operations officially ended over North Vietnam on January 27, 1973, tactical reconnaissance missions continued until August 15, 1973.

The Hazards of Tactical Aerial Reconnaissance in Southeast Asia

Sources tend to vary on the number of reconnaissance aircraft lost during the Vietnam War. It can be estimated that approximately eighty-three RF-4Cs and thirty-nine RF-101s were lost between 1964 and 1972. USAF tactical photographic reconnaissance aircrews, as well as the crews of other aircraft, faced numerous hazards on their missions during the Vietnam War. However, the reconnaissance crews probably faced a greater combination of these problems and this might help explain their higher-than-average rates of being listed as KIA or MIA over North Vietnam.

First, the environment of Southeast Asia presented many obstacles for photographic reconnaissance pilots. Coastal areas of both Vietnams were flat, but the interiors of the countries were hilly, with many twisting valleys. While such terrain presents a challenge to any pilot flying ground support missions, this obstacle is magnified for the photographic reconnaissance pilots, who frequently flew at night. The objectives of photographic missions often lay within these valleys, forcing pilots to fly with precision between peaks and over ridges while relying on radar to keep them aloft.

The tropical rains of Southeast Asia proved to be another obstacle to aircraft. Storms and clouds often prevented clear photographs of targets. In addition, the rain simply made flying difficult. Lt. Col. John Bull Stirling, the commander of the 20th TRS between 1966 and 1967, vividly recalled the rain that swept through Thailand, where his RF-101 squadron was based. During the monsoon season, RF-101s taxied through standing water while oil and tire residue mixed with the water to leave the runway slick. Stirling remembered watching an RF-101 land on the wet runway: "The wheels were hurling pools of standing water into the air in clouds of spray, at times completely obscuring the oscillating drag chute behind it from view." The jet drifted from the runway and onto the soft, red mud. Stirling related that "the landing gear struts and wheels, which were torn from the fuselage, sailed through the air, skipping over the surface and coming to rest on the runway. The airplane plunged over the surface of the mud and slammed into a dike, tearing the fuselage in half directly behind the cockpit." Fortunately, the pilot walked away from the landing.[28]

During low-altitude photographic runs, reconnaissance aircraft could be hit by anything the enemy could shoot into the sky. Antiaircraft fire came from small arms, large automatic weapons, and radar-directed, larger-caliber guns. Gunners managed to hit many reconnaissance aircraft that were photographing targets at low altitude. One RF-101 pilot, Capt. Thomas O'Meara, was even hit by 37 or 57 mm guns in August 1962 at an unusually high altitude, somewhere between 8,000 and 10,000 feet. Enemy antiaircraft gunners could be very efficient at their job. Lt. Col. Clark Taylor, an RF-4C pilot, noted, "They were really great gunners, in fact both optically and by radar."[29]

While antiaircraft guns were an obvious hazard to pilots, they also had to be aware of small-arms fire from soldiers on the ground. The more bullets fired into the flight path of an oncoming jet, the greater the chances that the plane would be hit. A single bullet striking the right location on a jet can bring down the plane. On March 27, 1967, enemy forces in South Vietnam forced an RF-4C of the 12th TRS, based at Tan Son Nhut, to make an emergency landing at Danang. The pilot, Capt. James Menees, and his back-seater, Capt. Ralph Barclay, were on a photographic mission in the I Corps area of South Vietnam when they encountered ground fire. Several .50-caliber rounds struck the nose of the aircraft, causing extensive damage, according to maintenance reports. One bullet lodged in Menees's right hand, rendering him incapable of controlling the aircraft. Barclay assumed control of the plane from his backseat position and directed the aircraft to Danang, the nearest American airfield, where he managed to land the damaged RF-4C.[30]

Flying at low altitudes meant maintenance crews had to carefully check each reconnaissance aircraft for small-arms damage after a mission because pilots did not always know whether they had been hit. SSgt. Edgar M. Mays, a maintenance crew chief with the 16th TRS, recalled an RF-4C that returned to Tan Son Nhut in South Vietnam from a night reconnaissance mission over North Vietnam early one morning in 1966. The pilot advised the maintenance personnel, saying, "Better check this one close guys, it was rough up there tonight. I could hear the tracers burning as they passed the canopy." Mays related that a document given to the pilots indicated that if they could hear tracers, the rounds were passing within 3 inches of the canopy. Mays and the other mechanics inspected the plane and noted that it had not received any damage during the mission. However, as they began refueling the aircraft, one of the airmen yelled, "Shut off the fuel, shut off the fuel," as the liquid began pouring onto the ramp. After removing the fuel, a more detailed inspection found a single hole from a small-arms round in the bottom of the 370-gallon tank where it was difficult to spot since it hung low to the ramp. The damage is testimony to the fact that a single small-arms round could damage a jet moving at high speed.[31]

Reconnaissance aircraft, like all American aircraft over North Vietnam, faced the menace of surface-to-air missiles (SAM). Most of the North Vietnamese SAM sites were located in Route Package VI, the area designated around Hanoi and Haiphong. Flying in pairs helped daylight RF-101 pilots watch for the SAM threat. The North Vietnamese tended to fire their SAMs in multiple salvos. While a pilot might be able to dodge one missile, trying to avoid several could prove to be a formidable challenge. Lt. Col. Stirling recalled this tactic. "I counted at least twenty 35-foot-long missiles trailing fire and rocketing into the sky around our formation, but none came closer than a mile in front of me. Still, these were more missiles than I had ever seen at one time."[32]

North Vietnamese MiG fighters were an infrequent nuisance for the RF-4C and RF-101 aircraft. Finding and catching the speedy reconnaissance aircraft, especially the RF-4C at night, proved to be a challenge for the MiG pilots. Despite many questionable and inflated boasts of aerial victories during the war, North Vietnam has claimed that its pilots shot down only six tactical reconnaissance jets over the country during the entire war (four RF-4Cs and two RF-101s). According to North Vietnamese sources, all of their MiG victories over RF-4Cs and RF-101s occurred between April 1966 and September 1967.[33] Following the confirmed downing of an RF-101 over North Vietnam by a MiG 21 on September 16, 1967, the USAF directed that all RF-101s would not fly missions into that country. After September 1967, the RF-4Cs continued their missions over North Vietnam while the RF-101s flew missions over South Vietnam and other areas of Southeast Asia.

The precise number of reconnaissance aircraft shot down by North Vietnamese fighters is still disputed to this day. Some aircraft losses credited by the United States to SAMs, antiaircraft guns, or "unknown" are claimed by North Vietnamese pilots as aerial victories. Sometimes, the North Vietnamese could not accurately distinguish between an F-4 fighter and an RF-4C photo reconnaissance Phantom. Naturally, it is the same aircraft variant on a different mission.

If one were to accept all North Vietnamese claims for aerial victories over RF-4C and RF-101 aircraft, one would still have a small number of claims compared to other conflicts. American reconnaissance pilots contended with North Vietnamese MiG fighters, but attempts to bring down the MiGs by aircraft were much rarer than in World War I, World War II, and the Korean War. This can be attributed to better fighter cover for the reconnaissance planes and to the speed and agility of their aircraft. Two MiG-17 Fresco aircraft tried to ambush a pair of RF-101s in late 1966, approximately 7 miles east of Yen Bay, North Vietnam. William Greenhalgh, in his official Air Force assessment, noted:

The [RF-101] wingman spotted two MiG's passing behind them at 15,000 feet. Because the flight leader had begun his photo run and was concentrating on his navigation, he did not see the MiG's, even after his wingman reported them. As the MiGs dove on the leader, the wingman called to him to break and slid his aircraft between the leader and the MiGs. The enemy switched their attention to the wingman while the leader finished his photo run and broke down and away. Twisting and turning, the wingman found the nimble MiG's turning inside of him and gradually forcing him in the wrong direction. His fuel was nearing the critical point and it was time to stop maneuvering and use the Voodoo's superior speed. He slithered down to 500 feet, rolled out level on a heading toward the city of Yen Bay, and dove to 100 feet, virtually in the treetops. As he streaked across the roofs of the city, every anti-aircraft battery opened fire, but all were firing well behind the Voodoo. The MIGs thought better of flying through their own flak and broke off the pursuit.[34]

MiG-17s made another attempt to ambush two RF-101s on November 26. The RF-101s were also on a mission in the Yen Bay area during the incident. This time the North Vietnamese dispatched four MiG-17s which allowed a pair to intercept each reconnaissance jet. The North Vietnamese pilots commenced firing when 4,000 feet from the RF-101s, forcing them to break and dive to an altitude of approximately 200 feet. The American pilots then increased speed and departed the area. One should remember that this was a time when reconnaissance aircraft flew unarmed, as during the Korean War, and a quick departure could be the best defense. In this case, an RF-101 could outrun a MiG-17.[35]

Two months later, on January 1, 1967, a pair of RF-101s were on a mission over North Vietnam, when their electronic warning system alerted them to the presence of enemy aircraft in the area. The RF-101 pilots immediately turned to the west to head home. The MiG fighters discontinued the pursuit when the reconnaissance aircraft crossed into Laos and into denser cloud cover. The American pilots noted later that the pursuing MiGs were flying at an unusually high speed, and they believed the North Vietnamese had dispatched MiG-21 Fishbed aircraft rather than MiG-17s. This more advanced plane could keep up with and catch an RF-101 under the right conditions.[36]

The North Vietnamese claimed one MiG-21 victory over an RF-101, and this is corroborated by the United States. On September 16, 1967, North Vietnamese Nguyễn Ngọc Độ (an ace with six kills at the end of the conflict) of the 921st Fighter Regiment claimed an RF-101 flown by Robert Bagley in the area of Sơn La, North Vietnam. Bagley flew one of two RF-101s, making a postbombing strike photographic assessment of the Northwest Railroad in North Vietnam. As the pair departed the area, the MiG-21 arrived and fired at least one air-to-air missile, which struck Bagley's aircraft. The American pilot successfully ejected and remained in North Vietnam as a POW until 1973. North Vietnamese pilot Phạm Thanh Ngân also claimed a 20th TRS RF-101 on the same day, but the United States officially attributes the loss to a SAM. [37]

A North Vietnamese MiG-21 pilot claimed the downing of an RF-4C flown by Maj. Gilland Corbitt with Capt. William Bare of the 16th TRS during a night mission on July 16, 1967. The crew made one final radio transmission before radar lost contact with the RF-4C. Visual searches did not locate any wreckage, and as of 2021, the pair is listed as "MIA–Presumptive Finding of Death." The United States does not list an official cause of the loss.[38]

On August 10, 1967, another North Vietnamese MiG-21 pilot claimed the downing of an RF-4C flown by Capt. Lauren Lengyel with Lt. Glen Myers. Both Americans ejected successfully and were immediately captured and held as POWs until 1973. The United States officially lists the loss as a result of antiaircraft fire rather than an air-to-air missile.[39] A third North Vietnamese MiG-21 claim against an RF-4C, unacknowledged by the United States, occurred on September 11, 1967. John Stavast and his navigator Gerald Venanzi were near Hanoi when a missile hit and downed their aircraft. Both men ejected and were captured and held as POWs until 1973. The United States officially credits a SAM for the loss of the RF-4C based on debriefing of the crew after the conflict. Venanzi stated, after his release as a POW:

On the 17th of September 1967 while navigator on an RF-4C aircraft, I was hit by a Surface-to-Air missile and ejected from my aircraft about 25 miles southwest of Hanoi. After spending 45 minutes on the ground, I was captured by the enemy, thus starting my internment.[40]

RF-4C and RB-57 crews flew many night missions. RF-4Cs flew over North and South Vietnam while the RB-57s covered South Vietnam. Although RF-101s were capable of night photography, they remained primarily in a daylight role. Most of the aircraft on night missions carried photoflash cartridges that could emit a very bright light after being dropped from the aircraft. Cameras located on the aircraft would take pictures as the intense bursts of light turned night into day. In 1967, reconnaissance tactics called for the use of photoflash cartridges by RF-4Cs at 3,500 feet due to enemy defensive fire. Lt. Col. Barnard Watts, the commander of the 12th TRS during this period, noted that photoflash picture quality tended to deteriorate above 2,500 feet, forcing some targets to be photographed more than once and increasing the chance of a plane being hit in a hostile area. Although the photoflash cartridges provided fairly good illumination for photography, the series of flashes also served to indicate the flight path of the jet as they were ejected from the aircraft. Watts warned in February 1967, "The present photoflash cartridges place the aircrew in the most vulnerable environment to enemy fire that is possible."[41]

Reconnaissance aircraft frequently flew without wingmen. For many years, the motto of the USAF tactical reconnaissance crews was "Alone, Unarmed, and Unafraid." However, flying alone led to unique problems for pilots, and most daylight missions were flown as pairs by 1966. A wingman provided an extra set of eyes to search for antiaircraft fire, North Vietnamese MiG fighters, or just to inspect the damage on the other aircraft if hit. If downed alone, especially over North Vietnam, aircrew members often simply "disappeared" without a wingman to report on what happened. Did they encounter stiff antiaircraft fire, or did they fly into the side of a mountain due to weather, faulty radar, or confusion brought on by night flying? In many cases, we will never know the fates of many tactical reconnaissance crews.

An example of this problem can be seen with the second RB-57 lost during the Vietnam War. The RB-57s provided day and night, high- and low-altitude, photographic and infrared reconnaissance. Its subsonic speed generally relegated it to missions over South Vietnam. Although the RB-57 carried an infrared camera that was similar to the one in the RF-4C, the RB-57 produced higher-quality photos due to vibration problems in the RF-4C. In addition, the RB-57 could utilize the infrared camera at a higher altitude than the RF-4C and cover a greater amount of terrain in a shorter amount of time. An RB-57 assigned to Detachment 1, 460th TRW, disappeared in the early morning hours of September 19, 1966, near Chu Lai, South Vietnam. A search discovered the crash site, and a Marine rescue helicopter arrived first to the scene. The Marine rescue crew recovered one deceased crew member and two flight helmets but could not find the second crew member. The Marines departed the crash site with the one body, and an Air Force rescue helicopter arrived thirty minutes later. The Air Force crew made a low pass over the site and found the second crew member's body. The search-and-rescue report states, "The other pilot was spotted in a rice paddy about 175 yards from the wreckage and only 20 yards away from his ejection seat. Since we did not draw any ground fire on the low pass, I decided to land near the body for recovery. It was apparent the pilot could not have survived the crash as he was still in his half-opened parachute."[42] Apparently, one of the crew members made an unsuccessful attempt to eject from the RB-57 before it struck the ground. The author had the pleasure of meeting one of the Air Force rescue crew members who participated in this mission, which provided an opportunity to chat about the loss of this RB-57.

Lt. Col. Morgan Beamer, commander of the 16th TRS 1965–1966. *Mays family*

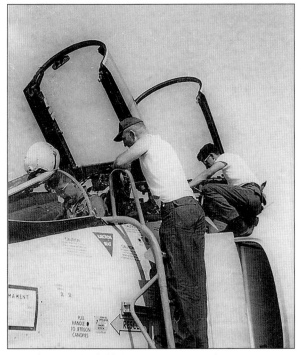

SSgt. Edgar Mays (*on ladder*) assisting an RF-4C pilot prior to a reconnaissance mission. *Mays family*

Flying in pairs helped the USAF account for pilots who otherwise would have been listed as missing in action due to an unknown cause. Capt. Jack Weatherby of the 45th TRS and his wingman, Capt. Jerry Lents, flew their RF-101s on a photographic mission to a suspected SAM site in the Phú Thọ area on July 29, 1965. Weatherby made a low-level run through the target area and attracted heavy ground fire in the process. His plane received a direct hit and exploded in midair. Lents witnessed the destruction of the aircraft and was able to return and report the incident.[43] If Weatherby had been flying alone on the mission, he would have become another reconnaissance pilot who had disappeared on a mission over hostile territory and listed as missing in action. In such a scenario, his family, like those of so many reconnaissance pilots, would have probably never known the facts behind his death.

Hazards also included the personal toil faced by the crews as humans. Aircrew members, especially those deploying to Southeast Asia as a unit, were too few in number for the type of sustained operations required to gather photographic intelligence. The 16th TRS was not an exception when it arrived in October 1965 with the first RF-4Cs in Southeast Asia. Aircrew members were quickly overwhelmed by the number and intensity of their missions as well as the usual hazards of operating in a tropical environment under combat conditions. Illness added to the problems faced by the aircrews. During a period when several aircrew members were ill, Lt. Col. Morgan Beamer flew additional day and night missions despite the many demands of his position as squadron commander. SSgt. Mays, while serving as the crew chief for Beamer, remembered the arrival of his RF-4C from a mission over North Vietnam.

155

After landing, Beamer turned to his Guy in Back (GIB) and offered a string of sincere apologies. Following Beamer's departure from the area, Mays asked the GIB what led to the apologies. The back-seater replied that shortly after takeoff, an exhausted Beamer fell asleep. The GIB then navigated to the operational area, flew the photograph run, and returned to Tan Son Nhut. As he approached the airfield, he awakened Beamer so that the aircraft commander could land the RF-4C. The GIB confided to Mays that he did not understand how Beamer kept going under such conditions.[44]

The Role of Maintenance Crews in Reconnaissance Operations

The USAF tactical reconnaissance aircrews who flew during the Vietnam War certainly deserve recognition for their exploits. They may not have downed MiGs or placed their ordnance directly onto an enemy target. However, the photographs they obtained helped pinpoint enemy troop movements, identify new SAM or antiaircraft gun sites, and collect battle damage assessments of previous targets. By risking their lives during unarmed missions, they saved the lives of others. Aviation stories tend to examine pilots and their aircraft. While there is nothing wrong with this approach, one should not forget the many individuals who work day and night to keep those planes and pilots in the air, especially the crew chiefs and their maintenance staff. The 16th TRS arrived at Tan Son Nhut, South Vietnam, from Shaw AFB, South Carolina, in the fall of 1965. Not only was the unit short of qualified maintenance supervisors but they had to operate from two old hangars. Initially, the maintenance crews of the 16th TRS worked twelve-hour shifts, seven days a week.

Crew chiefs had to demonstrate maintenance expertise on their (i.e., not the pilot's) aircraft, often going beyond what they learned in technical school or Air Force manuals to keep the planes flying. Most of all, they had to be resourceful in areas where resources were scarce. SSgt. Edgar M. Mays proved to be a good example of the type of crew chief who kept the RF-4Cs of the 16th TRS flying day after day in the tropical climate of Southeast Asia. Mays served as the crew chief for Lt. Col. Beamer, the commander of the 16th TRS, during the unit's transfer to South Vietnam in October 1965. The aircrews flew the RF-4Cs, while the maintenance personnel traveled in USAF C-135 transport aircraft. On the leg between California and Hawaii, Beamer's aircraft developed a fuel system problem during an in-flight refueling attempt. A fuel system specialist in Hawaii declared that he would have to order the necessary parts for the aircraft, and this process would take two to three weeks. Rather than allow *his* airplane to be left behind in Hawaii, Mays sought an alternative. Spying an F-4 fighter from George Air Force Base, California, parked nearby, Mays developed a plan to get his RF-4C airborne for the journey to South Vietnam. That night, he towed the F-4 and parked it alongside his RF-4C, while the other crew chiefs removed the damaged parts. They completed the replacement of the parts in the early hours of the next morning. Mays then tagged the F-4 as being inoperative and placed the damaged RF-4C parts on the back seat of the fighter so that its crew could turn them in and have their plane repaired. Nearly forty years later, Mays remembered with a smile that he left the inoperative F-4 sitting on the spot where he had removed the parts. He heard later that the transit alert crew of the F-4 was quite upset to discover the midnight requisition of their parts and then learn the culprit had made a clean getaway. The next morning, Beamer climbed into the cockpit and continued his journey to South Vietnam—thanks to a resourceful crew chief.

Crew chiefs also knew how to have fun with their pilots. In South Vietnam, Mays changed shifts and became the crew chief on a different RF-4C. This particular plane was the only one in the squadron without a 600-gallon centerline fuel tank due to a broken shackle. A newly arrived replacement pilot was assigned to fly the plane one night. When the pilot returned from the mission, he taxied to the squadron area. Mays hooked a ladder to the side of the aircraft and climbed up to help the pilot remove his harness strap and get out of the plane. The pilot, not realizing this particular plane did not carry a centerline fuel tank like the other RF-4Cs, turned to Mays and reported, "Chief, I really hate to be the bearer of bad news, but I recycled the centerline fuel switch four or five times and the tank wouldn't feed any fuel to the aircraft." Mays, noting the pilot's confusion, decided to have some fun with the situation. He pretended to look at the centerline area and replied, "Sir, you lost my centerline fuel tank." The pilot sank into the cockpit seat and replied, "Oh boy, I'll be writing reports to try to explain this to everybody." (An unintentional explosive release of a centerline

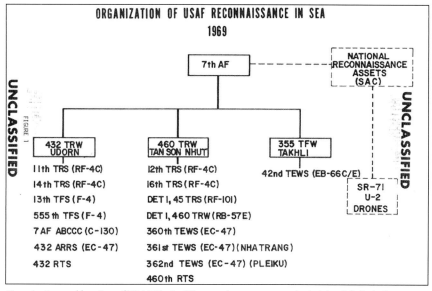

Organization and location of USAF Tactical Reconnaissance assets at the height of their deployment to Southeast Asia in 1969

Aerial photograph of a North Vietnamese SA-2 surface-to-air missile site taken on February 20, 1970, with a KS-72 camera at 500 feet in altitude

tank had to be reported up the chain of command during this period.) It took a couple of minutes to convince the pilot that it was a joke and that he had not accidentally jettisoned the fuel tank during the mission. Mays remembers that the other maintenance personnel standing around the airplane and the GIB ("Guy in Back" of the aircraft) were howling with laughter at the exchange between the pilot and crew chief. When he finally realized that he had been trying to feed fuel from a nonexistent fuel tank and had not lost it, the pilot began laughing and shaking his head. SSgt. Mays related that the incident traveled throughout the squadron and made everybody's week.[45] Behind every story of a combat pilot, there is a crew chief who has worked day and night to keep him in the air.

RF-4C struck by shrapnel and on fire from an SA-2 surface-to-air missile over North Vietnam on August 12, 1967. Captains Edwin Atterberry and Thomas Parrott were captured after ejecting. Atterberry died at the hands of the North Vietnamese after an escape attempt, and Parrott was released at the end of the war.

May 1972–January 1973: Linebacker I and II

Operation Linebacker I moved the United States into a fourth stage of the air war in Vietnam. The United States did not suffer any combat losses of RF-4Cs in 1971 or the first half of 1972, with the reduction in flights over North Vietnam. This changed as of May 9, 1972 with the launch of Operation Linebacker I, which represents the first sustained American bombing campaign of North Vietnam since the halting of Operation Rolling Thunder in November 1968. North Vietnam launched a major offensive against South Vietnam in March 1972 as

American forces were withdrawing from the area and preparing to turn over the military efforts to Saigon under the Vietnamization program. North Vietnam hoped for a clear victory over South Vietnam, but if not, Hanoi wanted to use gains on the battlefield as bargaining chips in the Paris Peace Talks with the United States.

The United States responded to what is known as the 1972 Easter Offensive with the Linebacker I bombing campaign to support the South Vietnamese military. This included flying approximately 200 combat aircraft into Southeast Asia from other locations. Approximately 125 B-52 bombers deployed to Guam for the operations. RF-4Cs supported the bombing raids with pre- and poststrike photography as well as reconnaissance of SAM and antiaircraft artillery sites, logistical facilities, and airfields.

Three of the reconnaissance aircraft did not return due to combat damage. The 14th TRS lost an RF-4C to 57 mm antiaircraft artillery on August 13, 1972. The pilot, Capt. William Gaunt, ejected and was captured and his GIB, Lt. Francis Towsend, died in the incident. A North Vietnamese SA-2 SAM brought down a second 14th TRS RF-4C on August 19, 1972. Capt. Roger Behnfeldt, the pilot, died and his GIB, Capt. Tomatsu Shingaki, successfully ejected to be captured and held as a POW until the next year. Behnfeldt and Shingaki were on a weather reconnaissance mission when they were downed. The pilot's remains were returned to the United States and identified in 1987. A third 14th TRS RF-4C failed to return from a mission on September 22, 1972, following being hit by antiaircraft artillery near Xuan Noe. The pilot, Capt. James Watts, and his GIB, Lt. John Pomeroy were rescued after ejecting.

The stalling of the North Vietnamese offensive and the sustained air campaign forced North Vietnam back to the bargaining table at the Paris Peace Talks. Linebacker I achieved the military successes that eluded Operation Rolling Thunder because of newer, precision air-to-ground weapons and a political administration that allowed the military commanders to conduct operations rather than imposing political restraints. Linebacker I officially ended on October 23, 1972, and President Nixon won reelection the following month.

The last combat loss of an RF-4C during the conflict occurred on December 9, 1972, when a SA-2 SAM struck a 14th TRS aircraft near Ngãi Hùng. Pilot Capt. Billie Williams died in the incident and his GIB, Lt. Hector Acosta, ejected and was captured. Three RF-4Cs were on a mission when the North Vietnamese launched SA-2 SAMs. One struck the aircraft flown by Capt. Williams. The plane burst into flames and the crews of the other aircraft reported seeing two parachutes. Acosta landed and made radio contact with a rescue team but was captured before he could be extracted. Williams died at some point between the missile strike and parachute landing. Acosta actually ejected both himself and Williams. He said after release as a POW that he thought Williams was already dead when ejected, and that he did not want to leave the body in the burning airplane. The next day, the North Vietnamese attempted to lure a rescue helicopter into an ambush by using the body of Williams as bait. When the rescue crew came under fire and noticed the body did not move despite being close to the weapons, they departed. The North Vietnamese did not return his body until December 1990.[46]

Negotiations in Paris broke down again on December 16, and the North Vietnamese refused to set a date for their resumption. President Nixon wanted an agreement before the United States Congress returned from Christmas break, and he attended his second inauguration in January. Two days after the North Vietnamese walkout, the United States commenced a new bombing campaign against North Vietnam. This time, the emphasis was placed on B-52 strategic bombing with 207 bombers, either in Thailand or in Guam. The air campaign of Operation Linebacker II began on December 18 and lasted eleven days until a ceasefire on December 29.

The Collapse of South Vietnam and the Mayaguez Incident

As in earlier conflicts, the Vietnam ceasefire, signed in January 1973, did not end the requirement for tactical air reconnaissance. At the time of the actual ceasefire, the Joint Chiefs of Staff ordered a halt to all tactical photo intelligence of North Vietnam and its territorial waters. MACV complied with the order, but four days later dispatched a request for Buffalo Hunter drone coverage to observe North Vietnamese military movement along the DMZ. The JCS approved the request permitting drone flights and, on the same day, strategic manned RC-135 reconnaissance flights over the Tonkin Gulf. The RC-135 is a four-jet-engine aircraft constructed by Boeing and operated by the Strategic Air Command (SAC) until 1992, when it was transferred to Air Combat Command. The RC-135 can perform a variety of strategic missions, including ELINT. Surveillance missions increased with the reinstatement of daily tactical reconnaissance missions over North Vietnam. Weekly SR-71 operations over North Vietnam began again in April 1973. The return of, and increases in, manned tactical reconnaissance flights supported the statements of President Nixon and Secretary of Defense James Schlesinger that the United States would militarily intervene if North Vietnam launched a full-scale offensive against South Vietnam. The reconnaissance flights observed the movement of equipment and personnel to and from North Vietnam.

Tactical reconnaissance missions over South Vietnam began soon after the ceasefire and increased to eighteen missions per day. Each had to be officially approved by the South Vietnamese government. SAM sites near Khe Sanh were frequent targets of these reconnaissance flights. North Vietnamese antiaircraft fire damaged an RF-4C during a reconnaissance mission to Khe Sanh, prompting the Air Force to add restrictions to the flights for safety. As with the flights over North Vietnam and the Tonkin Gulf, the missions over South Vietnam monitored the movement of personnel and equipment.

Tactical reconnaissance flights over Laos were not halted by the 1973 ceasefire. Reconnaissance aircraft flew with armed escorts and antiaircraft suppression planes, except in northern Laos and in areas known or suspected to be occupied by Chinese troops. The flights surveyed logistics networks and depots in order to spot ceasefire violations by the North Vietnamese. Reconnaissance flights continued on a limited basis over Cambodia and increased to eight per day by February 1973. Many missions performed bomb damage assessment along the eastern and southern borders of Cambodia and, by June, switched to monitoring the movement of North Vietnamese forces. By the summer of 1973, nearly 75 percent of all American manned tactical reconnaissance missions in Southeast Asia were being flown over Cambodia. Naturally, as most Americans assumed the United States had ceased conducting military operations in Southeast Asia following the 1973 ceasefire with North Vietnam, few realized that Air Force reconnaissance pilots were still in the air and being fired upon by hostile forces.

In 1974, the United States found itself trapped between the political realities of the growing assertion of power by Congress and the pending removal of President Nixon. Although newly appointed President Gerald Ford stated his support for South Vietnam, many people in Asia and the United States realized time was expiring for the Saigon government. Hanoi planned for a general offensive that could possibly defeat South Vietnam in the 1975–1976 time frame, before the expected completion of training and rearmament under the Vietnamization program. Therefore, they opted for a more meager offensive in 1974, with the hopes of gaining some areas lost in South Vietnam during the 1973 dry season. However, unexpected military successes in 1974, along with the political crisis in the United States and the continued impact of the global economic decline lingering from the 1973 "oil shock," prompted the North Vietnamese government to press their advances. The United States Congress refused a request for additional funding for South Vietnam in December 1974, as Hanoi's forces and the Viet Cong continued to advance within the country. The United States reduced its commitment to manned tactical reconnaissance in the fall of 1974. A declassified summary noted:

> In July, the JCS decided that, effective in November, all Southeast Asia reconnaissance would be submitted, approved, and accounted for under the Peacetime Aerial Reconnaissance Program, including RC-135s, UJ-2ls, and RF-4s, as well as other platforms flying in the area. Earlier, on May 15, another reconnaissance program had been phased down. EC-47 Airborne Radio Direction Finding missions, flown continuously since 1966, were discontinued and the responsibility for this task was assumed by the 7th Radio Research Field Station at Ramasun Station in Thailand.[47]

After the 1973 ceasefire, much of the American tactical air assets, including the one remaining RF-4C reconnaissance squadron, were based in Thailand. As North Vietnamese forces increased their gains in 1974, political disagreements and a coup in Thailand prompted the United States to begin withdrawing military forces from that country. Declassified documents from 1974 meetings between members of Congress and the military detailed the drawdown in Thailand as South Vietnam neared its collapse:

> In mid-December, Senate Armed Services Committee members visiting PACAF asked how many air squadrons were left and what the plans were for their withdrawal. They were advised that eight tactical fighter squadrons, one tactical reconnaissance squadron, two special operations squadrons, and one tactical air support squadron remained. The current program called for withdrawal down to two tactical fighter squadrons by fall of 1975. Asked about the rationale behind the withdrawal plans, the visitors were told that the force was sized to maintain a sortie capability as directed by the Secretary of Defense. Takhli Air Base, as planned, was returned to the Thai government (ahead of schedule) on September 12. On November l, Ubon Royal Thai Air Force Base was placed on standby status by the USAF. All US tactical aircraft departed Ubon as of August 4, 1974, and a standby force of 350 US personnel remained to maintain the facilities and provide the initial capability to receive aircraft units back at the base. At the end of the year, the 13th Air Force had identified 114 facilities as excess and approved for transfer to the Royal Thai Air Force.[48]

The South Vietnamese military collapsed in the Central Highlands by March 1975. Hue and Da Nang fell to the North Vietnamese before the end of March. As South Vietnam continued to fold in on itself, Cambodia fell to the Khmer Rouge. The capital of Phnom Penh fell on April 12, and the United States initiated Operation Eagle Pull to evacuate citizens and others to safety. Four RF-4C sorties from Thailand provided weather reconnaissance to support air missions associated with American Operation Eagle Pull.[49]

North Vietnamese forces launched a new offensive against Saigon as the South Vietnamese army continued to collapse. President Ford announced the cessation of all American aid to South Vietnam in April. Saigon and the government of South Vietnam fell on April 30, 1975. During Operation Frequent Wind to remove Americans and others deemed at risk from Saigon, at least two US Navy RF-4B aircraft were aboard USS *Midway* to provide tactical reconnaissance. Although Air Force assets were located in Thailand, and some strike aircraft did make the journey to provide any required protection during the evacuation, they were limited in their loiter time over Saigon and the coast due to distance. RF-4C reconnaissance aircraft are not listed among the American Air Force assets participating in Operation Frequent Wind.[50]

The final act of the Vietnam Conflict played out in Cambodia after naval elements of the Khmer Rouge seized the American transport ship SS *Mayaguez*, which was sailing to Thailand. There is still some speculation as to who actually ordered the seizure of the American vessel, but President Ford and his administration knew they had to act quickly to rescue the crew and recover the ship. Air Force RF-4C aircraft from Thailand flew twelve photographic reconnaissance sorties over the area in support of US Navy and Marine Corps operations to locate, track, and rescue the vessel and crew. An Air Force AC-130 Spectre Gunship crew conducting night commando operations encountered an RF-4C dropping flash cartridges for night photography of the island:

Gunship crews flew blacked out as a matter of routine, so when an RF-4 Phantom II tactical reconnaissance aircraft unexpectedly flew over the island dispensing photo-flash cartridges it was more than a little surprising. SSgt Joe Percivalle, the Illumination Operator on Spectre 31 remembered, "I was hanging off the ramp when out of nowhere an RF-4 flew from 7 to 4 o'clock shooting out a line of very bright flares. It being pitch dark and not knowing they were coming scared the crap out of me. He was close.[51]

With the retrieval of the SS *Mayaguez* and its crew, the 1961–1975 US military involvement in Southeast Asia and its associated Air Force manned tactical reconnaissance missions ended.

Gulf War and the Transformation of Tactical Reconnaissance

The [RF-4C] photos showed that the Iraqis had taken their MiGs and distributed them in urban housing areas. We were the first to see and report that.

—Capt. Ken Riser, 38th TRS

Gulf War

The United States Air Force dispatched twenty-four of its remaining RF-4C Phantom II tactical photographic reconnaissance aircraft to the Middle East for the Gulf War. Eighteen were based in Saudi Arabia and six in Turkey. The two-seat RF-4C Phantom II served as the primary tactical photographic reconnaissance aircraft of the Air Force since its introduction into the Vietnam Conflict in the fall of 1965, and the Gulf War signaled its curtain call. As a modification of the famous F-4 series of aircraft, the RF-4C boasted two General Electric J79 turbojet engines that provided the plane with a maximum speed of over 1,600 miles per hour and a range of over 1,600 miles with external fuel tanks. A total of 503 RF-4Cs were produced by McDonnell Douglas. The first models entered service with the Air Force in September 1964 and were utilized in Vietnam a year later.

The Gulf War in 1991 was the last military engagement in which the Air Force employed its RF-4C workhorse. The RF-4C was capable of carrying photographic equipment in three stations within the nose of the aircraft. One station could house a forward oblique or vertical camera. A low-altitude station could carry one of several different cameras designed specifically for taking photographs as the aircraft flew by quickly just above the treetops. A high-altitude station could be utilized for specialty cameras with optics and film designed to record targets as the aircraft flew out of range of most antiaircraft weaponry. RF-4Cs employed optical and infrared film-based sensors during the Gulf War. RF-4Cs were too few in number to adequately meet the tactical photographic needs of the United States military, and the aircraft required armed escorts. Photographs taken by the aircraft needed to be returned and processed, resulting in a time lag before commanders could evaluate them.

Post-Vietnam RF-4C

Post-Vietnam RF-4C front camera bay

Six Alabama National Guard RF-4Cs of the 106th Tactical Reconnaissance Squadron (TRS) deployed to Shaikh Isa Air Base, Bahrain, after the initial Iraqi invasion of Kuwait. In November 1990, the personnel of the 192nd TRS (Nevada National Guard) deployed to Bahrain to replace the 106th TRS. The RF-4Cs remained, and only the personnel were exchanged to reduce the "wear and tear" of the flight time of at least 15 hours on the aircraft and air crews. A second group of RF-4Cs arrived from the 38th TRS at Zweibrücken, Germany, in January 1991, and a third from the 12th TRS at Bergstrom Air Force Base, Texas. The latter group arrived late in the short war.

Although the RF-4Cs had carried upgraded cameras since the Vietnam War, they still utilized "wet" film which required to be manually downloaded on the ground and transported to a technical facility for processing into photographs. Technology and time were quickly eroding the reconnaissance assets of the RF-4C, which had been the primary tactical reconnaissance platform of the Air Force since 1965 . . . an incredible twenty-five years or more of service.

The Bahrain-based RF-4Cs flown by the 192nd TRS flew tactical reconnaissance operations over occupied Kuwait and Iraq during the conflict, on the commence of Allied military response on January 17, 1991. After the first night, the 192nd primarily flew day missions, performing the standard tactical reconnaissance operations developed in World War I and modified over the years. The pilots searched for Iraqi military units, rocket fuel facilities, command and control structures, critical infrastructure such as dams and power plants, and chemical weapons plants. Later in the war, the RF-4Cs spent many hours over Iraqi territory searching for rumored missile sites in the western desert. One of the last RF-4C missions of the war involved photographing the fires set by the Iraqis in the Kuwaiti oil fields. Iraqi ground and air defenses never touched an RF-4C on a reconnaissance mission, but the Air Force did lose one in an accident on March 31, 1991. Both crew members ejected safely.[1]

The *Gulf War Air Power Summary Report* of 1993 did not offer high praise to the RF-4Cs and their continued use as manned tactical air reconnaissance platforms. The report states:

> Tactical reconnaissance aircraft, this third category, proved deficient. The US Air Force employed twenty-four RF-4Cs (six of them flying from İncirlik, Turkey), and even these were a late addition to the force. The six aircraft at İncirlik did not arrive until February 1991, and twelve of the other RF-4Cs did not arrive in the theater until just before the beginning of the air war; more were not sent, reportedly, because of a lack of ramp space." This "lack of ramp space" argument suggests that these assets were assigned an extremely low priority, resulting in a short-age of tactical reconnaissance during the war. The Marine Corps had retired its own version of this aircraft, the RF-4B, only months prior to the war and before an operational replacement was available.[2]

Gulf War basing of American aircraft. The initial RF-4Cs were based in Bahrain (but written across Qatar on the map).

The Air Force retired the RF-4C, its last aircraft designed specifically for tactical photographic reconnaissance, in October 1995.

It is worth mentioning the Lockheed U-2 "Dragon Lady," perhaps the most famous of the American reconnaissance aircraft ever developed, for its high-level reconnaissance missions prior to and during the Gulf War. While a strategic rather than a tactical reconnaissance platform, the U-2 flew for the first time in 1955, and variations of the aircraft are still flying in the early twenty-first century. A U-2 carries a single General Electric F-118-101 engine and has a reported speed of over 400 miles per hour and a range of over 7,000 miles. The aircraft provides photographic reconnaissance from very high altitudes and is often known as a strategic rather than tactical asset. It did support reconnaissance operations in the Cuban Missile Crisis and the conflicts in Southeast Asia.

The Air Force also utilized the TR-1, a tactical version of the U-2, during the Gulf War. The TR-1 first flew in August 1981 and carried a reconnaissance pod under each wing, permitting it to conduct standoff tactical missions. Winter cloud cover reduced the effectiveness of the TR-1 during many Gulf War photographic missions, forcing the Air Force to rely heavily on the already overtaxed RF-4C aircraft. Six U-2 and six TR-1 aircraft supported the American effort, making the Gulf War the largest U-2 operation conducted by the United States.

Reconnaissance Pods and Drones

Manned tactical reconnaissance designated units and aircraft were replaced by reconnaissance pods and drones after the Gulf War. While a detailed examination of the two is not within the scope of this book, it is worth taking a brief look at these two systems which have been perfected—and continue to be perfected—over the years.

During Operation Iraqi Freedom in 2003 and 2004, the Air Force deployed the Theater Airborne Reconnaissance System (TARS) pods on F-16 Fighting Falcon aircraft, supporting ongoing military operations over Iraq. TARS is an "under the weather" system housed in a pod that is attached to the centerline underneath the aircraft. The system includes digital cameras, which eliminate the need for film processing and speed up the process time between taking the pictures and analyzing them. A recorder housed in the pod can store over 12,000 images. Pods such as TARS allow nearly any aircraft to perform tactical reconnaissance missions. The use of reconnaissance pods on fighter aircraft eliminates the problems associated with returning and processing film but still cost more than drones and still place the pilot in harm's way.[3]

The TARS pod, mounted on the centerline of the F-16 Fighting Falcon, contains a sophisticated photographic system that records high-resolution images that can be exploited by users on the ground within hours of landing. Because the pod is mounted on the centerline, the aircraft can still carry a variety of munitions under the wings to perform close air support for ground forces and air-to-air missions if necessary.

TARS imagery helps ground forces with their mission planning, providing them with up-to-date images of roads, houses, structures, neighborhoods and other areas of interest. TARS imagery is the equivalent of a 36-megapixel camera. In comparison, the average hand-held digital camera produces 2-to-5-megapixel imagery. Thus, these pods can provide very high resolution and high-quality images for the ground commanders. In addition to helping with mission planning, TARS images are being used extensively in "comparative detection" or "change detection" missions. In this role, F-16s photograph areas of interest repeatedly over time, looking for changes that would indicate insurgent activity, a function that has become increasingly important, as insurgents have made improvised explosive devices—their weapon of choice against coalition forces. TARS-equipped F-16s can also provide battle damage assessment of targets struck from the air. A TARS-equipped jet has the ability to photograph a target before a strike, drop a GPS-guided munition, and then perform its own high-resolution BDA.

Unmanned reconnaissance drones were mentioned in the chapter on Southeast Asia and Vietnam where they played an ever-increasing role in the reconnaissance over North Vietnam at the end of the conflict. Modern drones maintain the valuable human element of the operation, although remotely. At the same time, the human operators are kept safer than those reconnaissance pilots who displayed "grit and determination" to fly alone and unarmed to secure visual and photographic intelligence. They are also less expensive than a manned aircraft.

The two most common drones employed by the Air Force today are the MQ-1B Predator and the MQ-9 Reaper. The latter's primary function is to eliminate targets, as directed by its human operators, in a distant location. It does include a secondary function for intelligence gathering, including real-time video and still imagery. The primary function of the smaller Predator drone is real-time intelligence with the advantages of safety for the operators and real-time data collection via video and still photography.

The MQ-1B Predator is an armed, multimission, medium-altitude, long-endurance remotely piloted aircraft with excellent loiter time over the objective. While armed and available to launch weapons against targets, they are well designed to gather intelligence and perform surveillance and reconnaissance missions. It can be operated via line-of-sight or remote flying via a satellite link. The reconnaissance features of the drone include an infrared sensor, color/monochrome daylight TV camera, and an image-intensified TV camera. With real-time reconnaissance capability, the intelligence material is transmitted immediately to where it is required, and the loss of the drone to accident or combat does not mean the loss of its reconnaissance data.[4]

While there is considerable innovation and excitement surrounding both reconnaissance drones and pods, I trust that those who flew the tactical air reconnaissance missions from World War I to the Gulf War will not be forgotten.

Endnotes

Chapter 1

1. William H. Greenhalgh, *The RF-101 Voodoo 1961–1970* (United States Air Force, Office of Air Force History, 1979, declassified).

2. 67th Tactical Reconnaissance Group, Operations Report 67/231, Mission No. 17, June 6, 1944.

Chapter 2

1. ESG G-3, Memorandum, August 16, 1918.

2. Captain Daniel P. Morse, *The History of the 50th Aero Squadron* (New York: Blanchard, 1920), 1.

3. Ibid., 13–14.

4. H. A. Toulmin, *Air Service: American Expeditionary Force 1918* (New York: D. Van Nostrand, 1927).

5. Morse, *The History of the 50th Aero Squadron*, 13.

6. Lieutenant Lawrence L. Smart, *The Hawks That Guided the Guns* (self published, 1968), 37 and 40.

7. Morse, *The History of the 50th Aero Squadron*, 13.

8. Ibid., 37.

9. Leland F. Carver, Gustaf A. Lindstrom, and A. T. Foster, *The Ninetieth Aero Squadron: American Expeditionary Forces* (Hinesdale, IL: E. H. Griest, 1920), 22.

10. Smart, *The Hawks That Guided the Guns*, 37.

11. Ibid.

12. William B. Mitchell, *Memoirs of World War I* (New York: Random House, 1960; reprinted from original 1928 edition).

13. General Orders: War Department, General Orders No. 44 (1919).

14. Maurer, ed., *The US Air Service in World War I, vol. 1, The Final Report and a Tactical History* (Maxwell AFB, AL: Albert F. Simpson Historical Research Center, 1978).

15. 2nd Division: 202-20, 4 Intelligence Report, 2nd Division AEF, Genevrots, France, June 29, 1918.

16. General Orders: War Department, General Orders No. 44 (1919).

17. Headquarters 1st Army, AEF, August 6, 1918, Memorandum 8.

18. Ibid.

19. Headquarters, Air Service First Army, August 20, 1918, memorandum for commanding general, 1st Army, William S. Mitchell, colonel, A.S.S.C. C.A.S., 1st Army.

20. Headquarters, First Pursuit Wing Air Service, American E.F., August 29, 1918 Operations Memorandum 3, by order of Major Atkinson; Philip J. Roosevelt, captain, A/S. C. operations officer.

21. Headquarters Ninth Aero Service Squadron, Operations Report for September 12, 1918, Harold W. Merrill, 1st lieut., 103/F.A., operations officer.

22. Headquarters, 91st Aero Squadron, Operations Report for September 12, 1918, John W. Cousins, 1st lieut., operations officer.

23. Office of the Chief of Air Service, Headquarters First Army Corps, American Expeditionary Forces, Sept. 13, 1918, Summary of Operations for the day of Sept. 12, 1918. No. 3. By order of Major M. A. Hall, C. A. S., and 1st A. C. Paul D. Meyers, 2nd lieut., C.A. C. operations officer.

24. Headquarters, 90th Aero Squadron Observation Group–Fourth Army Corps, Sept. 12, 1918.

25. Headquarters, Ninth Aero Service Squadron, Operations Report for September 12, 1918, Harold W. Merrill 1st lieut., 103/F.A., operations officer.

26. Headquarters, 91st Aero Squadron, Operations Report for September 12, 1918, John W. Cousins, 1st lieut., operations officer.

27. 1st Aero Squadron, September 12, 1918, Summary of Operations.

28. Office of the Chief of Air Service Headquarters, First Army Corps American Expeditionary Forces, Sept. 13, 1918, Summary of Operations for the day of Sept. 12, 1918, no. 3. By order of Major M. A. Hall, C. A. S., and 1st A. C. Paul D. Meyers, 2nd lieut. C.A. C., operations officer.

29. 8th Aero Squadron, statement by 1st Lieutenant Horace W. Mitchell, no date listed.

30. 8th Aero Squadron, statement by Second Lieutenant John W. Artz, no date listed.

31. Headquarters, Air Service, First Army American Expeditionary Forces Operations Report No. 13, 1900 hrs., September 11–1900 hrs., Sept. 12, 1918.

32. General Orders: War Department, General Orders No. 15 (1919) Action Date: September 12, 1918.

33. General Orders: War Department, General Orders No. 126 (1919).

34. 94th Aero Squadron, 9/13/18 Reconnaissance Report, J. Bayard H. Smith 1st lieut., A.S. U.S.A., acting operations officer.

35. Percival Gray Hart, *History of the 135th Aero Squadron From July 25 to November 11, 1918* (Chicago: no publisher listed, 1939), 71.

36. Ibid., 72.

37. Brookhart, as recorded in Hart, *History of the 135th Aero Squadron from July 25 to November 11, 1918,* 66.

38. Carver, *The Ninetieth Aero Squadron: American Expeditionary Forces*, 24–25.

39. Office of the Chief of Air Service Headquarters First Army Corps American Expeditionary Forces, Sept. 13, 1918, Summary of Operations for the day of Sept. 12, 1918. No. 3.

40. Headquarters, 24th Aero Squadron, First Army Observation Group, Operations Report for September 13, 1918, John W. Cousins, 1st lieut., inf. operations officer.

41. 1st Aero Squadron, September 13, 1918, Summary of Operations.

42. 12th Aero Squadron, September 13, 1918, Summary of Operations.

43. 50th Aero Squadron Operations Report, September 13, 1918; Office of the Chief of Air Service Headquarters, First Army Corps American Expeditionary Forces, Sept. 14, 1918, Summary of Operations for the day of Sept. 13, 1918. No. 4. By order by Major M. A. Hall, C.A.S., and 1st A.C. Paul D. Meyers, 2nd lieut., C.A. C., operations officer.

44. 9th Aero Squadron, September 13, 1918, Missions Carried Out.

45. 104th Aero Squadron, September 13, 1918, Summary of Reports.

46. Headquarters, Air Service Fifth Army Corps, American E.F. Operations Report Number 38, 19:00 Sept. 12 to 19:00 Sept. 13, 1918. By order of Major Christie Fraser Hale, 1st lieut., FA USA, operations officer.

47. Ibid.

48. Headquarters, Ninth Aero Service Squadron, Operations Report for September 14, 1918.

49. Headquarters, 24th Aero Squadron, First Army Observation Group, Operations Report for September 14, 1918.

50. 12th Aero Squadron, September 14, 1918, Summary of Operations.

51. Headquarters, Air Service Fifth Army Corps, American Expeditionary Forces, Operations Report No. 39, 19:00 Sept. 13 to 19:00 Sept. 14, 1918.

52. George C. Kenney and Horace Moss Guilburt, *History of the 91st Aero Squadron: Air Service USA* (Coblenz, Germany: privately published, 1919), 11.

53. 104th Aero Squadron, September 15, 1918, Summary of Reports.

54. Richard S. Faulkner, *Meuse-Argonne, 26 September–11 November 1918* (Washington, DC: Center of Military History United States Army, 2018).

55. Carver, *The Ninetieth Aero Squadron: American Expeditionary Forces*, 30.

56. Morse, *The History of the 50th Aero Squadron*, 37.

57. Kenney, 40.

58. Ibid., 45.

59. General Orders: War Department, General Orders No. 56 (1922).

60. Morse, *The History of the 50th Aero Squadron*, 55.

61. Smart, *The Hawks That Guided the Guns*, 59.

62. Ibid., 61.

63. Ibid., 62.

64. Hart, *History of the 135th Aero Squadron from July 25 to November 11, 1918,* 154.

Chapter 3

1. 67th Tactical Reconnaissance Group, Historical Records of Headquarters, 67th Tactical Reconnaissance Group, June 1944.

2. 7th Photographic Reconnaissance Group, Group History Report, June 1944.

3. Ibid.

4. Ibid.

5. Ibid.

6. Ibid.

7. Headquarters, Ninth Air Force. Unit Commendation for Distinguished Service, April 13, 1944.

8. Historical Records of Headquarters, 67th Tactical Reconnaissance Group, June 1944.

9. Ibid.; and Clyde B. East, personal interview with the author, February 13, 2005.

10. Ibid.

11. Ibid.

12. Ibid.

13. 7th Photographic Reconnaissance Group, Group History Report, June 1944.

14. 111th Tactical Reconnaissance Squadron, Squadron History, April 1945.

15. Ibid.

16. 5th Photographic Squadron, Fotoron Five, Resume of Activities since Departure from Home Station for Field Service.

17. 5th Photographic Squadron, Fotoron Five, Resume of Activities from May 28, 1943, to October 9, 1943.

18. Ibid.

19. 5th Photographic Squadron, Squadron History, 5th Photo Squadron (Advanced Unit for Fifth Army), November 1943.

20. 5th Photographic Squadron, Squadron History Report, January 3, 1944.

21. Ibid.

22. 5th Photographic Squadron, Squadron History, April 1944.

23. 5th Photographic Squadron, Close Intelligence Support Furnished Outside Units, May 1944.

24. 5th Photographic Squadron, Squadron History, June 1944.

25. 5th Photographic Squadron, General Summary, June 1944.

26. 5th Photographic Squadron, Squadron History, August 1944.

27. 5th Photographic Squadron, Historical Records, April 1945.

28. Ibid.

29. 5th Photographic Squadron, Historical Records, May 1945.

30. 8th Photo Reconnaissance Squadron, Narrative, November 1944.

31. Marvin G. Gardner, "Target Buka," 8th Photographic Reconnaissance Squadron, March 1944.

32. 8th Photo Reconnaissance Squadron, Historical Report for the Month of December 1944.

33. Headquarters, US Army Forces in the Far East, General Orders No. 77 (1943).

34. 8th Photo Reconnaissance Squadron, Historical Report for the Month of December 1944.

35. Ibid.

36. Ibid.

37. Ibid.

38. Ninth Photographic Reconnaissance Squadron, *Squadron History for the Month of December 1942*.

39. Ninth Photographic Reconnaissance Squadron, *Squadron History for the Month of January 1943*.

40. Ibid.

41. Ninth Photographic Reconnaissance Squadron, *Squadron History for the Month of June 1943*.

42. Ibid.

43. Ibid.

44. Ninth Photographic Reconnaissance Squadron, *Squadron History for the Month of August 1943*.

45. Ninth Photographic Reconnaissance Squadron, *Squadron History for the Month of August 1943*.

46. Ibid.

47. Ibid.

48. Ninth Photographic Reconnaissance Squadron, *Squadron History for the Month of November 1943*.

49. Ninth Photographic Reconnaissance Squadron, *Squadron History for the Month of October 1943*.

50. Ninth Photographic Reconnaissance Squadron, *Squadron History for the Months of November and December 1943*.

51. Ninth Photographic Reconnaissance Squadron, *Operations of the Ninth Photographic Reconn Squadron for January 1944*, 7 April 1944, page 1. These dates are correct. The 9th PRS Commander's Office wrote more-detailed summaries of the January, February, and March 1944 unit operational reports from his perspective in April 1944.

52. Ibid.

53. Ibid.

54. Ninth Photographic Reconnaissance Squadron, *Operations of the Ninth Photographic Reconn Squadron for February 1944*, April 7, 1944.

55. Ninth Photographic Reconnaissance Squadron, *Operations of the Ninth Photographic Reconn Squadron for April 1944*, June 1, 1944.

56. Ninth Photographic Reconnaissance Squadron, *Operations of the Ninth Photographic Reconn Squadron for May 1944*, June 18, 1944.

57. Seventy-First Reconnaissance Group, Historical Record and History of the 71st Reconnaissance Group, September 14, 1945,5–6.

58. Ibid.

Chapter 4

1. Wayne Thompson and Bernard C. Nalty, *Within Limits: The US Air Force and the Korean War, 1–6.*

2. George Stratemeyer, *The Three Wars of Lt. Gen. George E. Stratemeyer: His Korean War Diary*, edited by William T. Y'Blood (Air Force History and Museums Program, 1999), 45–46.

3. Ibid., 6.

4. Curtis Peebles, *Shadow Flights: America's Secret Air War against the Soviet Union* (Novato, CA: Presidio, 2000), 4–39.

5. Richard P. Hallion, ed., *Silver Wings, Golden Valor: The USAF Remembers Korea* (Washington, DC: Air Force History and Museums Program, 2006), 69–70.

6. Stratemeyer, *The Three Wars of Lt. Gen. George E. Stratemeyer*, 45–46.

7. Ibid., 70.

8. Headquarters, Far East Air Forces, General Orders No. 73 (February 25, 1951).

9. Ibid., 71.

10. Stratemeyer, *The Three Wars of Lt. Gen. George E. Stratemeyer*, 261.

11. Ibid., 355.

12. Ibid., 357.

13. Ibid., 364.

14. Ibid.

15. 45th Tactical Reconnaissance Squadron, Unit Historical Report, December 1950.

16. Stratemeyer, *The Three Wars of Lt. Gen. George E. Stratemeyer*, 355.

17. J. B. Smith, "Bruce Shawe & JB Smith, 8th Tac Recon (Photo Jet), Korean War, 1950–53," 15th Tactical Reconnaissance Squadron, http://yocumusa.com/sweetrose/everymanatiger/waryalu. htm, accessed October 20, 2020.

18. General John A. Shaud, "Air Pressure: Air-to-Ground Operations in Korea," in *Silver Wings, Golden Valor: The Air Force Remembers Korea*, edited by Richard Hallion (Washington, DC: Air Force History and Museums Program, 2006), 71.

19. 45th Tactical Reconnaissance Squadron, Unit Historical Report, January 1951.

20. Ibid.

21. Ibid.

22. Ibid.

23. Ibid.

24. Clyde B. East, personal interview with the author, February 13, 2005.

25. Headquarters, Far East Air Forces, General Orders No. 569, December 4, 1951.

26. 45th Tactical Reconnaissance Squadron, Unit Historical Report, March 1951.

27. Ibid.

28. East, personal interview.

29. Stanley R. Sebring, "I Was Wrong about That," 15th Tactical Reconnaissance Squadron, http://yocumusa.com/sweetrose/everymanatiger/warenterthedragon.htm, accessed October 20, 2020.

30. James R. Hanson, "Korea," 15th Tactical Reconnaissance Squadron, http://yocumusa.com/sweetrose/everymanatiger/warairbattles.htm, accessed October 20, 2020.

31. Ibid.

32. James W. Nimmo, "Break, Break," 15th Tactical Reconnaissance Squadron, http://yocumusa.com/sweetrose/everymanatiger/warairbattles.htm, accessed October 20, 2020.

33. Hanson, "Korea."

34. Ibid.

35. Shaud, "Air Pressure: Air-to-Ground Operations in Korea," 71.

36. Ruffin W. Gray, "Code Name: Honeybucket," 15th Tactical Reconnaissance Squadron, http://yocumusa.com/sweetrose/everymanatiger/warairbattles.htm, accessed October 20, 2020.

37. Ibid.; and Norman E. Duquette, "587 Days of Communist Incarceration," Recce Reader, Winter 2004.

38. Ibid.

39. Ibid.

40. Ibid.

41. Ibid.

42. Richard Chandler, "Mission to China," 15th Tactical Reconnaissance Squadron, http://yocumusa.com/sweetrose/everymanatiger/wartrenches.htm, accessed October 20, 2020.

43. John M. Duquette, "The Loss of Major Jack P. Williams," 15th Tactical Reconnaissance Squadron, http://yocumusa.com/sweetrose/everymanatiger/wartrenches.htm.

44. Ibid.

45. Headquarters, Far East Air Forces, General Orders No. 216 (May 2, 1953).

46. Headquarters, Far East Air Forces, General Orders No. 372 (September 10, 1953).

Chapter 5

1. Major General Henry Viccellio, "The Composite Air Strike Force 1958," Air University Quarterly Review 11, no. 2 (Summer 1959): 4.

2. Robert D. Little and Wilhelmine Burch, "Air Operations in the Lebanon Crisis of 1958," USAF Historical Division Liaison Office, October 1962. Declassified. It is interesting to note this originally classified Air Force study on CASF Bravo was prepared during the same month as the Cuban Missile Crisis. For more information on the utilization of ground troops in Lebanon 1958, see "Not War but Like War: The American Intervention in Lebanon," by Roger J. Spiller, Leavenworth Papers 3 (Fort Leavenworth, KS: Combat Studies Institute, January 1981).

3. Bernard C. Nalty, *The Air Force Role in Five Crises, 1958–1965: Lebanon, Taiwan, Congo, Cuba, Dominican Republic*, USAF Historical Division Liaison Office, June 1968; and Jacob Van Staàveren, Air Operations in the Taiwanese Crisis of 1958, US Air Force Historical Division Liaison Office, November 1962, declassified.

4. Nalty, *The Air Force Role in Five Crises*; and Lawrence M. Greenberg, *United States Army Unilateral And Coalition Operations in the 1965 Dominican Republic Intervention*, CMH Pub 93-5 (Washington, DC: Analysis Branch, US Army Center of Military History, 1987).

5. Bill Bernert, interviews with the author, July 17, 2004 and April 27, 2005.

6. United States, 397. Memorandum prepared by acting director of Central Intelligence Carter, *Foreign Relations of the United States, 1961–1963, vol. 10, Cuba, January 1961–September 1962*. It should be noted that according to an undated memorandum to the director of Central Intelligence from Executive Director Lyman B. Kirkpatrick, it was Acting Director Carter who called General Lemnitzer on August 27 to discuss low-level photography over Cuba, not McCone (Ibid., box 17, Mongoose, Cuban Reconnaissance/Overflights).

7. United States, Summary Record of the 11th Meeting of the Executive Committee of the National Security Council, *Foreign Relations of the United States, 1961–1963, vol. 11, Cuban Missile Crisis and Aftermath*.

8. Lawrence Freedman, *Kennedy's Wars* (New York: Oxford University Press, 2000), 190–192.

9. B. J. Martin, interview with the author, July 16, 2004.

10. Jerry Rogers, interview with the author, July 17, 2004.

11. Gene Morris, interview with the author, July 2004.

12. James Blight, *On the Brink* (New York: Hill and Wang, 1989), 367.

13. Robert F. Kennedy, *Thirteen Days* (New York: W. W. Norton, 1969), 96–97.

14. Clyde East, interview with the author, February 13, 2005.

15. Joe O'Grady, interview with the author, July 16, 2004.

16. Edgar M. Mays, interview with the author, February 22, 2005.

17. 363rd TRW, Historical Report, November and December 1962, 57–60.

18. Clyde East, interview with the author, February 13, 2005.

19. Doug Yates, interview with the author, July 16, 2004.

20. Howard Davis, interview with the author, July 16, 2004.

21. Charles Lustig, interview with the author, July 16, 2004.

22. John Leaphart, interview with the author, February 24, 2005.

23. United States, Memorandum for Record, *Foreign Relations of the United States, 1961–1963, vol. 11, Cuban Missile Crisis and Aftermath*.

24. United States, Summary Record of the 40th Meeting of the Executive Committee of the National Security Council, *Foreign Relations of the United States, 1961–1963, vol. 11, Cuban Missile Crisis and Aftermath*.

25. Tom Curtis, interview with the author, February 20, 2005.

Chapter 6

1. William H. Greenhalgh, *The RF-101 Voodoo: 1960–1971* (Office of Air Force History, 1979, declassified), 24–25.

2. Ibid.

3. Ibid., 26–28.

4. Leland Olson, "Able Mable: The Secret Mission That Wasn't," https://lelandolson.com/2018/04/01/able-mable-the-secret-mission-that-wasnt/, accessed January 29, 2021.

5. Greenhalgh, *The RF-101 Voodoo: 1960–1971,* 53–67.

6. Lou Drendel and Paul Stevens, *Voodoo* (Carrollton, TX: Squadron Signal, 1985), 31–32.

7. 80 TFS Historical Report, July 1–Dec. 31, 1964.

8. PACAF, "USAF Reconnaissance in Southeast Asia (1961–1966)," Directorate of Tactical Evaluation, October 15, 1966, 37–42.

9. https://www.pownetwork.org/bios/m/m119.htm, accessed January 29, 2021.

10. https://www.pownetwork.org/bios/s/s134.htm, accessed January 28, 2021.

11. Peter Davies, *RF-101 Voodoo Units*, Combat Aircraft 127 (Oxford: Osprey, 2019), 59.

12. Note that some military records misspelled his name as "Mervin Lindsey." However, it should be "Marvin Lindsey," as listed in this publication.

13. John L. Frisbee, "Valor: Valiant Volunteer," *Air Force Magazine*, April 1, 1998, https://www.airforcemag.com/article/valor-valiant-volunteer/.

14. https://www.16af.af.mil/News/Legacy/Article/1680133/20th-is-airmen-welcome-home-one-of-their-own/, accessed January 29, 2021.

15. http://veterantributes.org/TributeDetail.php?recordID=294, accessed January 30, 2021.

16. https://media.defense.gov/2011/Mar/23/2001330100/-1/-1/0/AFD-110323-013.pdf, accessed February 2, 2021.

17. Peter E. Davies, *RF-101 Voodoo Units in Combat* (Oxford: Osprey, 2019), 69.

18. https://www.pownetwork.org/bios/g/g061.htm, accessed January 29, 2021.

19. https://www.pownetwork.org/bios/b/b106.htm, accessed January 29, 2021.

20. https://www.pownetwork.org/bios/a/a016.htm; https://www.dpaa.mil/portals/85/VietnamAccounting/pmsea_una_AIR%20FORCE_20210205.pdf; and personal conversations with Senior Master Sergeant Edgar Mays.

21. Greenhalgh, *The RF-101 Voodoo: 1960-1971.*

22. 432nd Tactical Reconnaissance Wing, *History*, October–December 1969, 1.

23. US Air Force, *Trends Indicators and Analysis (TIA)*, vol. 12, 1970, 1–11.

24. Ibid., 1–14.

25. Wayne Thompson, *To Hanoi and Back: The USAF and North Vietnam, 1966–1973* (Washington, DC: Air Force History and Museums Program, n.d.), 156.

26. Colonel Don Dessert (ret.), personal interview, August 20, 2002.

27. US Air Force, Briefing, Subject: Mission of the 716th Reconnaissance Squadron AFAT-1, undated, 5.

28. John Bull Stirling, "Voodoo Reconnaissance in the Vietnam War, 1966–1967," edited by Albert J. Redway Jr., *Air Power History* 43, no. 4 (1996):18–19.

29. Robert F. Door and Chris Bishop, *Vietnam Air War Debrief* (London: Aerospace Publishing, 1996).

30. 460th Tactical Reconnaissance Wing, "460th Historical Report, 1 January 1967–31 March 1967," 6.

31. Senior Master Sergeant Edgar M. Mays (ret.), personal interview, July 23, 2001.

32. Stirling, "Voodoo Reconnaissance in the Vietnam War, 1966–1967," 25.

33. Istvan Toperczer, *Air War over North Vietnam: The Vietnamese People's Air Force, 1949–1977* (Carrollton, TX: Squadron Signal, 1998).

34. Greenhalgh, *The RF-101 Voodoo: 1960–1971,*90–91.

35. Ibid.

36. US Air Force, *Trends Indicators and Analysis (TIA)*, vol. 12, 1970, 1–11.

37. https://valor.militarytimes.com/hero/24072, accessed February 6, 2021; and Istvan Toperczer, MiG-21 Units of the Vietnam War (Oxford: Osprey, 2001), 85 and 91.

38. https://dpaa-mil.sites.crmforce.mil/dpaaProfile?id=a0Jt0000000KYOXEA4, accessed February 6, 2021.

39. https://www.pownetwork.org/bios/l/l018.htm, accessed February 6, 2021.

40. https://www.pownetwork.org/bios/v/v007.htm, accessed February 6, 2021.

41. 432nd Tactical Reconnaissance Wing, *History*, October–December 1969.

42. Detachment 7, 38th ARSq, "Mission Narrative Report #1-3-66," September 22, 1966.

43. 45th Tactical Reconnaissance Squadron, "History of the 45th Tactical Reconnaissance Squadron, 1 July–31 December 1965," 4.

44. Edgar M. Mays, interview, July 23, 2001.

45. Ibid.

46. https://airforce.togetherweserved.com/usaf/servlet/tws.webapp.WebApp?cmd=ShadowBox Profile&type=Person&ID=81916, accessed February 6, 2021.

47. E. H. Hartsook, *The Air Force in Southeast Asia: The End of the US Involvement,1973–1975*, Office of Air Force History, Headquarters USAF, 1980.

48. Ibid.

49. Daniel L. Haulman, "Cambodian Airlift and Evacuation: Operation Eagle Pull," in *Short of War: Major USAF Contingency Operations, 1947–1997*, edited by A. Timothy Warnock (Air Force History and Museums Program in association with Air University Press, 2000).

50. Hartsook, *The Air Force in Southeast Asia*.

51. Daniel L. Haulman, "Crisis in Southeast Asia: Mayaguez Rescue," in *Short of War: Major USAF Contingency Operations, 1947–1997*, edited by A. Timothy Warnock (Air Force History and Museums Program in association with Air University Press, 2000).

Chapter 7

1. Robert F. Door, *Gulf War: RF-4C Phantom II in Desert Storm*, Defense Media Network, February 14, 2011, https://www.defensemedianetwork.com/stories/gulf-war-rf-4c-phantom-ii-in-desert-storm/. This is a very good short article on the RF-4Cs in the Gulf War. See also United States Government, Gulf War Air Power Survey, vol. 4, Weapons, Tactics, and Training and Space Operations, 1993.

2. United States Government, *Gulf War Air Power Survey*, Summary Report, 1993, 194–195.

3. Major John S. Hutcheson, "Tactical Recon Paying Dividends with TARS," United States Air Force press release, April 25, 2006.

4. United States Air Force, "MQ-9 Reaper Fact Sheet," September 23, 2015.

Bibliography

Personal Interviews

Bernert Bill, personal interviews with the author, July 17, 2004, and April 27, 2005.

Curtis, Tom, personal interview with the author, February 20, 2005.

Davis, Howard, personal interview with the author, July 16, 2004.

Dessert, Don, personal interview with the author, August 20, 2002.

East, Clyde B., personal interviews with the author, February 13, 2005; February 15, 2005.

Leaphart, John, personal interview with the author, February 24, 2005.

Lustig, Charles, personal interview with the author, July 16, 2004.

Martin, B. J., personal interview with the author, July 16, 2004.

Mays, Edgar M., personal interviews with the author, July 23, 2001; February 22, 2005.

Morris, Gene, personal interview with the author, July 16, 2004.

O'Grady, Joe, personal interview with the author, July 16, 2004.

Rogers, Jerry, personal interview with the author, July 17, 2004.

Yates, Doug, personal interview with the author, July 16, 2004.

United States Government and United States Air Force Documents, Publications, and Reports

1st Aero Squadron, September 12, 1918, Summary of Operations.

1st Aero Squadron, September 13, 1918, Summary of Operations.

2nd Division: 202-20, 4 Intelligence Report, 2nd Division AEF, Genevrots, France, June 29, 1918.

5th Photographic Squadron, Fotoron Five, Resume of Activities since Departure from Home Station for Field Service.

5th Photographic Squadron, Fotoron Five, Resume of Activities from May 28, 1943, to October 9, 1943.

5th Photographic Squadron, Squadron History, 5th Photo Squadron (Advanced Unit for Fifth Army), November 1943.

5th Photographic Squadron, Squadron History Report, January 3, 1944.

5th Photographic Squadron, Squadron History, April 1944.

5th Photographic Squadron, Close Intelligence Support Furnished Outside Units, May 1944.

5th Photographic Squadron, Squadron History, June 1944.

5th Photographic Squadron, General Summary, June 1944.

5th Photographic Squadron, Squadron History, August 1944.

5th Photographic Squadron, Historical Records, April 1945.

5th Photographic Squadron, Historical Records, May 1945

7th Photographic Reconnaissance Group, Group History Report, June 1944.

8th Aero Squadron, statement by 1st Lieutenant Horace W. Mitchell, no date listed.

8th Aero Squadron, statement by Second Lieutenant John W. Artz, no date listed.

8th Photo Reconnaissance Squadron, Narrative, November 1944.

8th Photo Reconnaissance Squadron, Historical Report for the Month of December 1944.

9th Aero Squadron, September 13, 1918, Missions Carried Out.

12th Aero Squadron, September 13, 1918, Summary of Operations.

12th Aero Squadron, September 14, 1918, Summary of Operations.

45th Tactical Reconnaissance Squadron, Unit Historical Report, December 1950.

45th Tactical Reconnaissance Squadron, Unit Historical Report, January 1951.

45th Tactical Reconnaissance Squadron, Unit Historical Report, March 1951.

45th Tactical Reconnaissance Squadron, "History of the 45th Tactical Reconnaissance Squadron, 1 July–31 December 1965".

50th Aero Squadron Operations Report, September 13, 1918; Office of the Chief of Air Service Headquarters, First Army Corps American Expeditionary Forces, Sept. 14, 1918, Summary of Operations for the day of Sept. 13, 1918. No. 4. By order by Major M. A. Hall, C.A.S., and 1st A.C. Paul D. Meyers, 2nd lieut., C.A. C., operations officer.

67th Tactical Reconnaissance Group, Operations Report 67/231, Mission No. 17, June 6, 1944.

67th Tactical Reconnaissance Group, Historical Records of Headquarters, 67th Tactical Reconnaissance Group, June 1944.

80 TFS Historical Report, July 1–Dec. 31, 1964.

94th Aero Squadron, 9/13/18 Reconnaissance Report, J. Bayard H. Smith 1st lieut., A.S. U.S.A., acting operations officer.

104th Aero Squadron, September 15, 1918, Summary of Reports.

111th Tactical Reconnaissance Squadron, Squadron History, April 1945.

363rd TRW, Historical Report, November and December 1962.

432nd Tactical Reconnaissance Wing, History, October–December 1969.

460th Tactical Reconnaissance Wing, "460th Historical Report, 1 January 1967–31 March 1967".

Detachment 7, 38th ARSq, "Mission Narrative Report #1-3-66," September 22, 1966.

ESG G-3, Memorandum, August 16, 1918.

Gardner, Marvin G. "Target Buka." 8th Photographic Reconnaissance Squadron, March 1944.

General Orders: War Department, General Orders No. 15 (1919) Action Date: September 12, 1918.

General Orders: War Department, General Orders No. 44 (1919).

General Orders: War Department, General Orders No. 126 (1919).

General Orders: War Department, General Orders No. 56 (1922).

Greenberg, Lawrence M. *United States Army Unilateral And Coalition Operations in the 1965 Dominican Republic Intervention.* CMH Pub 93-5 Washington, DC: Analysis Branch, US Army Center of Military History, 1987.

Greenhalgh, William H. *The RF-101 Voodoo 1961–1970* United States Air Force, Office of Air Force History, 1979, declassified.

Hartsook, E. H. *The Air Force in Southeast Asia: The End of the US Involvement,1973–1975.* Office of Air Force History, Headquarters USAF, 1980.

Headquarters 1st Army, AEF, August 6, 1918, Memorandum 8.

Headquarters, 24th Aero Squadron, First Army Observation Group, Operations Report for September 13, 1918, John W. Cousins, 1st lieut., inf. operations officer.

Headquarters, 24th Aero Squadron, First Army Observation Group, Operations Report for September 14, 1918.

Headquarters, 90th Aero Squadron Observation Group–Fourth Army Corps, Sept. 12, 1918

Headquarters, 91st Aero Squadron, Operations Report for September 12, 1918, John W. Cousins, 1st lieut., operations officer.

Headquarters, Air Service First Army, August 20, 1918, memorandum for commanding general, 1st Army, William S. Mitchell, colonel, A.S.S.C. C.A.S., 1st Army.

Headquarters, Air Service, First Army American Expeditionary Forces Operations Report No. 13, 1900 hrs., September 11–1900 hrs., Sept. 12, 1918.

Headquarters, Air Service, Fifth Army Corps, American E.F. Operations Report Number 38, 19:00 Sept. 12 to 19:00 Sept. 13, 1918. By order of Major Christie Fraser Hale, 1st lieut., FA USA, operations officer.

Headquarters, Air Service, Fifth Army Corps, American Expeditionary Forces, Operations Report No. 39, 19:00 Sept. 13 to 19:00 Sept. 14, 1918.

Headquarters, Far East Air Forces, General Orders No. 73, February 25, 1951.

Headquarters, Far East Air Forces, General Orders No. 569, December 4, 1951.

Headquarters, Far East Air Forces, General Orders No. 216 (May 2, 1953).

Headquarters, Far East Air Forces, General Orders No. 372 (September 10, 1953).

Headquarters, First Pursuit Wing Air Service, American E.F., August 29, 1918 Operations Memorandum 3, by order of Major Atkinson; Philip J. Roosevelt, captain, A/S. C. operations officer.

Headquarters Ninth Aero Service Squadron, Operations Report for September 12, 1918, Harold W. Merrill, 1st lieut., 103/F.A., operations officer.

Headquarters, Ninth Aero Service Squadron, Operations Report for September 14, 1918.

Headquarters, Ninth Air Force. Unit Commendation for Distinguished Service, April 13, 1944.

Headquarters, US Army Forces in the Far East, General Orders No. 77 (1943).

Hutcheson, Major John S. "Tactical Recon Paying Dividends with TARS." United States Air Force press release, April 25, 2006.

Maurer, Maurer, ed. *The US Air Service in World War I. Vol. 1, The Final Report and a Tactical History* Maxwell AFB, AL: Albert F. Simpson Historical Research Center, 1978.

Nalty, Bernard C. *The Air Force Role in Five Crises, 1958–1965: Lebanon, Taiwan, Congo, Cuba, Dominican Republic.* USAF Historical Division Liaison Office, June 1968.

Ninth Photographic Reconnaissance Squadron, Squadron History for the Month of December 1942.

Ninth Photographic Reconnaissance Squadron, Squadron History for the Month of January 1943.

Ninth Photographic Reconnaissance Squadron, Squadron History for the Month of June 1943.

Ninth Photographic Reconnaissance Squadron, Squadron History for the Month of August 1943.

Ninth Photographic Reconnaissance Squadron, Squadron History for the Month of November 1943.

Ninth Photographic Reconnaissance Squadron, Squadron History for the Month of October 1943.

Ninth Photographic Reconnaissance Squadron, Squadron History for the Months of November and December 1943.

Ninth Photographic Reconnaissance Squadron, Operations of the Ninth Photographic Reconn Squadron for January 1944, 7 April 1944. *These dates are correct. The 9th PRS Commander's Office wrote more-detailed summaries of the January, February, and March 1944 unit operational reports from his perspective in April 1944.*

Ninth Photographic Reconnaissance Squadron, Operations of the Ninth Photographic Reconn Squadron for February 1944, April 7, 1944.

Ninth Photographic Reconnaissance Squadron, Operations of the Ninth Photographic Reconn Squadron for April 1944, June 1, 1944.

Ninth Photographic Reconnaissance Squadron, Operations of the Ninth Photographic Reconn Squadron for May 1944, June 18, 1944.

Office of the Chief of Air Service, Headquarters First Army Corps, American Expeditionary Forces, Sept. 13, 1918, Summary of Operations for the day of Sept. 12, 1918. No. 3. By order of Major M. A. Hall, C. A. S., and 1st A. C. Paul D. Meyers, 2nd lieut., C.A. C. operations officer.

PACAF, "USAF Reconnaissance in Southeast Asia (1961–1966)," Directorate of Tactical Evaluation, October 15, 1966, 37–42.

Seventy-First Reconnaissance Group, Historical Record and History of the 71st Reconnaissance Group, September 14, 1945.

United States, Memorandum for Record, *Foreign Relations of the United States, 1961–1963*, vol. 11, Cuban Missile Crisis and Aftermath.

United States, 397. Memorandum prepared by acting director of Central Intelligence Carter, *Foreign Relations of the United States, 1961–1963*, vol. 10, Cuba, January 1961–September 1962.

United States, Summary Record of the 11th Meeting of the Executive Committee of the National Security Council, *Foreign Relations of the United States, 1961–1963*, vol. 11, Cuban Missile Crisis and Aftermath.

United States Government, *Gulf War Air Power Survey*, Summary Report, 1993.

US Air Force, "MQ-9 Reaper Fact Sheet," September 23, 2015.

US Air Force, Briefing, Subject: Mission of the 716th Reconnaissance Squadron AFAT-1, undated.

US Air Force, *Trends Indicators and Analysis (TIA)*, vol. 12, 1970.

Van Staaveren, Jacob *Air Operations in the Taiwanese Crisis of 1958*. US Air Force Historical Division Liaison Office, November 1962, declassified.

Books and Articles

Blight, James. *On the Brink* New York: Hill and Wang, 1989.

Carver, Leland F., Gustaf A. Lindstrom, and A. T. Foster. *The Ninetieth Aero Squadron: American Expeditionary Forces* Hinesdale, IL: E. H. Griest, 1920.

Chandler, Richard. "Mission to China." 15th Tactical Reconnaissance Squadron. http://yocumusa.com/sweetrose/everymanatiger/wartrenches.htm, accessed October 20, 2020.

Davies, Peter. *RF-101 Voodoo Units*. Combat Aircraft 127 Oxford: Osprey, 2019.

Door, Robert F. and Chris Bishop. *Vietnam Air War Debrief* London: Aerospace Publishing, 1996.

Door, Robert F. "Gulf War: RF-4C Phantom II in Desert Storm." Defense Media Network, February 14, 2011. https://www.defensemedianetwork.com/stories/gulf-war-rf-4c-phantom-ii-in-desertstorm/.

Drendel, Lou and Paul Stevens. *Voodoo* Carrollton, TX: Squadron Signal, 1985.

Duquette, John M. "The Loss of Major Jack P. Williams." 15th Tactical Reconnaissance Squadron. http://yocumusa.com/sweetrose/everymanatiger/wartrenches.htm.

Duquette, Norman E. "587 Days of Communist Incarceration." *Recce Reader*, Winter 2004.

Faulkner, Richard S. *Meuse-Argonne, 26 September–11 November 1918.* Washington, DC: Center of Military History United States Army, 2018.

Freedman, Lawrence. *Kennedy's Wars.* New York: Oxford University Press, 2000.

Frisbee, John L. "Valor: Valiant Volunteer." *Air Force Magazine*, April 1, 1998. https://www.airforcemag.com/article/valor-valiant-volunteer/.

Gray, Ruffin W. "Code Name: Honeybucket." 15th Tactical Reconnaissance Squadron. http:// yocu-musa.com/sweetrose/everymanatiger/warairbattles.htm, accessed October 20, 2020.

Hallion, Richard P., ed. *Silver Wings, Golden Valor: The USAF Remembers Korea.* Washington, DC: Air Force History and Museums Program, 2006.

Hanson, James R. "Korea." 15th Tactical Reconnaissance Squadron. http://yocumusa.com/sweetrose/everymanatiger/warairbattles.htm, accessed October 20, 2020.

Hart, Percival Gray. *History of the 135th Aero Squadron from July 25 to November 11, 1918.* Chicago: no publisher listed, 1939.

Haulman, Daniel L. "Cambodian Airlift and Evacuation: Operation Eagle Pull." In *Short of War: Major USAF Contingency Operations, 1947–1997.* Edited by A. Timothy Warnock. Air Force History and Museums Program in association with Air University Press, 2000.

Haulman, Daniel L. "Crisis in Southeast Asia: Mayaguez Rescue." In *Short of War: Major USAF Contingency Operations, 1947–1997.* Edited by A. Timothy Warnock. Air Force History and Museums Program in association with Air University Press, 2000.

Kennedy, Robert F. *Thirteen Days.* New York: W. W. Norton, 1969.

Kenney, George C., and Horace Moss Guilbert. *History of the 91st Aero Squadron: Air Service USA.* Coblenz, Germany: privately published, 1919.

Little, Robert D., and Wilhelmine Burch. "Air Operations in the Lebanon Crisis of 1958." USAF Historical Division Liaison Office, October 1962.

Mitchell, William B. *Memoirs of World War I.* New York: Random House, 1960; reprinted from original 1928 edition.

Morse, Captain Daniel P. *The History of the 50th Aero Squadron.* New York: Blanchard, 1920.

Nimmo, James W. "Break, Break." 15th Tactical Reconnaissance Squadron. http://yocumusa.com/sweetrose/everymanatiger/warairbattles.htm, accessed October 20, 2020.

Olson, Leland. "Able Mable: The Secret Mission That Wasn't." https://lelandolson.com/2018/04/01/able-mable-the-secret-mission-that-wasnt/, accessed January 29, 2021.

Peebles, Curtis. *Shadow Flights: America's Secret Air War against the Soviet Union.* Novato, CA: Presidio, 2000.

Sebring, Stanley R. "I Was Wrong about That." 15th Tactical Reconnaissance Squadron. http:// yocu-musa.com/sweetrose/everymanatiger/warenterthedragon.htm, accessed October 20, 2020.

Shaud, General John A. "Air Pressure: Air-to-Ground Operations in Korea." In *Silver Wings, Golden Valor: The Air Force Remembers Korea.* Edited by Richard Hallion. Washington, DC: Air Force History and Museums Program, 2006.

Smart, Lieutenant Lawrence L. *The Hawks That Guided the Guns.* Self-published, 1968.

Smith, J. B. "Bruce Shawe & JB Smith, 8th Tac Recon (Photo Jet), Korean War, 1950–53." 15th Tactical Reconnaissance Squadron. http://yocumusa.com/sweetrose/everymanatiger/waryalu. htm, accessed October 20, 2020.

Stirling, John Bull. "Voodoo Reconnaissance in the Vietnam War, 1966–1967." Edited by Albert J. Redway Jr. *Air Power History* 43, no. 4 (1996).

Stratemeyer, George. *The Three Wars of Lt. Gen. George E. Stratemeyer: His Korean War Diary*. Edited by William T. Y'Blood. Air Force History and Museums Program, 1999.

Thompson, Wayne, and Bernard C. Nalty. *Within Limits: The U.S. Air Force and the Korean War.*, Air Force History and Museums Program, 1996.

Thompson, Wayne. *To Hanoi and Back: The USAF and North Vietnam, 1966–1973*. (Washington, DC: Air Force History and Museums Program, n.d..

Toperczer, Istvan. *Air War over North Vietnam: The Vietnamese People's Air Force, 1949–1977*. Carrollton, TX: Squadron Signal, 1998.

Toulmin, H. A. *Air Service: American Expeditionary Force 1918*. New York: D. Van Nostrand, 1927.

Viccellio, Major General Henry. "The Composite Air Strike Force 1958." *Air University Quarterly Review* 11, no. 2 (Summer 1959).

Index

A